Crime Prevention
Through Environmental
Design

Crime Prevention Through Environmental Design

Applications of Architectural Design and Space Management Concepts

Second Edition

Timothy Crowe

National Crime Prevention Institute

Butterworth-Heinemann
An Imprint of Elsevier
Boston   Oxford   Auckland   Johannesburg   Melbourne   New Delhi

Elsevier supports the efforts of American Forests and the Global ReLeaf program in its campaign for the betterment of trees, forests, and our environment.

Library of Congress Cataloging-in-Publication Data

Crowe, Timothy D.
   Crime prevention through environmental design : applications of architectural design and space management concepts / by Timothy D. Crowe. — 2nd ed.
      p.   cm.
   "National Crime Prevention Institute."
   Includes bibliographical references and index.
   ISBN-13: 978-0-7506-7198-9   ISBN-10: 0-7506-7198-x (alk. pbk.)
   1. Crime prevention and architectural design.
   I. National Crime Prevention Institute
   (University of Louisville)   II. Title.
   HV7431.C79 1999
   364.4'9 — dc21   99-045731

British Library Cataloguing-in-Publication Data

A catalogue record for this book is available from the British Library.
The publisher offers special discounts on bulk orders of this book.

For information, please contact:
Manager of Special Sales
Butterworth-Heinemann
225 Wildwood Avenue
Woburn, MA 01801-2041
Tel: 781-904-2500
Fax: 781-904-2620

For information on all Butterworth-Heinemann publications available, contact our World Wide Web home page at:
http://www.bh.com

Transferred to Digital Printing 2009

Contents

Preface

We have reached the brink of the 21st century and buildings continue to be built, communities continue to be planned, and technical developments continue to be conceived. Astronauts are regularly shuttled to outer space and back and unmanned spacecraft are probing even deeper. Medical science continues to make remarkable discoveries about the human body. Advances in technology have put us on the verge of being able to replace human body parts with synthetic devices. Future developments will enable the blind to see through video cameras attached to nerve endings that will transmit images to the brain.

For over 5,000 years, architects have used design and space management concepts to manipulate human behavior. History has recorded these methods. Yet, for the past several decades, mistakes have been made in community development, urban planning, and architectural design that belie our ever having had a historical knowledge of such design concepts. It may be that the incredible gains in technology may have corrupted our thinking, because many environmental conditions (but not all) can now be controlled by machines.

Schools now close when temperatures get too high, because our children are now too acclimated to air-conditioned environments. This rarely occurred 30 years ago. Mass media and modern transportation systems have had a profound impact on our lives, but may have resulted in our failure to think explicitly about the relationship between the environment and human behavior. The Crime Prevention Through Environmental Design (CPTED) program has rejuvenated an interest in age-old concepts of environmental psychology. The program has helped to redefine strategies and concepts that had become lost in a morass of conflicting opinions and beliefs about planning and design. Many of these beliefs were generated by radical trends in social policy emanating from urban unrest and political conflict associate with the broad movement for civil rights and the war in Vietnam.

The renewed interest in CPTED has resulted in a wide range of activity that has suffered from a lack of direction. Persons who are actively attempting to implement CPTED concepts have experienced difficulty in obtaining up-to-date materials and guidelines. Many are using outdated material.

Others are being misdirected by hybrid versions of CPTED concepts that are incomplete or confusing. This book was prepared to provide a fundamental introduction to the history and development of CPTED. It establishes a common basis for the orientation and education of those who are trying to incorporate CPTED concepts into their ongoing planning and development activities.

Acknowledgments

The National Crime Prevention Institute (NCPI) is more than just an organization or agency. Over 40,000 graduates of its many programs and seminars will attest to the fact that NCPI becomes a part of each person who attends its courses. NCPI has become a home in the purest sense of the word. It is a foundation or focal point for many professionals who rely upon substance, history, and principles of crime and loss prevention to sustain them through both the good and bad times of their careers. Ardent alumni of any educational institution share the same commitment for the mission of their institution that only another alumnus of that organization may appreciate.

NCPI has its own spirit. Otherwise, why would so many people share as a common bond the sense of pride in where they learned about crime and loss prevention? The spirit of NCPI is there—everyone acknowledges it—but no one has described it better than long-time faculty member Richard Mellard, who told me when I interviewed for the director's position that he could not explain why he stayed for the low pay and the bureaucratic nonsense, except for the fact that he "just loved the place!" It has been a decade since I stepped down as director of NCPI, and there is not a day that goes by that I do not miss it.

1

Introduction to CPTED

BACKGROUND

The purpose of this book is to provide challenging questions and practical advice to people who make decisions that affect the physical environment and the human functions in the community. This book is not intended to be an academic study of the environment, of crime prevention, or of environmental psychology. Because of the pervasiveness of its potential influence, it would be impossible for this book to be a complete study of all of the fields and disciplines that its topics encounter.

The book is a summation of my experience with the concept of Crime Prevention Through Environmental Design (CPTED). The CPTED concept, coined by Dr. C. Ray Jeffery in his book by the same title, expands upon the assumption that *the proper design and effective use of the built environment can lead to a reduction in the fear of crime and the incidence of crime, and to an improvement in the quality of life*. This translates to many practical and useful applications.

The contents bring together the observations, consulting work, and lectures and teaching materials that I have amassed in over 30 years of experience. These experiences have included major events, such as the 1979 Pan American Games, the 1982 World's Fair, and the 1972 political conventions held in Miami Beach. A considerable amount of time has been spent in schools and public housing projects. Shopping centers, malls, fast food restaurants, and downtown street systems have been part of my consultative practice. Hotels and residential housing have also been a significant part of my professional experience.

A practical guide to the use of CPTED concepts is necessary because the research literature has yet to thoroughly investigate the considerable small-scale applications of the CPTED concept. Controlled research and evaluation activities are required to make CPTED a fully definitive concept. However, buildings must be built, major events must be conducted, and communities must continue to grow without the benefit of perfect scientific knowledge. Accordingly, this book contains some simple concepts and a variety of examples to assist the builder, planner, architect, or police and security consultant who will be making decisions about individual projects and human functions.

The intention of this book is not to tell people how to design buildings or what decisions to make about the future of the properties that they manage. It is rather to share concepts and ask questions that may never have been asked, with the hope that these concepts and questions will improve decisions and stimulate greater creativity in designing and managing human activities.

ASKING THE RIGHT QUESTIONS

CPTED concepts, at least as used in this work, are largely self-evident. Most of the time recipients of CPTED assistance exclaim, "I should have thought of that!" Too often, after it is too late to undo the damage, an individual will say, "I thought of that, but was afraid to ask." It is quite common for police officers and security consultants to withhold their comments because they feel that they would be overstepping the boundaries of their security role. Yet the performance of architects, developers, and facility managers can only be as good as the information they are given from all quarters.

Once the basic principles of CPTED are understood, it is difficult to look at the environment again without asking, "What if. . . .." At the beginning of each CPTED seminar we stress the following three points:

1.   Never look at the environment the same way again.
2.   Question everything, no matter how trivial.
3.   Learn the language of the professions you are working with and you will understand their motivations.

Elizabeth Meehan, a color and light consultant, and a visiting lecturer of the National Crime Prevention Institute (NCPI), summarized the problem with interior design. She said that illumination consultants are always looking up. Floor covering consultants are always looking down. Wallpaper consultants are always looking at the walls. But no one usually looks at the whole interior as the sum of its parts. Each profession is trained to focus attention on its unique objectives. For instance, police officers are trained to look at openings — doors and windows. Not until they have had CPTED training do they begin to see the property as a whole, as it was intended to be. And it is not until this happens that a good crime prevention officer or security consultant can contribute to meeting the objectives of the human function. *Never look at the environment the same way again.*

The old expression, "If I had a nickel for every time something happened that I knew would happen and didn't stop, I'd be rich," too often applies in CPTED experience. Designers and planners need help in identifying the little problems, which are often their undoing. For instance, the city of Louisville, Kentucky, replaced a portion of the failed River City pedestrian mall with a cobblestone street that was intended for people to walk on. Instead, people fell down. In Jacksonville, Florida, a River Walk project with a pier was installed along a transitional site across from its downtown river front improvement program. But the designer got so involved in the aesthetics of his boardwalk that he installed boards that were separated to allow the pedestrian to see, as well as hear, the water lapping underneath. This was great for water drainage, but not for high-heeled shoes! *Question everything.*

Many agencies and professions learn to stick to their own bailiwick and avoid direct conflict. At least in direct conflict, they are still talking, albeit somewhat loudly. It is not until someone is able to cross over the disciplines that common interests are found. This is perhaps the hardest lesson for law enforcement officers and security consultants to learn. It is too easy to allow buildings to be built and events to be planned before thinking about security. There is a tendency to feel out of place in insisting that security be considered in the design and layout of the human function or activity. Conversely, event managers, architects, and planners often view the security and law enforcement consultants as myopically concerned with what can go wrong, not with what can go right. CPTED enthusiasts know that planning ahead to make things go right is the key to reducing or eliminating security problems. *Learn the language.*

THE NEED FOR CPTED

Do you currently have review and approval authority for all physical changes occurring in your jurisdiction? Are you involved at the concept stage in event planning, or are you last in line to comment on a completed plan? Are you tired of hearing about new crime prevention efforts that are abandoned after several years? Are you willing to take a calculated risk, one that presents great promise for the future role of your organization or community?

CPTED is a new approach that has an old background. Trends are pointing to a resurgence of interest in CPTED. The National Association of Convenience Food Stores highlighted CPTED as a feature panel in its 1987 convention in Toronto. This association has an average attendance of 8,000 people at each convention. Designers and merchandisers have discovered new store configurations that reportedly have increased sales as much as 33% and decreased security problems by 50%.

The American Society for Industrial Security (ASIS) featured a CPTED session in its store security segment at the 1987 convention in Las Vegas. CPTED concepts in commercial, convenience, and fast food stores were covered at length. The National Association of Urban Planning Educators scheduled a CPTED session as a major panel at its 1987 conference. One key issue was the need for CPTED training at the academic level.

The state of Florida has passed a CPTED-related law, the "Safe Neighborhoods Act," which provides funding for CPTED planning in residential and business areas. The city of Gainesville, Florida, has passed a CPTED-related ordinance that places special requirements on the convenience industry. The ordinance requires, among other things, that the stores provide security training, remove signs from windows, increase the number of store employees after 9:00 P.M., and increase internal lighting at night. The ordinance has reduced robberies alone by 65%.

Nearly every journal related to the planning and architectural business is beginning to feature articles that challenge popular design and planning assumptions. Downtown pedestrian malls and those horrible downtown one-way street systems are under the gun. In the latter case, critics are finding that the one-dimensional value of enhanced traffic flow is not worth the loss of traditional business areas. The loss of on-street parking and the diversion of traffic has hurt a lot of business areas. We have given up a lot for the sake of moving commuters through traffic a little faster. Why don't we just divert them instead?

The National Crime Prevention Institute's new CPTED Studio and one- and two-week courses present an excellent opportunity to initiate a team approach to CPTED, even for the corporate business person. Bring your facility planners and designers with you to a class that may change the way you do business. Learn how to merge your common interests and objectives, thus helping each member of the team do a better job of attaining his or her own goal.

One strong admonition is, "Don't hide CPTED from your boss, like you do everything else that you want to control." A friend of mine recently complained that I had caused his boss to "go off half-cocked and shoot his mouth off about CPTED." The official complaint was that the boss couldn't be protected unless what he saw was controlled. Perhaps the real problem was that *the boss couldn't be controlled when he understood what was going on.*

Both you and your bosses need to understand and practice CPTED. It will take all the support you can get to make it a success. Of course, you are only looking at something that has the potential, for the first time, of achieving some results over the long term for your community or organization. What we do right or wrong with our human and physical resources produces a lasting legacy.

COMPETING CRIME PREVENTION STRATEGIES

A number of related concepts have become confused with the CPTED operating theories and applications. While some of these concepts overlap with CPTED, others are very different in that they attempt to repackage and redefine the common sense approach of CPTED. An explanation of some of these related concepts follows:

CPTED-Organized and Mechanical Approach versus Natural Approach. There is some confusion and competition within the CPTED movement itself that boils down to one group that casually blends the three strategy areas (organized, mechanical, and natural approaches) as opposed to another group of specialists whose principal emphasis is on natural approaches. The former is more of a crime control model whereas the latter may be conceived as a planning model.

Defensible Space. This concept was developed in the public housing environment. It is similar to CPTED in that it shares the basic characteristics of natural surveillance, natural access control, and territorial concern. CPTED, in its modern form, was developed as an extension of defensible space concepts to commercial retail, industrial institutional, and low-density residential environments.

Environmental Security. This concept was developed on a parallel basis to CPTED. It was initially used in residential settings. Environmental security differs from CPTED in that it contemplates the use of a broad range of crime control strategies, including social management, target hardening, activity support, and law enforcement.

Security by Design. This concept is best understood as a repackaging of solid security engineering, physical security, and procedural security measures to provide improved emphasis in the design process.

Natural Crime Prevention. This concept grew out of the CPTED emphasis on natural strategies, those that factor behavior management and control into the design and use of the built environment.

Safer Cities. This is another spin-off of CPTED that attempts to define an approach to crime prevention that incorporates traditional crime prevention and law enforcement strategies with CPTED. Of course, CPTED planners know that CPTED does not replace other crime prevention strategies but that a high priority should be placed on natural strategies that take advantage of how human and physical resources are being expended.

Situational Crime Prevention. This concept is much more comprehensive than CPTED because it incorporates other crime prevention and law enforcement strategies in an effort that focuses on place-specific crime problems.

Place-Specific Crime Prevention. This is just another name for situational crime prevention and environmental security.

It is clear from a review of these apparently competing concepts that they actually overlap and are extremely compatible with CPTED. Many were developed to provide a vehicle for incorporating organized and mechanical strategies into a free-standing model. However, most long-time CPTED planners have always viewed CPTED as a small subset of the total set of measures required for effective crime prevention and control. Criminologists know that a comprehensive system must include strategies on a continuum that ranges from prenatal care to dementia among elderly persons. It would be unconscionable for anyone to think otherwise.

CPTED AND CONTEMPORARY PLANNING MODELS

There has been some controversy and misinformation about the role of CPTED in the contemporary planning models. These contemporary models include the Urban Village, Transportation-Oriented Development, Neotraditional Planning, Liveable Cities, and New Urbanism. Supporters of these planning approaches will often cite conflict with CPTED based upon a narrow perception that all CPTED planners do is "close streets and cut bushes."

A study of the concepts and beliefs associated with these contemporary planning models and the natural approaches to space management and design emphasized in CPTED reveals that there is very little conflict. Moreover, there is an overwhelming amount of compatibility. Perhaps an increase in education about all of these planning approaches will help to eliminate the myths. The key to overcoming the concern about conflicts is to understand that *CPTED is a process for improving planning decisions*. It is not about beliefs that grid streets are bad and curvilinear ones are better. Once the critic understands that CPTED is a process and not a belief system, it will be easy to use CPTED to improve upon decisions within the framework of whatever planning model that is adopted.

CPTED IN THE UNITED STATES

Early interest in CPTED began with the research of Jane Jacobs. Her book, *The Death and Life of Great American Cities*, published in 1961, described many observations of the relationships between the urban design and crime. Ms. Jacobs work stressed the importance of increasing territorial identity and natural surveillance.

Oscar Newman demonstrated the importance of natural surveillance, access control, and territorial concern in his 1972 book, *Defensible Space*. Newman proved that a relationship exists between space management and design and crime in public housing environments.

As mentioned earlier, Dr. C. Ray Jeffery coined the phrase, *Crime Prevention Through Environmental Design*, in his 1971 book by that title in which he described the relationship between urban design and crime. His book included excerpts from a 1968 report from the National Commission on the Causes and Prevention of Violence that warned the American public of the direct relationships between urban design and crime. This Commission studied the massive urban violence and racial unrest that had occurred in U.S. cities between 1964 and 1968. Richard Gardiner, a landscape architect and developer, successfully demonstrated the use of CPTED concepts in residential areas. His 1978 manual, *Design for Safe Neighborhoods*, presented the results of a successful project in a Hartford, Connecticut neighborhood, which significantly reduced crime and improved the quality of life.

The most significant CPTED developmental effort in the United States was conducted by the Westinghouse Electric Corporation through a massive contractual effort funded by the U.S. Department of Justice. Westinghouse managed a large group of consultants and subcontractors who were responsible for adapting CPTED concepts that had been proven effective in public housing environments to retail, transportation, and school environments. Much was learned from these efforts, which have formed the basis for current efforts in the United States.

Interest in CPTED at the federal government level waned during the 1980s. However, state and local units of government took the lead and produced a large number of successful projects. These led to the incorporation of CPTED principles into local building codes. Design review ordinances have been modified to require the use of CPTED in building design. Several state governments have passed legislation and developed new regulations governing the design and management of schools and the convenient food store industry. The state of Florida has taken the most steps by passing legislation and actively conducting training for the public and private sectors.

The National Crime Prevention Institute at the University of Louisville created the first CPTED training program in 1985. A design studio was created to assist in the teaching of CPTED concepts. This training program has been attended by several thousand participants who have spread the use of CPTED concepts in their communities throughout the world. The content of this training program formed the basis for the 1991 book, *Crime Prevention Through Environmental Design: Applications of Architectural Design and Space Management Concepts*, by Timothy D. Crowe. This book is the most widely used manual for CPTED at the present time in the United States.

The American Institute of Architects conducted the first national CPTED conference in December of 1993. The U.S. Conference of Mayors conducted a national CPTED conference in June of 1995 to report on the results of their nationwide survey of mayors. This survey documents the extent to which local governments have implemented CPTED concepts.

CPTED WORLDWIDE

Many of the concepts of CPTED are being practiced in countries throughout the world. It is interesting to note that the process in most cases is an evolution toward a simple model of CPTED that becomes integrated as part of a comprehensive planning process for crime control. It is impossible to describe all of these activities, let alone attempt to list them or identify all the individuals involved. Accordingly, the following is a sample of many of the outstanding activities that are presently being implemented.

Canadian provinces and cities have been very active in CPTED. In 1992, the city of Toronto published a manual for planners entitled *A Working Guide for Planning and Designing Safer Urban Environments*. The Peel Regional Police, in the suburbs of Toronto, have implemented CPTED in housing guidelines, school site plans, and in commercial and industrial site improvements. The city of Calgary, located in the province of Alberta, has used CPTED in downtown and transit improvements. Vancouver, British Columbia, has a formal CPTED program that has involved police and planning activities for many years.

The British Home Office conducted many demonstrations and evaluations in housing programs concurrently with the early efforts of the U.S. planners. Guidelines were developed for architectural liaison officers in the late 1987. The British Crime Prevention Center, in Stafford, has provided CPTED training to these officers since approximately 1980. A special instructor exchange program between the British Crime Prevention Center and the National Crime Prevention Institute, in Louisville, Kentucky, occurred between 1987 and 1990. Architect Barry Poyner published *Design Out Crime* in 1983 and engineer Graham Underhill published *Security of Buildings* in 1985. Dr. Ronald Clarke published *Situational Crime Prevention* in 1982. These books added to the wealth of research and developmental efforts that have been contributed by the British.

The Japanese Ministry of Justice has conducted CPTED research in housing and transportation. The privately funded Japanese Urban Security Research Institute has published a number of CPTED journal articles and conducted two major national symposia on CPTED. The first edition of this book, published in 1991, was republished in 1994 in a Japanese language translation. There is much interest in using CPTED concepts in the promotion of three-generation housing to increase territoriality and stability in neighborhoods.

A group of researchers in the Netherlands is actively involved in using CPTED to overcome high crime problems and poor quality of life issues in low-income housing and in small neighborhoods. The firm of Van Djk, von Soomeren and Partners located in Amsterdam has had considerable success in obtaining acceptance of CPTED in the community planning process.

The Australian Institute of Criminology has conducted numerous research projects involving CPTED. This organization produced a 1989 manual, entitled *Design Out Crime*. The city of Waverly published its CPTED planning guidelines. The planning committee for the 2000 Olympic Games in Sydney has adopted CPTED in planning for venues, housing, and transportation. The Transit Authority for New South Wales has conducted CPTED reviews of its stations and undergone a renovation program since 1995.

RESULTS OF CPTED

There are many case studies that demonstrate how the application of CPTED concepts have reduced the incidence of crime and fear of crime. Significant results have been produced in many places, including residential areas, convenient food stores, malls and shopping centers, transit stations, and parking structures. Journal and newspaper articles have reported on these successes.

Descriptive studies have reported on historical relationships between crime and the environment. The U.S. Department of Justice has published a number of bibliographies and documents about these observational studies. Small- to medium-size cities have also reported on considerable crime and fear reductions directly attributable to CPTED traffic management strategies.

The pertinent statistical results documenting the impact of CPTED are too numerous to list in this book, and any attempt to provide detailed case studies and research results would not only take up this whole volume but would duplicate many other published studies and annotated bibliographies. For example, the National Criminal Justice Reference Service in Rockville, Maryland, maintains an active database. Additionally, Internet sites provide access to public and private information sources worldwide. Finally, the historical basis of CPTED makes the success of the concepts self-evident.

Following is a sample of the many success stories that have resulted from the use of CPTED concepts:

- Convenience stores have used CPTED to increase sales and reduce losses from theft of up to 50% and from robberies of 65%.
- Malls in Sacramento and Knoxville have reduced incidents by 24% and noncrime calls to police by another 14% using CPTED parking management concepts; the largest mall in the world located in West Edmonton, Alberta, Canada, has used CPTED concepts with well-documented success; the Mall of America in Bloomington, Minnesota, used CPTED from the initial conceptual stage of design; the same or better results have been obtained by many other malls.
- Corporations, including Westinghouse, Mobil, Trinova, Macy's, Disney World, and Sam's/Pace, have reduced losses and improved productivity using CPTED strategies.
- Neighborhoods in Ft. Lauderdale, Tallahassee, Bridgeport, Knoxville, Jacksonville, Dayton, North Miami Beach, Calgary, Toronto, and many others have produced dramatic reductions in drug sales, burglaries, and general crime by 15–100%.

- Schools using CPTED throughout the world are reducing construction costs, lowering conduct and crime violations, and improving achievement and matriculation levels.
- Design research on office environments has determined that the lack of territorial identity in the office space contributes to lower morale, less productivity, and greater tolerance of dishonesty among fellow workers.
- Transportation authorities in Washington, D.C., Houston, Toronto, Sydney (Australia), and for the Canadian Pacific Railway and many others have produced cost savings and crime reductions using CPTED.
- Various levels of government in the United States, Canada, Japan, France, Germany, Australia, Turkey, United Kingdom, and many other countries have initiated CPTED programs; provincial and state governments have developed legislative requirements; many cities throughout the world have adopted ordinances or bylaws in which CPTED design review processes were established.

SCOPE AND CONTENT

The goals of this book on Crime Prevention Through Environmental Design (CPTED) are to alter and expand the reader's perception of the immediate physical environment. This, in turn, increases the capacity to understand the direct relationship of the environment to human behavior and to crime. An increase in this basic understanding should result in the greater likelihood of the individual's confidently questioning or challenging decisions that affect her immediate environment — particularly those that may have a direct bearing on the safety of the individual, her family, neighborhood, or place of business.

An understanding of the direct relationship of the design and management of the environment to human behavior is a prerequisite to increasing the success of efforts in crime prevention. It is the key to effective community organization because it gives the citizen the power to protect and control the physical environment and quality of life. CPTED is not the total answer to community problems, but it does provide the community with the means to eliminate or reduce environmental obstacles to social, cultural, or managerial control.

An understanding of the direct relationship of the design and use of the environment to human behavior is a prerequisite to increasing productivity and profit in the commercial and industrial sectors. Loss prevention and profit are linked. Loss prevention, as a concept, goes far beyond crime prevention and its focus upon legally defined criminal behavior.

The contents of this book largely represent my own observations and experiences. Most of the historical discussions are composed of generally accepted knowledge. A selected bibliography is included for the reader who seeks additional research support. As a practical guide to CPTED concepts, the book has been written in an open narrative style. It is intended to challenge many contemporary notions of security and loss prevention, and to stimulate a reassessment of contemporary space management and design concepts, with which it shares a variety of strategies that may be useful to the reader. The book contains many down-to-earth observations of the interaction between human behavior and their environment. It is the task of the reader to relate these examples and ideas to his own life experiences and observations and to determine their usefulness and application to the reader's vocation or professional activity.

2

Crime and Loss Prevention

INTRODUCTION

The challenge of crime to society changes with the advance of civilization, particularly as technology continues to improve. Advancing technology brings greater opportunity and human comforts. But it also introduces new opportunities and temptations for human greed.

In the preface to the original printing of *Oliver Twist*, Dickens described 19th-century criminals in London:

> I had read of thieves by scores — seductive fellows, amiable, fault-less in dress, plump in pocket, choice in horseflesh, bold, great at song and fit companions for the bravest...
>
> But I had never met with the miserable reality. It appeared to me that to draw a knot of associates in crime as they really do exist; to paint them in all their deformity, in all their wretchedness, in all the squalid poverty of their lives; to show them as they are...
>
> It appeared to me that to do this would be to attempt something which was greatly needed, and which would be a service to society.

Dickens wrote this defense in the preface to his book after intense public criticism for his audacity in openly describing criminal conditions in England. The so-called good society was shocked that Dickens would publicly describe the actual conditions of crime, but his work served to reinforce the notion that criminal behavior is limited solely to the lower classes of society.

Although Dickens's works forced the upper classes to acknowledge the existence of criminal conditions, this sentiment has prevailed into the 20th century. Societal and scientific concepts of crime are related to the antisocial behavior of bad people or career criminals. It is popular to associate criminal behavior with the poor physical and social conditions of the impoverished segments of our population. Social scientists persist in identifying the origins of criminal behavior with lack of opportunity and improper education.

Some attempts have been made to legitimize criminal behavior as the only means of existence for individuals who would otherwise be law-abiding citizens, if only they were given the chance in life that is enjoyed by the middle and upper classes. A small number of individuals, who are loosely associated with an ideology labeled radical criminology, believe that crime is caused by the military-industrial establishment through its denial of opportunity to all but the upper classes. The popular musical stage show and subsequent film *West Side Story* implanted this notion, at least in American society, by characterizing delinquent behavior as the product of a disadvantaged environment.

Unfortunately, much of the contemporary theory about criminal behavior and rehabilitation focuses on what may be a limited view of human behavior. The many diverse sociological, psychological, and biological theories of criminal behavior do not explain the known, but officially unacknowledged, realm of criminal behavior that relates to dishonesty, cheating, and breach of duty that may be pervasive in all societies, at all levels of class and social position. The problems of white collar crime, organized crime, insurance fraud, financial fraud, and evasion of duty (e.g., tax cheating) may actually be greater than ordinary crime, in terms of overall social, economic, and political effect.

Studies of individual honesty reveal the surprising fact that a great proportion of our society may be prone to dishonesty. Dr. W. Steve Albrecht of Brigham Young University's School of Business has conducted numerous studies of white-collar crime. In a recent film about the subject, *Red Flags*, Dr. Albrecht cites the results of studies of honesty among the general public that reveal the following:

- 30% of the public will steal or be dishonest on a regular basis.
- 30% of the public will steal or be dishonest depending on the situation (and risk).
- 40% of the public will never steal or be dishonest, regardless of the situation.

Where does the definition of criminal behavior start and stop? Should we continue to limit our concerns to the individuals who are responsible for the reported crime rate and those arrested for ordinary crimes? Is it desirable to uncover the true extent of criminal behavior and fraud in our society, and its impact upon our lives? Is it worth the risk?

CRIME

Crime is so common to human existence that it is taken for granted. That is, everyone knows what it is, so it needs no definition. But does the general public really know what crime is? Do legislative and governmental bodies know?

Few persons have a clear idea about the true nature and scope of crime and criminal behavior. The following definition of crime from *Webster's Ninth New Collegiate Dictionary* provides some insights into a broader understanding of the problem. Crime is "an act or commission of an act that is forbidden or the omission of a duty that is commanded by a public law and that makes the offender liable to punishment by that law." This definition provides a broad description of crime that includes behavior that is *prohibited*, as well as behavior or acts that are required by law.

What is the level and importance of crime to society? A special report by the United Nations summarized reported crime statistics from 64 nations between 1970 and 1975.

crimes against property	72%
crimes against persons	20%
crimes related to drugs	8%

These proportions come from a combined data base revealing a rate of crime for these countries that averaged 1,311.2 offenses per 100,000 persons. This international average is much lower than the approximate 5,000 offenses per 100,000 population in the United States of America. A separate study of reported world crime trends in James Q. Wilson's *Crime and Human Nature* presents a clear distinction between proportions of crime in developing countries versus developed countries. *Developing* countries experience a more even breakdown between crimes against persons (43%) and property (49%). *Developed* countries experience a higher proportion of crimes against property (82%) than crimes against persons (10%). However, drug-related crimes do not vary proportionally between developing and developed countries.

The crime figures for the United States do not provide a true picture of crime because unreported crime and minor crimes are not included in official reports. United States statistics on reported crime reveal a level of nearly 12 million serious crimes in 1988. These serious crimes are murder, rape, robbery, aggravated assault, burglary, larceny, theft, and motor vehicle theft. These crime levels do not include a wide range of minor offenses. However, a breakdown of the major crimes reveals that approximately 89% are crimes against property and 11% are crimes against persons.[1]

It is common for the general public and government officials to have a very limited understanding of the true nature and extent of crime, criminal behavior, fraud, dishonesty, and failure or neglect of duty. Most public policies are founded upon the basis of officially reported, major offenses, which to many experts are but the tip of the iceberg in regard to actual

---

[1] Federal Bureau of Investigation, *FBI Uniform Crime Reports*. Washington, DC: U.S. Department of Justice, 1988.

numbers of offenses and the losses they cause. Retail business operators have a much better idea about the impact of crime and dishonesty, particularly in terms of the impact upon the costs of consumer goods. But even the business person may not be aware of the magnitude of the effect of crime and dishonesty on business liability.

LEVELS OF CRIME

Many decisions about what to do about crime are based upon the levels of crimes or security incidents that are reported to authorities. Knowledge of offenders is limited to those persons who are caught and the offenses that they were either caught committing, or the ones that they are willing to divulge to authorities.

There are four levels of crime that must be considered in understanding the impact of crime in our communities and in making rational judgments about public responses.

1. *Reported crime* is measured by the FBI Uniform Crime Reports and by security incident reports. About 12 million major crimes are reported nationally each year. Twenty-one percent of these crimes are solved. Most are crimes against property, but they still produce fear of crime.

2. *Unreported crime* is measured by the National Crime Surveys. These surveys reveal that only 35% of all individual victimizations are reported to law enforcement agencies. The remainder are not reported for a number of reasons. These crimes include everything from the most minor offenses to the most serious. The results of this annual survey demonstrate that law enforcement's overall success rate is approximately 7% when the unreported crimes are added into the base.

3. *Unacknowledged crime* is another large category of crime that is committed against individuals and organizations. These crimes are measured, albeit poorly, by "shrinkage" data that is maintained in accounting and inventory control systems. The levels of loss are enormous. A commonly accepted level of shrinkage in property inventories is 10%. That is, about 10% of all products and goods disappear from inventories. Shoplifting and employee theft dominate these areas. The ratio of employee theft to shoplifting runs at 7:1 to 5:1 depending on the product line. Reported and unreported crime amount to about $37 billion annually. Unacknowledged crime costs the public another $100 to $200 billion.

4. *Undetected losses* are those that have yet to be discovered. Theft of time and illegal loans against insurance policies that are not authorized by insurees are examples of a nearly unlimited list of crimes. The losses in this category drive total loss levels in all four categories up to about $650 billion

annually. The impact on the American public is staggering. The net effect economically may be equal to at least 15% of the Gross National Product (GNP). Loss of confidence in business and government affects programs. These losses drive the cost of consumer products so high that they become unattainable (e.g., health insurance, auto insurance, consumer products).

Most individuals are aware of reported crime. Few are aware of the actual extended level of crime that includes unreported victimizations, as well as unacknowledged or undetected losses.

Victimization surveys in many countries reveal that many offenses are never reported, for a variety of reasons. Here are some general facts about the problem:

- Annual surveys in the United States indicate that only 35% of all victimizations are reported to police.
- The Firemen's Fund Insurance Company reported that one-third of all business failures in the United States are due to employee theft.
- The U.S. Chamber of Commerce found that 15% of the cost of consumer goods is due to employee theft.
- The same study (U.S. Chamber of Commerce) found that losses due to employee theft were five times higher than due to customer shoplifting.
- Dr. Steve Albrecht, of Brigham Young University in the United States, found in studies of honesty among the general public that 30% of the public will steal or be dishonest on a regular basis, another 30% will be dishonest depending upon the situation, and 40% will never steal or be dishonest, regardless of the situation.
- The U.S. Internal Revenue Service estimates annual losses of $100 billion dollars (U.S.) due to income tax cheating.
- The Hallcrest Report on private security in the United States estimates that "theft of time" costs U.S. industry nearly $125 billion dollars each year.
- Fraud and abuse of the insurance system account for a range of 10 to 20% of premiums paid throughout the world, which translates into an annual loss of $48 to $96 (U.S.) per person in Europe and $110 to $220 per person in the United States.

The cost of crime and dishonesty to business, especially to the retailer, has many direct and indirect effects. Direct losses may be measured in terms of "shrinkage" and apparent business decline. Indirect losses may be measured in terms of reduced productivity, increased overhead, employee absenteeism, and neglect-related capital costs for repair and replacement of equipment and buildings.

The costs of customer and employee victimization may be added on to the total. Positive community image and marketing opportunities suffer. Finally, declining business success reduces the local tax base, resulting in the further decline of public services and loss of confidence in government. Accordingly, business areas that begin to decline lose their "clean, well-lighted" image, producing a negative impression on potential business investors.

Admittedly, some of these shocking trends in crime losses and dishonesty may be unique to the U.S. culture. Nevertheless, it must be assumed that some level of unreported or undetected economic crime transcends all nations and societies. Some important conclusions may be drawn from these findings:

- Most crime statistics are limited to reported crimes without counting the higher levels of unreported, unacknowledged, or undetected crime.
- Public policy and public attitudes about crime, crime control, and criminal behavior continue to be limited to the popular notions about violent crimes and common offenses against property.
- The potential impact of true crime levels upon the economy and the quality of life may be much more negative than imagined.
- The continued acceptance of dishonesty and cheating among the general public and government serves only to legitimize this behavior for future generations, thus guaranteeing the continuing existence of public corruption, personal dishonesty, and high crime levels.
- Contemporary social, psychological, and biological theories of crime and criminal behavior do not explain the pervasiveness of economic crime throughout all levels of society and culture.

EXPLANATIONS OF CRIME

Criminologists have attempted for years to develop explanations of crime and delinquency. Theories have been created to explain the origin of criminal behavior. Other theories have been used to identify approaches to treatment or rehabilitation. None have proven successful in providing a comprehensive understanding of crime and delinquency. Accordingly, public policy has been guided by a succession of philosophies about the causes of crime.

Most of the philosophies may be organized and summarized around five categories: legal, social, psychological, biological, and political.

Legal theorists have argued for many years that the decision to commit crime is rational. That is, the offender weighs the circumstances and makes a decision to commit an offense based upon his or her perception of the amount to be gained versus the risk of punishment. This belief has its basis in the so-called pleasure-pain principle. Crime control under this model is oriented around certainty of punishment and making the punishment fit the crime.

Social theorists believe that criminal behavior is related to and is the result of social conditions. Criminologists and the criminal justice system have spent countless time and resources attempting to validate social explanations of crime. Many of these theories hover around some compelling arguments that social conditions, such as lack of opportunity, improper associations, and poor environmental conditions, cause people to commit crime. Social theories helped to bring about urban reform and contemporary public housing programs. The now defunct Model Cities and Planned Variations Programs were massive experiments in social engineering. Social theories seem to possess the greatest appeal as explanations of crime for public policymakers, although interest has waned with the failure of these programs.

Psychological theorists prefer to explain crime in individual terms, whereas the sociologist focuses on group dynamics and segments of the population. The psychologist searches for explanations associated with individual choices to commit crime or with mental pathologies that result in dysfunctional behavior. Learning theories have emanated from this area of research and hold some promise for treating and controlling certain behaviors.

Biological explanations of criminal behavior range from the bizarre to some that are scientifically valid. Nineteenth- and early twentieth-century researchers attempted to prove relationships between body types and criminal behavior. These included everything from degrees of musculature to the numbers and locations of "bumps" on the head. Some contemporary biological researchers have established relationships between chemical deficiencies and behavior. Others have demonstrated hereditary relationships between violent fathers and their offspring, hence offering somewhat scary support for what was thought to be the archaic belief in "bad blood."

Political theorists skip the behavioral explanations. They believe that crime and criminal behavior are natural societal reactions to oppressive capitalistic government. The so-called military-industrial establishment is at fault. These radical criminologists espouse a Marxist view that says that society is wasting its time attempting to treat criminal behavior. Anarchy and violent overthrow of the system are the preferred methods of crime prevention. Some other political theories are based in a belief that class or power conflict, the clash between the "haves" and "have nots," is the cause of criminal behavior.

Research findings are dismal, at least if one is looking for evidence to validate a pet theory. Some weak evidence still exists for a few social theories. Stronger evidence is available to support learning theories, which are subsumed under the psychological umbrella. Only rhetorical support exists for most of the political theories. Hundreds of years of experience with the legal theories that form the basis of our criminal justice system have not provided any answers to the causes of crime. However, it is clear from the research that although we know how to control behavior through legal restraints and supervision, we do not know how to treat misbehavior, or how to prevent what causes it in the first place.

Criminologists and public policymakers have failed to acknowledge and deal with this total level of criminal behavior and loss. Public policy continues to be based upon "common" crime that is committed by persons who, because of their environmental limitations, are confined largely to the lower socioeconomic segments of our population. Self-reporting studies and common knowledge reveal that criminal behavior occurs at all levels of society, possibly at the same rate. The only differences are the type of offenses and the payoff.

IMPLICATIONS FOR PUBLIC ACTION

First, it is clear that programs must be founded in fact. Information must be used to enhance cooperative efforts. Facts must replace unsubstantiated beliefs in determining program approaches. Second, popular theories of criminal behavior have to be viewed in terms of the failure of social, psychological, and biological theories to explain the broad range of criminal activity throughout all levels of our society. This means that what we do know has to be used, while we await further information from science. Supervision, control, interagency cooperation, and environmental management are known capabilities. Finally, the statistics about crime and victimization in public housing must be considered to be the tip of the iceberg in terms of a real understanding of the problem. This also means that the relationship between the developmental activities and the contiguous neighborhood has to be defined and taken into account in planning.

Uncontrolled criminal activity in public areas, especially housing, affects the quality of life in the project. It affects the perceptions and the subsequent development of attitudes and behavior of the children who grow up in these places. It affects the neighborhood. Can a healthy neighborhood absorb a public housing project and make it part of its social fabric? Can a project reach out to a troubled neighborhood and become the focal point for neighborhood development? These questions must and can be answered in a well-controlled and fundamentally CPTED neighborhood project.

Young people experience problems that go beyond traditional concepts of crime and victimization. Young people under 24 years account for about 51% of all arrests. Young people under the age of 18 account for 17% of all arrests and about 40% of all arrests for serious property crimes. Some more startling facts include:[2]

- Persons under age 18 are the most highly victimized segment of our population.

---

[2] National Crime Prevention Council. *Crime and Crime Prevention Statistics*. Washington, DC: U.S. Department of Justice, 1986.

- Persons under age 18 are the least likely segment of our population to report a criminal victimization.
- Persons under age 18 are seven times more likely to be victimized by another young person than by an adult.
- Suburban youth experience a school dropout rate of 25% and urban youth a dropout rate of 35%.
- Child molestation and abuse is immeasurable, but it is estimated that 1,100 children died as a result of neglect in 1986.
- Drug and alcohol use are common for elementary, middle, and high school students — 7% of 8th grade students used marijuana by grade 6; 62% of 8th grade students who reported having tried cocaine said that they tried it first in grade 7.
- High school seniors reported (1986) having used drugs in 57% of all interview responses.
- Thirty-five percent of all boys age 0–18 will be arrested at least once; 18–21% of these young men will become career offenders.[3]

Young people under age 18 represent only 27% of the American population. Yet this same age group is commonly more than 50% of the population of public housing projects. Habitual offender programs have estimated that a disproportionate number (per capita) of officially identified habitual juvenile offenders reside in public housing, in contrast to other housing forms.

CONTEMPORARY CRIME PREVENTION AND INTERAGENCY CONCEPTS

There has been a proliferation of crime prevention, delinquency control, and community organization projects and programs that have been pushed and sold throughout the past 30 years. Many of these programs were based on a number of compelling social theories that did not pan out in the implementation stage. Accordingly, local units of government, criminal justice agencies, and public housing authorities are worn out with many of the tried and failed program approaches and philosophies.

Fortunately, two areas of crime prevention and control have continued to surface positively in evaluations and in common experience. These are interagency program approaches and Crime Prevention Through Environmental Design (CPTED). This does not mean that other programs have not been successful, but that these two areas present greater opportunities for success than others.

---

[3] Wolfgang, Marvin E. "Delinquency in Two Birth Cohorts." *American Behavioral Scientist*, 1983, 37(1), 75–86.

Moreover, these concepts provide an organizational and environmental basis for the use of other, more socially oriented programs, giving them a better chance of successful implementation.

There is a growing belief among mental health and youth development professionals that young persons who grow up in large, undifferentiated environments fail to learn respect for property and property values. It is believed that these children will have greater difficulties in controlling their behavior as they mature. Likewise, children who grow up in large undifferentiated environments, with little or sporadic supervision and control, will also experience more difficulties. The CPTED emphasis on promoting territorial behavior and natural approaches to behavioral control fit well into these emerging child development concepts. The emphasis on interagency cooperation and collaboration enhances these strategies.

CRIMINAL JUSTICE — A MISPERCEIVED CONCEPT

Many persons in the public and private sectors have a limited viewpoint of law enforcement and security operations. A highly placed official in a major oil company recently told me that he thought the security people were there to screen employees and provide protection against terrorist attacks. Many criminologists, criminal justice practitioners, and security administrators suffer from the same delusion.

"Catching thieves" is the most visible and popular role for law enforcement and security operations. Crime fighting is synonymous with images of the "hound dog detective" who always gets his man. McGruff "taking a bite outa crime" is a symbolic reference to the traditional watchdog who catches crooks by the seat of their pants. Catching "bad guys" seems to be the focal point of most law enforcement and security programs, yet it is the one thing that we fail to do most of the time!

There is clearly a misplaced emphasis upon apprehension. In practice, we solve only about 20% of all serious crimes.[4] The National Crime Surveys have found that only about 38% of all victimizations are reported to authorities. Children are victimized more often than any other age group. Habitual juvenile offenders account for a disproportionate share of all crime committed by young people. We know all of this, but it doesn't seem to have much impact on our overall public policies and priorities.

NCPI's definition of crime prevention provides some insight into a new focal point for law enforcement and security programs. "The anticipation, recognition, and appraisal of a crime risk, and the initiation of some action to remove or to reduce it" may seem to be an awkward way of saying it, but it says to me, "If it ain't apprehension, it's gotta be crime prevention."

---

[4] Federal Bureau of Investigation. *FBI Uniform Crime Reports.* Washington, DC: U.S. Department of Justice.

The crime-related aspects of law enforcement and security include at least six major functions. It is useful to examine each element individually to see how it relates to crime prevention.

1.   *Crime prevention* in this limited context is that process of eliminating or reducing the opportunity to commit an offense, or the denial of access to crime targets.

2.   *Detection* is the critical process of monitoring the activities and functions of the community to gather intelligence about the activities and associations of known offenders, and to identify and discover criminal activity that would have gone unnoticed. This process is fundamental to crime prevention and crime control. You can't prevent it if you don't know about it!

3.   *Suppression* is the act or method of restraining or controlling the activities of would-be or known offenders. A simple example of suppression is the monitoring and intense supervision of habitual juvenile offenders. Another example is the practice of active warrant service, particularly for repeat adult offenders. The objective of these community control strategies is to prevent crime.

4.   *Investigation* is the follow-up procedure for examining a criminal incident with the objective of solving the crime and resolving the problem. Contemporary case management systems are limited to solving the crime and arresting the offender, instead of the traditional practice of following up on an offense to resolve the situation, prevent it from happening again, or to bring the offender to justice. Contemporary case management systems focus upon solvability factors that are valid for no more than the 20% of all serious crimes that are solved, thus overlooking effective case resolution for the 80% of the crimes that will not be solved. Case resolution and victim follow-up are good crime prevention.

5.   *Apprehension* is the first step in the application of legal sanctions to accused offenders. Traditional police values called for the use of prevention and suppression of crime, using the arrest and prosecutive process only where punishment was required. That is, apprehension and prosecution were traditionally viewed as a final resort when other methods of crime control failed, not the primary solution.

6.   *Prosecution* is the official presentation of fact to the court with the intent of denying an individual's basic right of freedom because of criminal activity. The courts are used where other social controls fail. Crime prevention can be enhanced by providing special support for the prosecution of habitual offenders, who have proven themselves to be career offenders. Offenders do not have to be locked up to be incapacitated. All that has to be done is to effectively control them, either through close supervision or residential treatment programs. The effective control of repeat offenders is good crime prevention. Prosecution programs can assist in crime prevention.

Crime prevention may now be perceived as something that special unit people do to divert the public from the basic ineffectiveness of law enforcement and security programs. As long as this continues, crime prevention will still be relegated to a gadget orientation.

An objective study of any law enforcement or security operation will reveal that the primary requirement for crime-related services is prevention, in its broadest sense. Each of us must ask the following three questions before we continue in our present activities, or allow our organizations to proceed within the limited understanding of the role of crime prevention:

1.   What is the requirement for our services?
2.   How do we spend our time and resources?
3.   What are the results?

Crime prevention and security personnel can help their organizations develop department-wide crime prevention programs. These may include the integration of covert intelligence gathering activities aimed at property crime with a joint public and private information sharing and suppression effort. Expanded case management systems designed for 100% follow-up using a range of resolution methods may be initiated along with improved patrol productivity programs such as Directed Patrol. Interagency programs may be developed which increase the monitoring and supervision of troubled, problem, and delinquent youth. In essence, crime prevention needs to become more visible and assertive and accept its integral role in the functions of prevention, detection, suppression, investigation, apprehension, and prosecution.

PRODUCTIVITY FOR THE CRIME AND LOSS PREVENTION SPECIALIST

Do you, as a loss prevention or crime prevention specialist, desire to expand or improve your program? Do you wish that the rest of your organization would take your program seriously? Do you feel, at times, that what you are doing is "pyramiding?" That is, does it seem that the harder you work, the more work there is? If your answer is yes to these questions, then you are probably suffering from an acute case of "special-unit-itis." Some symptoms of this malady are:

- feeling like a mushroom, being kept in the dark and fed "organizational waste"
- feeling like when everything else fails, they give it to you to fix
- representing the organization when it's clear the audience is going to shoot the messenger

- feeling that everyone in your organization is either brain-dead or conspiring to screw up anything that relates to your job, so that you will have to take it over to make sure that it is done well
- laboring under the assumption that your devotion to carrying the organization will lead to an improved life as a consultant or "icon" of crime prevention in the year 2000

Do you recognize these symptoms? If so, then you are probably terminally ill with the admirable but quixotic trait of being a professional crime prevention/loss prevention officer. Bless you, your reward will come in the end!

The crime prevention/loss prevention field is faced with the need to move past the developmental years of establishing the technology of our profession to the integration of prevention concepts into how we run our organizations and communities.

As a full-time police intern in 1968 I had the unique opportunity to experience firsthand a number of major shifts in public and law enforcement technology. The need to control the actions of personnel resulted in the practice of having special units or functions run interference while the rest of the department remained at the station. This worked so well that many chiefs and sheriffs embraced it through the late sixties and early seventies. Unfortunately, it diverted attention away from the growing lack of productivity of the bulk of the organization — the operations division. It was simply easier to manage special units for special problems than it was to achieve compliance behavior or improved performance from the rest of the organization.

The public and private sectors have suffered from this shift in organizational thinking. Stringent security procedures impede private sector productivity and labor relations. High-volume, hands-on service in the public sector are still being delivered by specialists who are outnumbered 7 to 1 by operations personnel. Specialists achieve productivity levels of 85–92%, while operations personnel function at 10–40%. Yet a time and task analysis reveals that crime prevention services are pervasive. That is, the potential volume is such that only the operations division of a law enforcement agency, or the worker division of a company, can actually deliver crime prevention/loss prevention services.

There is nothing wrong with the specialist functions. The absurd debate in the early seventies about generalist versus specialist functions missed the point that both are required. However, the specialist functions need to manage and coordinate services, rather than deliver them. The concept and role definition of program management has emerged from the realization that humans will take the path of least resistance. As long as a special unit is ready and willing to take on a problem, then why bother! It is easy to repress personal responsibility by reinforcing the escape route of "hold the scene and wait for the smart guys." The adoption of a program management system will help to eliminate, or lessen, the effects of the special unit versus operations conflict.

The special unit style of management usually undergoes four phases:

1. A unit or assignment is created to respond to a problem or a public policy decision. The staff members are hand-picked and quickly develop their program. High connections and considerable influence are enjoyed.
2. The normal turnover, promotion or burnout of staff results in the assignment of persons who are less controversial or charismatic. This is done to bring the unit into line and heal some internal difficulties.
3. Cutback management forces the reduction of resources in all special units and peripheral programs. Token positions are retained and unit responsibility is curtailed, usually under the guise of reorganization.
4. The unit or function disappears quietly, after a key staff member retires or resigns.

Contemporary administrators must develop a more functional viewpoint of the organization. City or market-wide service needs demand organizational approaches that produce volume. The source of major productivity potential has to be where the greatest investment in resources is placed. Finally, the competence of the organization is the major factor in developing citizen satisfaction and consumer support.

Consider the following example. Twelve crime prevention officers are going to try to conduct surveys of 180,000 households so that the homeowners may receive a discount on their insurance. How long will it take? Each officer will have to survey 15,000 homes. At a normal pace, the job will be complete in 10 to 15 years. What do you think the city manager will have to say about this? How long would it take the patrol division, even though they would be limited to uncommitted time? Clearly, the key to productivity is to match resources with demand. Thus, the program management role of the special unit becomes paramount.

Program management may be defined as an approach to improved organizational effectiveness that identifies the importance of fixing responsibility for coordinating each major activity at a single point. These activities are either top priorities of the organization, or are, most often, requirements for service that cross-cut unit lines. The concept behind program management is that the major functions or service need areas are identified formally as programs. Special units or individuals may then be assigned to plan, manage, and monitor the organization's performance in carrying out the goals and objectives of the program area.

The mission of a special unit changes significantly when it assumes a program management function. Time has to be allocated properly among the following functions:

- planning, managing, and monitoring the program
- delivering the highly complex or unique services that require specialist attention
- conducting internal and external liaison and problem solving services

The temptation to take on large caseloads must be avoided. Clear guidelines and procedures must be developed for assuring that work is distributed properly according to the volume and substantive requirements of the program. The program management unit has to be perceived by line personnel in a collaborative role, instead of evaluative. Experience has shown that clear goals, objectives, and performance reporting are the keys to the successful implementation of program management.

Even a person whose position in the organization is not very powerful can try some or all of these strategies:

- Develop a long-term program plan for crime/loss prevention.
- Conduct an analysis of present productivity levels of your operations personnel and identify alternatives that will save or recover time.
- Present a comparative analysis of the value of a new program that increases and improves crime/loss prevention services versus the existing approaches.
- Find an alter ego in your organization and enlist this person's support.
- Change the way you do business personally. Stop trying to carry the whole load.
- Practice delayed gratification: each day do something for the future of your program, instead of working in one more speech.

It is the contention of the author that the crime and loss prevention specialist should promote his role in the CPTED process. Participation in the local or organizational review process of the design and use of the environment we build may lead to greater productivity and reduced losses. It will definitely bring the mushroom out of the dark and help to redefine crime and loss prevention as a program management function rather than a technical services specialty.

CRIME VERSUS LOSS PREVENTION

The use of the terms *crime* and *loss prevention* seem redundant to many people. Criminologists and criminal justice specialists do not perceive the difference between the concepts of crime prevention and loss prevention. The general public probably does not distinguish between these terms either. Moreover, there is considerable controversy among social scientists and criminologists about the definition of crime prevention.

Some criminologists have attempted to develop classifications of definitions of crime prevention. The following are common descriptions that differentiate approaches to crime prevention:

1. Punitive approaches are based upon legal assumptions that crime may be controlled or prevented through punishment that fits the crime. The theory is that criminals will not commit a crime if they will receive one more unit of pain than the amount of pleasure or value derived from a criminal act. This concept depends upon the creation of a system where it is apparent that a criminal will be apprehended and punished for committing a crime. This is a classical criminal justice model that relies upon the perception that an offense will be detected and punishment will be swift.

2. Mechanical approaches are defined as measures that are taken to deny the opportunity for an offender to commit a crime. These methods depend on the denial of access to vulnerable properties or individuals. They also include the use of natural strategies to increase the perception of surveillance and access control, to ward off the potential offender.

3. Corrective approaches are aimed at eliminating the motives for committing crime. These concepts are usually associated with focusing attention on the so-called social, economic, and political causes of crime. It has always been socially desirable to advocate attention to the root causes of crime.

Other criminologists have reversed the order of these typologies of crime prevention by referring to primary, secondary, and tertiary approaches. Primary approaches are concerned with creating barriers or obstacles to criminal activities (i.e., mechanical). Secondary approaches emphasize the implementation of a criminal justice and crime control system that guarantees the likelihood of detection, apprehension and punishment (i.e., punitive). Tertiary approaches focus on dealing with the cause of criminal behavior and the treatment or rehabilitation of offenders (i.e., corrective).

It is clear from both of these approaches to defining crime prevention that the corrective and the related tertiary approaches are the most socially desirable. But time has run out on attempts to control and successfully treat criminal behavior. Many of the theories relating to causes of crime and treatment have failed to explain the wide range of criminal behavior and dishonesty that occurs in our communities and within our institutions.

The National Crime Prevention Institute has adopted the following definition of crime prevention: "Crime prevention is the anticipation, recognition and appraisal of a crime risk and the initiation of some action to remove or reduce it (the risk)." This may seem to be an awkward definition. It may even seem to be limited to the primary or mechanical approaches, which may not seem to be socially desirable. After all, these approaches seem to deal only with creating barriers to criminal activity, without addressing the root causes. Yet this definition acknowledges the uneven and incomplete understanding of the causes of criminal behavior, the knowledge that crime and dishonesty is pervasive throughout all socio-economic levels and that people are motivated by a hierarchy of needs that starts with individual security.

Many people believe that the real priority is to deal with the popular root causes of crime, the so-called social, economic, and political causes. Block clubs and community organization approaches have been criticized by some as means of adult repression of young people. Self-help (e.g., personal safety practices and the use of locks and residential alarm systems) has been stigmatized by evaluators as dealing with the symptoms, but not with the causes. This criticism fails to take into account the self-centered nature of human behavior. Behavior change starts with the individual, then moves to the near group, before it emerges as a collective societal reaction. It is difficult to conceive of getting the citizens of a community, or the employees of an organization, to devote their attention to global change, or to demanding broad social, economic, and political metamorphosis until they progress through a continuum of steps ranging from self to family to neighborhood to community.

A person is not going to worry about changing the attitude of "city hall" until he feels safe in moving from his home to his automobile, or source of transportation to work. A person is not going to worry about the economic status of the world until he feels secure in paying the rent and covering the basic costs of sending his kids to school. A person is not going to be anxious about the neighborhood until he knows that the house is safe and the immediate neighbors are trustworthy.

A basic principal of medical treatment is to control and stabilize a situation before attempting treatment. It is basic to emergencies that the situation must be controlled before it may be resolved. An offender must be placed under the control of society, before he may be rehabilitated. Even an automobile that is in disrepair must be diagnosed before repairs may be accomplished. It is clear that steps may not be skipped in dealing with human activities. The world will not change until people change, and then set about changing their community, once their hierarchy of needs is met.

It is self-evident that most people will not be able to effect global change, especially when and until we can protect ourselves and our property. Accordingly, it makes the most sense to focus on the punitive and mechanical approaches to controlling crime, while we continue to support the corrective or tertiary approaches to finding solutions to the causes of criminal behavior and its treatment. Control of behavior must precede its treatment in any case.

Loss prevention is broader than crime prevention because it includes a wider range of behavior than that which is defined legally as criminal. Loss may be defined as the removal or taking of an object or asset of value. Loss may be due to crime, poor productivity, incompetence, inefficiency, and lack of management attention. Loss may result from poor employee morale or lack of motivation to complete a work task or to use resources properly. The loss of value may be financially measured, or it may be assessed in emotional terms. The improper use and management of talent may also become a loss category. Loss occurs on a broader scale through natural causes, such as storms or earthquakes.

Loss and loss prevention are related directly to the achievement of human functions and objectives. This concept is more important to the practical use of CPTED methods than to dealing merely with losses due to criminal behavior. There is a fine line that separates pure criminal behavior from the proper care of and responsibility for the expenditure and use of resources.

NCPI recasts its definition of crime prevention into the following one for loss prevention: "Loss prevention is the anticipation, recognition and appraisal of a risk of loss, and the initiation of some action to reduce it (the loss)." The old adage "if it ain't broke, don't fix it," is totally irrelevant to crime and loss prevention. The cost of prevention, although sometimes higher than the loss itself, is legitimate because of the secondary and tertiary costs. It is better to prevent the opportunity for employees to steal, than it is to arrest employees. It is preferable to prevent a loss or a crime from occurring than to handle it after the fact. Crime and loss result in higher costs for goods and services. They result in inconvenience and, at times, the removal of a valued or needed service. The pain, suffering, and denial that result from reactions to loss affect everyone. Medical bills are higher. Unnecessary and painful medical procedures result from doctors who are hesitant to incur liability because of the abuse of the insurance system and the related decisions of the courts and juries, which often set unconscionable settlements of claims.

Crime, and especially loss prevention, depends upon the concept of risk management. Most individuals and organizations encounter two types of risk—pure and dynamic. Pure risk is the potential for loss of value, with no possibility of gain. The risk is total. Dynamic risk is more like gambling, in that one is willing to chance the loss of money or resources for a potential profit or gain. A purchaser of a lottery ticket is willing to lose the cost of the ticket price, in exchange for the potential winning value. A store owner risks the cost of rent, salaries of employees, and the purchase of goods to make a profit. A police department attempts to project or predict areas where it will get the most value out of the investment of officer time. The acknowledgment of risk and the management of risk is inherent to management of resources. The most successful managers assume that risk management is a primary element of success. Poor managers assume that risk is a threat to survival. Unfortunately, many of these poor managers continue to thrive in bureaucracies.

RISK MANAGEMENT

Risk management involves five major functions: risk avoidance, risk reduction, risk spreading, risk transfer, and risk retention.

Risk avoidance is the process of limiting or eliminating opportunities for loss. This is accomplished by reducing the number of activities or exposures to loss. It is also accomplished by the complete alteration or cessation of human activities and functions which are vulnerable to risk. This is a negative approach that is justified only through cost-benefit analysis that indicates a greater potential loss than gain through the continuance of an activity.

Risk reduction occurs through what is referred to commonly as procedural security. Loss possibilities are offset through dramatic alterations of the process of accounting for or controlling human functions. Checks and balances are implemented to increase the likelihood of exposure or to reduce the opportunity for someone to steal or to break the law.

Risk spreading is the diversion of resources and assets for the purpose of lowering loss exposure. Distance, location and time are used to create the spreading of assets. Barriers are also included in this concept of risk management. Security engineering and physical security approaches are inherent in the spreading and denial of access.

Risk transfer is the fundamental aspect of insurance. A large group of individuals share a common risk, such as a property or casualty loss. Health insurance is a direct form of risk transfer.

Risk retention is the conscious acceptance of the potential for loss. Potential losses are not covered necessarily by insurance, nor by other means of security. The owner or individual simply assumes the possibility of a loss.

Risk management is inherent in the operation of any business. It is also inherent in the operation of a community or neighborhood. Without acknowledging it, most people assume the risk of criminal victimization. But they are less likely to continue to assume that risk once they have been victimized. Fear and concern about crime usually relates to a part of one's community that is distant, a place where the person is not likely to go. Avoidance behavior ensues, thus perpetuating the perception that a place is unsafe.

CONCLUSIONS

Criminologists and public policymakers have perpetuated a limited definition and understanding of crime and criminal behavior. Many myths about the causes of crime exist because they are socially desirable. However, criminal behavior is pervasive throughout all levels of society, although it is popular to focus upon common crime and common criminals.

The concept of loss adds to the magnitude of crime and criminal behavior. It also adds to the reality that conventional reactive approaches to crime and loss are failing. CPTED concepts integrate productivity and profit with security and loss prevention. Profit to a neighborhood is quality of life. A happy neighborhood does not tolerate, nor experience, crime and loss problems. A well-run business has fewer losses. A good school has higher achievement levels and a lower incidence of disruptive behavior and criminal incidents. A downtown or shopping center that is successful in attracting customers makes greater profits and has fewer losses.

Attention to crime and loss prevention will produce payoffs. Crime and loss prevention are inherent to human functions and activities, not just something that police or security people do.

3

CPTED Concepts and Strategies

BACKGROUND

Do you know that the signaling of the traffic light at the end of your block, or just down the street from your intersection, has a lot to do with the amount of control you and your friends have over your neighborhood? Are you concerned with the scheduling of park programs for youth and the locations of these activities? Were you aware of the fact that the placement of bus stops can help to make or break the businesses nearby, thus contributing to the perception that an area is unstable or unsafe? Everyone knows that zoning and business regulation contribute to a more controlled and safe community, but do they know that the size, shape, landscaping, and exterior design of local buildings have an impact, too? The design and management of parking lots, storefronts, parks, schools, and just about everything in your community have important connections to the problems of crime and the fear of crime.

What can you do about it? Does it take a lot of expertise to understand the relationship between the environment, the roles of noncriminal justice agencies, and crime? The answers to these questions are simple. All it takes is an awareness that there is a relationship between the things that people do naturally—just everyday things—and the amount of surveillance and access control that exists. Both offenders and normal users of space recognize the environmental cues that say, "This is a safe place—or an unsafe place." A lot of experts and sophisticated technology are not required to think about what is going on and to take advantage of natural opportunities to make your community safer. All that is required is good sense.

Environmental approaches to crime prevention and security were made popular by Oscar Newman in his book *Defensible Space*. These concepts have been successfully demonstrated in schools, commercial, residential, and transportation areas. They are now being widely adopted by industry because they contribute to productivity. City governments are finding out that it is a lot less expensive to design crime prevention into the way things are done than to hire extra police, or to pay for extra protection that can make the community look like a fortress instead of a nice place to live.

For several thousand years, an awareness of how the environment shapes human behavior has been used by architects, city planners, and residential dwellers to elicit desired behaviors. Greek temples in the large Sicilian colony were designed to produce fear through the absence of light. Early city-states, such as Florence, designed assembly chambers to create the impression that the roof would cave in, literally, to speed up the legislative process. Modern-day commercial establishments use sound, color, and furniture design to create the illusion of fast service (if not the reality). McDonald's restaurants and even eyeglass stores are using their physical environments to manipulate senses and behavior to enhance their sales.

At the national level, the CPTED Program is a synthesis and extension of reports, investigations, studies, and initial demonstrations sponsored by the National Institute of Law Enforcement and Criminal Justice (NILECJ). In turn, many of those activities trace their conceptual content to a variety of NILECJ-sponsored crime prevention and environmental design-related documents, texts, and articles that date back many years. The most significant antecedents of the CPTED Program, dating from 1969, related to the following areas:

- *Studies.* Crimes against small business, neighborhood design techniques for crime prevention, burglary prevention studies, public safety in urban dwellings, architectural design for crime prevention, private police, public housing, patterns of robbery and burglary, street lighting, hardware performance and standards, and "defensible space."
- *Programs.* The Federal Crime Insurance Program, development of Model Security Codes and Guidelines, equipment standards program, vertical policing programs in public housing, architectural design experiments in public housing and residential areas, and training in crime prevention.

These prior efforts led NILECJ to initiate the CPTED program as a comprehensive effort to create physical and social conditions through environmental design demonstrations in selected environments (residential, school, commercial, transportation) aimed at reducing crime and fear of crime and at improving the quality of life in these environments.

A selected bibliography, sources of information, and related research are found at the end of this volume.

CPTED CONCEPTS

The conceptual thrust of the CPTED program is that the physical environment can be manipulated to produce behavioral effects that will reduce the incidence and fear of crime, thereby improving the quality of life. These behavioral effects can be accomplished by reducing the propensity of the physical environment to support criminal behavior.

Environmental design, as used in the CPTED program, is rooted in the design of the human/environment relationship. It embodies several concepts. The term *environment* includes the people and their physical and social surroundings. However, as a matter of practical necessity, the environment defined for demonstration purposes is that which has recognizable territorial and system limits. The term *design* includes physical, social, management, and law enforcement directives that seek to affect positively human behavior as people interact with their environment. Thus, the CPTED program seeks to prevent certain specified crimes (and the fear attendant on them) within a specifically defined environment by manipulating variables that are closely related to the environment itself. The program does not purport to develop crime prevention solutions in a broad universe of human behavior but rather solutions limited to variables that can be manipulated and evaluated in the specified human/environment relationship.

CPTED involves design of physical space in the context of the needs of bona fida users of the space (physical, social, and psychological needs), the normal and expected (or intended) use of the space (the activity or absence of activity planned for the space), and the predictable behavior of both bona fide users and offenders. Therefore, in the CPTED approach, a design is proper if it recognizes the designated use of the space, defines the crime problem incidental to and the solution compatible with the designated use, and incorporates the crime prevention strategies that enhance (or at least do not impair) the effective use of the space. CPTED draws not only on physical and urban design but also on contemporary thinking in behavioral and social science, law enforcement, and community organization.

The emphasis on design and use deviates from the traditional target-hardening approach to crime prevention. Traditional target-hardening focuses predominantly on denying access to a crime target through physical or artificial barrier techniques (such as locks, alarms, fences, and gates). Target-hardening often leads to constraints on use, access, and enjoyment of the hardened environment. Moreover, the traditional approach tends to overlook opportunities for natural access control and surveillance. The term *natural* refers to deriving access control and surveillance results as a byproduct of the normal and routine use of the environment. It is possible to adapt normal and natural uses of the environment to accomplish the effects of artificial or mechanical hardening and surveillance. Nevertheless, CPTED employs pure target-hardening strategies, either to test their effectiveness as compared to natural strategies or when they appear to be justified as not unduly impairing the effective use of the environment.

As an example, a design strategy of improved street lighting must be planned and evaluated in terms of the behavior it promotes or deters and the use impact of the lighted (and related) areas in terms of all users of the area (offenders, victims, other permanent or casual users). Any strategies related to the lighting strategy (e.g., block-watch, 911 emergency service, police patrol) must be evaluated in the same regard. This reflects the comprehensiveness of the CPTED design approach in focusing on both the proper design and effective use of the physical environment. Additionally, the concept of proper design and effective use emphasizes the designed relationship among strategies to ensure that the desired results are achieved. It has been observed that improved street lighting alone (a design strategy) is ineffective against crime without the conscious and active support of citizens (in reporting what they see) and of police (in responding and conducting surveillance). CPTED involves the effort to integrate design, citizen and community action, and law enforcement strategies to accomplish surveillance consistent with the design and use of the environment.

CPTED STRATEGIES

There are three overlapping strategies in CPTED:

1.   Natural access control
2.   Natural surveillance
3.   Territorial reinforcement

Access control and surveillance have been the primary design concepts of physical design programs. At the outset of the CPTED program, access control and surveillance — preexisting as conspicuous concepts in the field of crime prevention through environmental design — received major attention. Access control and surveillance are not mutually exclusive classifications since certain strategies achieve both, and strategies in one classification typically are mutually supportive of the other. However, the operational thrust of each is distinctly different, and the differences must be recognized in performing analysis, research, design, implementation, and evaluation.

Access control is a design concept directed primarily at decreasing crime opportunity. Access control strategies are typically classified as organized (e.g., guards), mechanical (e.g., locks), and natural (e.g., spatial definition). The primary thrust of an access control strategy is to deny access to a crime target and to create a perception of risk in offenders. Surveillance is a design concept directed primarily at keeping intruders under observation. Therefore, the primary thrust of a surveillance strategy is to facilitate observation, although it may have the effect of an access control strategy by effectively keeping intruders out because of an increased perception of risk. Surveillance strategies are typically classified as organized (e.g., police

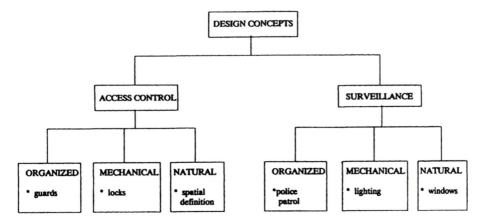

Figure 3-1:   Typical access control and surveillance concepts and classifications.

patrol), mechanical (e.g., lighting), and natural (e.g., windows). These typical concepts and strategies are illustrated in Figure 3-1.

Traditionally, access control and surveillance, as design concepts, have emphasized mechanical or organized crime prevention techniques while overlooking, minimizing, or ignoring attitudes, motivation, and use of the physical environment. More recent approaches to physical design of environments have shifted the emphasis to natural crime prevention techniques, attempting to use natural opportunities presented by the environment for crime prevention. This shift in emphasis led to the concept of territoriality.

The concept of territoriality (elaborated most fully to date in the public housing environment) suggests that physical design can contribute to a sense of territoriality. That is, physical design can create or extend a sphere of influence so that users develop a sense of proprietorship—a sense of territorial influence—and potential offenders perceive that territorial influence. At the same time, it was recognized that natural access control and surveillance contributed to a sense of territoriality, making it effective for crime prevention. Natural access control and surveillance will promote more responsiveness by users in protecting their territory (e.g., more security awareness, reporting, reacting) and promote greater perception of risk by offenders.

Further, the effort to achieve a balance between design for crime prevention and design for effective use of environments contributed to the shift in focus from organized and mechanical strategies per se to natural strategies. This was because natural strategies exploited the opportunities of the given environment both to naturally and routinely facilitate access control and surveillance, and to reinforce positive behavior in the use of the environment. The concept reflects a preference, where feasible, to reinforce existing or new activities, or to otherwise reinforce the behavior of environment users so that crime prevention flows naturally and routinely from the activity being promoted.

The conceptual shift from organized and mechanical to natural strategies has oriented the CPTED program to develop plans that emphasize natural access control and surveillance and territorial reinforcement. The conceptual relationship suggested by this shift is reflected in Figure 3-2.

Although conceptually distinct, it is important to realize that these strategy categories tend to overlap in practice. It is perhaps most useful to think of territorial reinforcement as the umbrella concept, comprising all natural surveillance principles, which in turn comprises all access control principles. It is not practical to think of territorial reinforcement, natural surveillance, and access control as independent strategies because, for example, access control operates to denote transitional zones, not necessarily impenetrable barriers. If these symbolic or psychological barriers are to succeed in controlling access by demarcating specific spaces for specific individuals, potential offenders must perceive that unwarranted intrusion will elicit protective territorial responses from those who have legitimate access.

Similarly, natural surveillance operates to increase the likelihood that intrusion will be observed by individuals who care but are not officially responsible for regulating the use and treatment of spaces. If people observe inappropriate behavior but do nothing about it, then the most carefully planned natural surveillance tactics are useless in terms of stopping crime and vandalism.

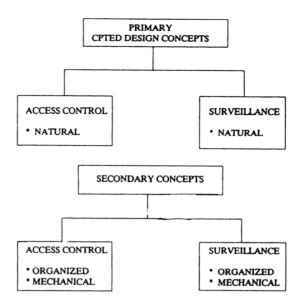

Figure 3-2:   The conceptual shift from organized and mechanical concepts has led to the natural CPTED concepts.

THE THREE-D APPROACH

For CPTED to be a success, it must be understandable and practical for the normal users of the space. That is, the normal residents of a neighborhood and the people who work in buildings or commercial areas must be able to use these concepts. Why? Because these people know more about what is going on in that environment and they have a vested interest (their own well-being) in ensuring that their immediate environment operates properly. The technologist or specialist, who may be a traffic engineer, city planner, architect, or security specialist, should not be allowed to shoulder the responsibility alone for safety and security. The specialist needs to follow the dictates of the users of the space, because he can often be swayed by misperceptions or by the conflicting demands of his professional competition.

The Three-D approach to space assessment provides a simple guide for the layperson to use in determining the appropriateness of how her space is designed and used. The Three-D concept is based on the three functions or dimensions of human space:

1. All human space has some designated purpose.
2. All human space has social, cultural, legal, or physical definitions that prescribe the desired and acceptable behaviors.
3. All human space is designed to support and control the desired behaviors.

By using the Three-Ds as a guide, space may be evaluated by asking the following types of questions:

Designation

- What is the designated purpose of this space?
- What was it originally intended to be used for?
- How well does the space support its current use? Its intended use?
- Is there conflict?

Definition

- How is the space defined?
- Is it clear who owns it?
- Where are its borders?
- Are there social or cultural definitions that affect how that space is used?
- Are the legal or administrative rules clearly set out and reinforced in policy?

- Are there signs?
- Is there conflict or confusion between the designated purpose and definition?

Design

- How well does the physical design support the intended function?
- How well does the physical design support the definition of the desired or accepted behaviors?
- Does the physical design conflict with or impede the productive use of the space or the proper functioning of the intended human activity?
- Is there confusion or conflict in the manner in which the physical design is intended to control behavior?

The three CPTED strategies of territorial reinforcement, natural access control, and natural surveillance are inherent in the Three-D concept. Does the space clearly belong to someone or some group? Is the intended use clearly defined? Does the physical design match the intended use? Does the design provide the means for normal users to naturally control the activities, to control access, and to provide surveillance?

Once a basic self-assessment has been conducted, the Three-Ds may then be turned around as a simple means of guiding decisions about what to do with human space. The proper functions have to be matched with space that can support them — with space that can effectively support territorial identity, natural access control and surveillance and intended behaviors have to be indisputable and be reinforced in social, cultural, legal, and administrative terms or norms. The design has to ensure that the intended activity can function well and it has to directly support the control of behavior.

EXAMPLES OF STRATEGIES IN ACTION

There are hundreds of examples of CPTED strategies in practice today. In each example there is a mixture of the three CPTED strategies that is appropriate to the setting and to the particular security or crime problem. Some of the examples were created in the direct application of CPTED concepts. Others were borrowed from real-life situations. The common thread is the primary emphasis on naturalness — simply doing things that you already have to do, but doing them a little better.

Some examples of CPTED strategy activities are:

- Providing clear border definition of controlled space
- Providing clearly marked transitional zones that indicate movement from public to semi-public to private space

- Relocating gathering areas to locations with natural surveillance and access control, or to locations away from the view of would-be offenders
- Placing safe activities in unsafe locations to bring along the natural surveillance of these activities to increase the perception of safety for normal users and risk for offenders
- Placing unsafe activities in safe spots to overcome the vulnerability of these activities with the natural surveillance and access control of the safe area
- Redesignating the use of space to provide natural barriers to conflicting activities
- Improving scheduling of space to allow for effective use and appropriate critical intensity
- Redesigning space to increase the perception or reality of natural surveillance
- Overcoming distance and isolation through improved communications and design efficiencies

USE OF INFORMATION

It goes without saying that all important decisions should be based on good information. Especially where the design and use of the physical environment is at stake, it is imperative that at least five basic types of information be collected and used. Unless a rational basis is used to make informed decisions, the same mistakes that generated the original problem will continue to be made.

The five basic types of information needed for good CPTED planning are crime analysis information, demographic information, land use information, observations, and resident or user interviews. This information does not have to be sophisticated. It exists in a fundamental form in every community or location. Moreover, unless it can be presented in its most basic form, it is of little value. For instance, very little can be done with a statistical measure that says burglaries are up by 5%. Much more can be done with a crime map that shows a clustering of burglaries in a specific block (see Figure 3–3). Even more can be done when one finds that the burglar used an alleyway as his approach to a series of related offenses because it afforded a good cover for his vehicle.

The other bits of information that are needed should be available in simple, usable formats. Following is a simple guide to each type of information:

- *Crime analysis.* This type of information is available in every police department; it is obtained by plotting offenses on a wall map and organizing the information on crime reports for the major purpose of

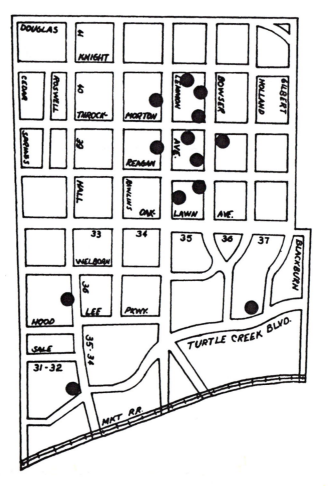

Figure 3–3: Geographic concentration pattern.

identifying patterns of criminal activity. There are two basic types of patterns: geographic and similar offense.

- *Demographic*. This is information that describes the nature of the population for a given city, district, or neighborhood. It is available through city planning departments or the city manager's or mayor's office. Another source of this type of information is the Census Bureau and the city and county data books that may be found in most public libraries.

- *Land use.* City planning departments, zoning boards, traffic engineering councils, and local councils of government have information and maps that describe and depict the physical allocations and uses of land. Simple wall maps with colored sections showing residential areas, commercial areas, industrial areas, parks, schools, and traffic flows can be of immeasurable assistance in understanding the physical setting. Natural boundaries and neighborhoods are easier to visualize on such maps, especially in relation to land use and pedestrian and traffic flows.

- *Observations*. It is very helpful to conduct either formal or informal visual reviews of physical space to get first-hand knowledge of how, when, and by whom that space is used, and where problems may arise. Environmental cues are the key to normal user and offender behavior. Observations may include pedestrian/vehicle counts, on- and off-street parking, maintenance of yards and fences, the degree of proprietary behaviors prohibited by residents and/or users, the presence of either controlling or avoidance behaviors, and other potential indicators of territorial concern such as the percentage of window blinds drawn in homes and businesses overlooking parks or schools.

- *Resident or user interviews.* This source of information is needed to balance the other data sources. People's perceptions of where they feel safe and where they feel endangered often vary from the locations on crime maps where the most offenses occur. It is vital to determine the residents' or users' perceptions and extent of identity with the surrounding space, what affects their behavior or reactions as they move about, and what they think the needs are.

Any attempt to skip the basics in favor of more complex forms of information gathering or analysis often obscures the picture. Professionals often suppress the active participation of residents or space users by relying on complex modes of analysis. This is dangerous because it can cause some very basic ideas or explanations to be overlooked. It is axiomatic that very little good will be accomplished without the full and active involvement of the users of space.

The best way to understand the information and present it to others is through visual means. Maps and transparent overlays are useful means of comparing the five types of information that are needed in CPTED planning. Figure 3–3 presents an example of a crime map.

SOME BENEFITS OF CPTED PLANNING ACTIVITIES

In addition to dealing with the reduction of crime and fear problems, other benefits of CPTED planning include the following:

- *Treatment of crime problems at various environmental scales.* The CPTED process for identifying crime/environment problems, selecting CPTED strategies, and initiating, implementing, and evaluating anti-crime projects can be applied to entire neighborhoods or types of institutional settings within a city, such as secondary schools, or the process can be applied equally well to a small geographic area or to one particular institution.

- *Integration of prevention approaches.* CPTED principles are derived from an opportunity model of criminal behavior that assumes that the offender's behavior can be accounted for by understanding how, and under what circumstances, variables in the environment interact to induce crime. Once an assessment of the opportunity structure is made, then appropriate strategies can be designed and integrated into a coordinated, consistent program.

- *Identification of short- and long-term goals.* Comprehensive broad-based programs like CPTED have ultimate goals that may take years to accomplish. Unlike CPTED, however, many programs fail to develop short-term or proximate goals and adequate ways to measure their success. The CPTED approach includes an evaluation framework that details proximate goals relating to increased access control, surveillance, and territorial reinforcement. The rationale is that the ultimate program success is directly related to its success in achieving the proximate goals.

- *Encouragement of collective responses to problems.* The CPTED emphasis is on increasing the capacity of residents to act in concert rather than individually. Strategies are aimed at fostering citizen participation and strengthening social cohesion.

- *Interdisciplinary approach to urban problems.* An explicit policy of interdisciplinary teaming ensures effective cooperation among diverse city departments such as public works, social services, economic development, police, and so forth. Each participant benefits from exposure to the responsibilities, jurisdiction, and skills of the others.

- *Encouragement of better police/community relations.* A key strategy is to coordinate law enforcement and community service activities with the result of improving police/community relations and developing an anticrime program that is not solely dependent on enforcement agencies.

- *Development of security guidelines and standards.* CPTED programming can lead to the creation of security criteria for newly constructed or modified environments to avoid planning and design decisions that inadvertently provide opportunities for crime.

- *Assistance in urban revitalization.* Through its impact on physical, social, and economic conditions, CPTED can be instrumental in revitalizing communities, including downtown areas. Once business leaders, investors, and other citizens perceive that a comprehensive effort is underway to reduce crime and fear, there will be an improvement in community identity and cohesiveness.

- *Acquisition of development funds.* The incorporation of CPTED into existing programs can provide additional jurisdiction for awarding grants, loans, and community development funds.

- *Institutionalization of crime prevention policies and practices.* CPTED projects can create a local management capability and expertise to maintain ongoing projects. This capability can be incorporated into existing citizen organizations or municipal agencies.

Not all of these situations will apply to every local jurisdiction; and there may be additional applications not covered by the above examples. It is important that local decision makers establish objectives that they hope to achieve through a CPTED project. These can range from a narrowly drawn goal that aims at a single purpose to a broad and comprehensive focus with multiple benefits. Hence, a decision about the project and its objectives will be an important determinant of the type of CPTED project to be initiated, its management requirements, its resource commitments, and similar policy decisions.

AN OUNCE OF PREVENTION: A NEW ROLE FOR LAW ENFORCEMENT SUPPORT OF COMMUNITY DEVELOPMENT

The well-worn cliche coined by Benjamin Franklin, "An ounce of prevention is worth a pound of cure," seems an appropriate way of introducing a new role for law enforcement agencies in supporting the public and private activities of communities. Law enforcement agencies are the only major community and governmental services that are not included in the review and approval process of planning, zoning, traffic, and environmental design decisions.

Why is it easy for a law enforcement officer who is visiting another city to pick out the problem neighborhoods and business areas? Because she has learned to associate certain environmental conditions with social, economic, and crime problems. The same is often true for non-law enforcement visitors.

The degree of attractiveness of any location says a lot about its owners and the type of people who frequent the place. But it can also say a lot about the mistakes committed by public agencies and private developers, mistakes that end up making victims (and sometimes hostages) out of the residents. Whatever the interpretation, the atmosphere of any area gives off environmental cues that tell an individual whether he is safe or unsafe.

There is a resurgence of interest in the concept of CPTED. The state of Florida has gone so far as to pass a law entitled the "Safe Neighborhoods Act," which provides legal authority and funding for the implementation of CPTED strategies. The CPTED concept calls for integrating natural approaches to crime prevention into building design and neighborhood planning rather than responding to crime problems after they materialize.

But what has this got to do with law enforcement? What right has law enforcement to be involved in planning, zoning, and architectural design decisions? Is it not true that law enforcement agencies are already too overburdened with calls for service and for investigations to take on another function? Isn't this really someone else's job? Couldn't law enforcement get sued for suggesting a change that does not work?

There are a number of compelling reasons for law enforcement to be involved in CPTED:

1.   CPTED concepts have been proven to enhance community activities while reducing crime problems.
2.   CPTED concepts are fundamental to traditional law enforcement values, in terms of helping the community to function properly.
3.   CPTED requires the unique information sources and inherent knowledge of the community that is endemic to the law enforcement profession.
4.   CPTED problems and issues bear a direct relationship to repeat calls for service and to crime-producing situations.
5.   CPTED methods and techniques can directly improve property values, business profitability, and industrial productivity, thereby enhancing local tax bases.

Law enforcement agencies, regardless of size, must be involved formally in the review and approval process of community and business projects. Their participation must be active and creative, rather than passive and reactive. Moreover, any such involvement should not be understood to expose the agencies to possible litigation, since it is the role of law enforcement in CPTED to provide additional information and concerns that may not have occurred to the persons who are responsible (and qualified) for making changes to the environment. The expression, "Pay me now, or pay me later," conveys the idea that the early involvement of a knowledgeable law enforcement agency in the conceptualization and planning of community projects can lead to improvements in the quality of life and to reductions in the fear and incidence of crime. This early involvement is one of the most cost-effective methods of crime prevention.

CPTED Definitions

The definition of CPTED used by the National Crime Prevention Institute (NCPI) is "the proper design and effective use of the built environment can lead to a reduction in the fear and incidence of crime, and an improvement in the quality of life." This definition says, basically, that the better we manage our human and physical resources, the greater our profit and the lower our losses. In a residential neighborhood, profit translates to the protection of property values and improved quality of life. In a business neighborhood, profit translates to a better bottom-line, to economic growth, and to attractiveness (as well as tax benefits). In both situations the byproduct is crime prevention.

CPTED Problems

One problem with all this is that the public and some law enforcement administrators assume that the role of the police is limited to "trail them, nail them, and jail them." Public administrators sometimes find it expedient to limit each local government agency to its most visible task, thereby reducing interagency conflict and avoiding consolidated or collective actions that may be hard to control. Crime and crime prevention cannot be restricted to the law enforcement function unless we wish to perpetuate the practice of closing the barn door after the horse gets out. Instead, we must acknowledge the necessity for integrated program planning and support.

A common misconception that is shared by the public, the media, and elected officials is that reactive law enforcement approaches are working. However, the facts do not support this notion. Reported crime figures are only the tip of the iceberg regarding the true extent of crime, fraud, cheating, and dishonesty in the United States. Clearly, it must be concluded that purely reactive law enforcement responses are inappropriate. Something more fundamental than public education and gadget-oriented crime prevention programs must be undertaken.

Many environmental issues have surfaced over the past 40 years that lead to the conclusion that CPTED may be one of the more important (but not exclusive) crime prevention initiatives for the next two decades. Perhaps the most basic of these issues is the discovery that so many of the environmental factors that we take for granted have something to do with crime. Moreover, it has been observed that many community and government functions seem to exist or co-exist in a mutually exclusive manner, even while appearing to cooperate. For instance, urban planners and traffic engineers are involved in approving new commercial construction projects. It has been found that many of their standards and requirements have gone unchallenged. Sometimes they agree on the same standard, but for different reasons.

Over many years of attempted collaboration, it has become commonplace for planners, transportation engineers, developers, public housing officials, and code enforcement authorities to seem to coordinate and cooperate through subtle conflict. That is, instead of openly fighting, they establish territories and stick to them, keeping their noses out of each other's bailiwicks. Consequently, many fundamental errors slip through, resulting in failed business areas and declining neighborhoods that stand as a permanent legacy to the failure to communicate.

Following are some environmental problems and issues that are a small sample of areas in which a CPTED effort may help:

- *One-way street systems* have been found to improve traffic flow, but also to create dead zones for business, with resulting crime or fear of crime that deters development efforts.

- *Through traffic in neighborhoods* has been found to be detrimental to residential housing values, stability, and crime rates.
- *Downtown projects* continue to fail by making fundamental errors that reduce natural surveillance and natural access control, resulting in the loss of desired users and domination by unwanted users.
- *Fortress effects* are produced by designers of convention centers, hotels, banks, senior citizen housing, and parking lot structures. These destroy the surrounding land uses and create a "no-man's land."
- *Bleed-off parking* enhances conflict between commercial and residential land uses; both lose.
- *Store design* and *management* can actually reduce business and increase victimization of employees and customers.
- *Mall and major event facility parking* areas with poorly planned access control and layout can produce traffic congestion and become magnets for undesirable activity.
- *School and institutional design* can inadvertently create unsurveillable and dysfunctional areas, resulting in increased behavioral and crime problems and overall impediments to successful operations (e.g., students' achievement in schools).
- *Public housing and affordable housing* can become projects that serve as magnets for transients, as opposed to local poor, with further detrimental effects on existing neighborhoods.

Nearly every environmental situation or location is amenable to the application of CPTED concepts. The law enforcement agency can assist in asking the right questions and in supplying the right kind of information to help the community to make more informed decisions.

Someone has to politely challenge the one-dimensional decisions that are too often made by those individuals with the responsibility to develop, manage, and control our environment. Someone also has to challenge the foundation for many of these decisions.

An example of this occurred several years ago in a northern Midwest community. The police department had been incurring excessive overtime costs for a number of years as a result of the popularity of jogging and bicycle events. Event organizers planned the routes and activities, and then relied on the police to secure the routes. Nobody questioned the basic routing until a police sergeant who was trained in CPTED asked the question, "Why are you racing on this street pattern?" The sergeant who asked this question had a personal motivation: he wanted to run in the planned event but could not because the chief of police had assigned him to extra duty to supervise a team of officers assigned to the race. The response to his question was, "It seems to be a good idea." After the initial shock of realizing that the police had been holding the bag for a number of years, the sergeant helped the event planners select a route that reduced police personnel requirements by one-half. The race was still a success!

What does a law enforcement agency have to do to conduct CPTED reviews without embarrassing itself? How does the agency go about getting anyone to listen, or even to allow the agency to get involved in the first place? First, the head of the agency needs to make the commitment. Second, someone has to study the CPTED concept. CPTED is much easier than it appears initially; many excellent training and orientation programs are available. Third, the agency head has to sell the concept and request formal involvement in the local review and approval process. This is the tricky part! It is easy to sell CPTED if it appears that it will help the other agencies or developers meet their own objectives. It is hard to sell if it appears to be simply another type of crime prevention activity.

The law enforcement administrator must adopt the attitude and priority system reflected in these basic CPTED questions:

1. What are you trying to accomplish in this space or project?
2. How may we help you do it better?

The law enforcement agency is not in the business of telling other professionals how to do their jobs. The role of law enforcement in CPTED is to ask questions, share ideas, and provide information that would otherwise be unavailable to the builders, designers, and planners.

"CLEAN, WELL-LIGHTED PLACES": A NATURAL APPROACH TO RETAIL SECURITY

"One to show and one to go" is a maxim of merchandising and good business accounting. Materials management experts have developed the art of knowing just how much inventory to order to meet merchandising needs while holding down carrying costs. It has also been a common assumption that merchandising and security concepts are contradictory. But is it good business to have a dirty, cluttered store with poor visibility and lighting? Do high gondolas and shelves actually increase sales, or are they really for employee convenience? After all, the job of constantly replenishing inventory is a boring and tedious task. Everyone knows that you have to store the inventory somewhere, so why not on the sales floor?

The generally unquestioned acceptance of shrinkage (the theft of merchandise) is justified on the basis of trade-off analysis and risk retention. Young business persons have this pounded into their heads, principally because it is assumed commonly that good business and good security are incompatible.

Unfortunately, many fundamentals of business and merchandising have continued to go unchallenged, much in the same manner as has the conventional wisdom in security and crime prevention reflected in the expression, "Trail them, nail them, and jail them." Nobody really wants a costumer frisked every time he comes in to buy a gallon of milk (or a fur coat). Many retailers are worried that the presence of armed guards and extensive security measures will turn away customers—and they are probably right.

Years of experiments and practical applications in the field have continually demonstrated that the CPTED concept works in all environmental scales. That is, it has direct applications to commercial, residential, transportation, recreational, and institutional environments. It has worked at scales as small as a single room and as large as an entire community. Its commercial and industrial uses have repeatedly supported the traditional notion that the better one manages human and physical resources, the greater the profit and the smaller the losses. Clearly, effective resource management, which leads to increased profitability, results in fewer security problems.

A store that is attractive, well-lighted, and open is more appealing to customers, especially in the convenience industry, which thrives upon impulse stopping and buying. A store that is profitable has to depend upon the enthusiastic and dedicated support of its staff. Pride in one's work and environment stimulates extended territorial concern. Honest customers and employees feel safer and more visible in clean, well-lighted places. They feel the presence and controlling behaviors of others. Conversely, a dirty and poorly managed store engenders little pride on the part of the honest employee, which reduces territorial concern and promotes avoidance behaviors.

A poorly managed and upkept store also introduces the possibility of civil negligence. The failure of proprietors to establish reasonable measures to protect their products, employees, and customers will be used against them in determining out-of-court settlements, as well as in trials. Poor inventory control and accounting may even suggest some liability in the area of product tampering or poisoning. A clean, well-lighted store in which the proprietors and customers are actively exhibiting controlling behaviors simply tells others that only accepted behaviors will be tolerated.

CPTED is a small part of the total set of concepts involved in loss prevention and assets protection, but it is an important concept for the business community because it emphasizes the integration of security concepts into what has to be done anyway, before additional funds are expended on guards or security devices.

CPTED planners classify security strategies into three categories:

1. *organized,* labor-intensive security where the cost is extracurricular to the normal functions and requirements of human space (e.g., guards),
2. *mechanical,* capital- or hardware-intensive security where the cost is, once again, extracurricular to the normal functions and requirements of space (e.g., fences, alarms, cameras), and

3. *natural,* the integration of security and behavior concepts into how human and physical resources are used (e.g., spatial definition, placement of work stations, location of windows).

The CPTED planner merely tries to maximize the use of natural strategies before using the more costly organized and mechanical ones that may actually serve as impediments to profitable operations. The conventional security concepts of access controls and surveillance are enhanced by the emphasis on natural approaches, with the added feature of increased territorial behavior and expanded proprietary concern.

It is fundamental to this behavioral approach that the CPTED planner seeks to expand the territorial concern of the owner and normal user of space. It is equally important to present behavioral and environmental cues that tell normal users of space that they are safe. The same cue has an inverse effect on the abnormal user, or potential offender, by increasing her perception of risk. That is, the design of the space and the way people are behaving gives the impression that the abnormal user will be observed, stopped, or apprehended. Accordingly, the CPTED planner learns to differentiate between the unique differences and values of various users. In the design or redesign of store layouts, the owner must focus on several kinds of individuals:

- *normal users,* persons whom you desire to be in a certain space,
- *abnormal users,* persons whom you do not desire to be in that space, and
- *observers,* those persons who have to be in that space to support the human function.

Strategies are aimed at only one, or sometimes all, of these categories of users, depending on the circumstances. Conditions that make the normal user feel safe make the other feel at risk of detection. Conversely, conditions that make the normal user feel unsafe make the abnormal user feel at low risk of detection. The CPTED planner must try to determine how space is defined for each of these groups.

Values can shift. For instance, when school lets out in the middle of the afternoon, three or four boys coming into a shopping mall would be desirable visitors. If the same boys came back at 9:30 when the mall was closing, and they'd taken off their school clothes, were dressed in strange ways, and had dyed their hair orange, they would be less than desirable.

Another example: Suppose you are a casual shopper at a convenience store. At one store, you see a group of kids with orange hair in the parking lot. You look down the street and see a well-lighted and appealing store with no one outside. Is there any doubt which store you would patronize?

This shows how the environment can affect the way people feel about your place of business. The physical environment affects people's behavior and perceptions, which impact not only on attitudes, but also on productivity and loss prevention.

Commercial and retail establishments have always used the physical environment to affect customer perceptions and behavior. CPTED adds a new dimension by incorporating these elements into space design and management:

- *Natural access control.* Your space should give some natural indication of where people are allowed and are not allowed. Don't depend just on locks and guards, but make security part of the layout.
- *Natural surveillance.* Again, traditional factors like good lighting are important, but don't overlook a natural factor such as a strategically placed window or the placement of an employee work station.
- *Territorial reinforcement.* This is an umbrella concept, embodying all natural surveillance and access control principles. It emphasizes the enhancement of ownership and proprietary behaviors.

These concepts can be more important than you suspect. There is one individual, for instance, who has owned five convenience stores for about 20 years. He always felt that environmental concepts were a lot of hogwash. But the neighborhood changed and disintegrated, and he failed to keep up with it. Now, almost too late, he realizes that you must design your space to cope with your environment.

There are many applications of CPTED to commercial environments. Perhaps the greatest and most valuable lesson being learned is that good store design and merchandising are not incompatible with effective security. Both objectives may be achieved and enhanced through space planning and behavioral concepts. Some examples:

- The convenience industry is using new building shapes to attract, but separate, the construction worker, the juvenile, and the adult impulse buyer.
- Gondolas, shelves, racks, and displays are being dropped to enhance visibility from and into the store, as well as within, to improve attractiveness and perceptions of security.
- Parking is being located in front of stores and shops with good landscaping to screen the unsightliness of autos and pavement, but improve perceptions of safe access for people and protection of the auto.
- Illumination is being increased inside stores, at night, to suggest a more welcome atmosphere for the customer who is driving or walking by.
- The location of employee work stations is being selected strategically to increase the perception of surveillance, improved customer convenience, and employee productivity. Employee work station location and orientation can help to increase proprietary concern and cut employee theft.

- Special lease and business license incentives may be used to extend a business owner's and employee's proprietary concern for multiple-purpose or adjacent public space, and to increase sales during special events.
- Shopping centers are enclaving parking areas with curbing and landscaping to make them more attractive, while limiting the number of access points to those that are perceived to be under surveillance, or that may be sealed off, thus cutting off perceived escape routes for abnormal users.
- Shopping centers and adjacent office complexes are using zoned parking based on user need, with systematic closings of zones by time of day, day of week, and other special factors. This increases the probable scrutiny of vehicles that are there at the wrong times.
- Business areas are getting local government to reroute excessive rush hour or through traffic that bleeds through nonarterial or high capacity streets. Through traffic has been found to suppress impulse buying (slow driving and parking) because of higher speed pressure and driver behavior, and it results in higher numbers of police service calls and crimes.
- Some excessive use of downtown one-way street systems and over-emphasis of street design for vehicle movement capacity is being questioned with an emphasis on providing a more effective balance between the desire to protect business areas versus the need to move commuter traffic.
- Social policies requiring the excessive use of amenities and landscaping in open downtown pedestrian malls is being questioned, in view of their tendency to attract unsightly vagrants and associated vandalism, as well as to reduce the amount of potential business space.

The list of CPTED applications to the retail environment is potentially endless. Design and use strategies may be used at any scale if there is the potential for positive effects on employee and customer behavior. Productivity and profit will be enhanced, while abnormal users are more visible and aware that they are under greater control and risk. CPTED concepts, creatively applied, can and will improve business, and they may just make it a lot more fun!

CPTED IN LOW-INCOME, PUBLIC, AND THREE-GENERATION HOUSING

Most of the concerns about crime problems relate to a high degree of accessibility to the housing communities from outside areas. Lighting has been identified as a potential problem, as well as space management and design deficiencies that may contribute to the perception of apathy on the part of management and residents.

CPTED concepts have been proven to reduce crime and increase the quality of life in many public housing communities. They also are effective in removing many obstacles that prevent law enforcement and social control mechanisms in communities from working effectively to control crime and drug abuse.

Low-income housing communities are victims of community attitudes. Many of the drug dealers and criminals who operate at housing locations are not residents there. The buyers of stolen products and drugs are attracted to public housing sites because of the general perception that these areas are associated with, and tolerant of, criminal activities.

The following examples of CPTED strategies for low-income and public housing are grouped under the three primary CPTED concepts of natural surveillance, natural access control, and territorial reinforcement:

Natural Surveillance

- Provide magnets for watchers, or gatekeepers, by increased outdoor use of space (e.g., porches, yard assignment, and gardening).
- Reduce light pollution on bedroom windows to influence residents to leave curtains and blinds open or partially open to create the reality and perception of surveillance.
- Install windows in dead walls on the sides of buildings.
- Install automatically controlled porch lights to create a sea of light at the human scale to allow for better visual identification of faces, and to reduce light pollution through the reduction of the use and intensity of overhead mast-mounted lights.
- Place car parking in line-of-sight of units, or preferably, immediately in front.
- Install central HVAC to eliminate the use of window units that block natural surveillance and audio monitoring of outdoor activities; this also significantly improves the quality of life.
- Remove walls and hedgerows that produce impediments to natural surveillance; replace dumpster enclosures and perimeter fencing with transparent materials.

Natural Access Control

- Control vehicle traffic to reduce nonresident through access; this may include closures, one way streets, or other designs.
- Install traffic chokers and speed bumps to reduce speed and to improve pedestrian safety.
- Install entry monuments to celebrate the identity of the community and to signify the movement from public to private space, as a warning to potential abnormal users.

- Segment parking areas to create enclaves for fewer cars in each, and to create one-way in and out to promote the perception of potential entrapment for abnormal users of space.

Territorial Reinforcement

- Reduce the number of people sharing a common entrance or stairwell.
- Reduce the number of people sharing a common balcony or gallery.
- Reduce the number of people sharing a common green area.
- Reduce the number of people sharing a common parking area.
- Increase the assignment and active use of yard space.
- Relocate parallel sidewalks away from close proximity to individual units, to create more defensible space for the residents.

Livability

Public housing may have to compete with privately owned housing if changes in federal housing policy are enacted. This will present a major problem in that public housing policy has typically stressed an "up and out" attitude and the tendency to exhibit a "barebones atmosphere" to appease the taxpayers perception that poor, often unemployed people should not have better housing than those who work regularly.

Many people expect the minimum of comforts in housing, which includes air conditioning in hot climates and easy access to laundry facilities and shopping. It is common for people to depend upon their automobile as a necessity for access to jobs, shopping, and leisure activities. Marketing research studies generally reveal that, in order to monitor and protect their investment in an automobile, people prefer to park immediately in front of or within line-of-sight of their dwelling units.

General Liability

Local governments have kept public housing at an "arms distance" as a matter of policy to reduce their involvement in the issue over ownership of, and hence responsibility and liability for, properties that are now reaching the end of their useful life. Many of these properties were built over 60 years ago. Deferred maintenance and capital improvement requirements present some major cost issues that have often resulted in a low priority for budget and policy concern for public housing.

Housing Recipients

American public housing has focused on the needs of the poor throughout most of its history. Other countries provide public housing for working families as well as the poor, which produces more social stability. American housing authorities are now planning for expansion of services to working families. This move will require more attention to livability and security to attract the working families.

Neighborhood Planning

Public housing and the immediate neighborhoods adjacent to them are linked economically and in quality-of-life issues. In spite of this link, public housing has quite often been viewed as "islands of despair" that divide neighborhoods and areas of cities. Many neighborhood improvement programs have functioned independently and, at times, competitively with public housing communities. Independent agencies within local governments have separate funding sources that they tend to protect. Public sentiment is often misguided regarding the plight of low-income neighborhoods, which can be reflected in local government's policies that do not incorporate public housing concerns within the broader investment in community development.

Law Enforcement

Domestic violence incidents are one of the most frustrating and dangerous events for police intervention. Civil unrest and urban violence that has continued to occur in inner cities has produced the perception that police are "occupying forces" in low-income and public housing neighborhoods. It is hard for police officers to feel that they are welcome in these communities, even though they perceive that they are exposing themselves to hazard by the very act of attempting to provide service and to protect the innocent in these areas. Accordingly, stereotypical images of public housing and of those who live there are common among police professionals, which results in slow responsiveness to and even avoidance of these communities.

Density

It is a general principle in the planning for all types of housing that densities should be limited to provide for the following:

- adequate daylight, sunlight, air, and useable open space for all dwellings
- adequate space for all community facilities
- a general feeling of openness and privacy
- a reasonable relationship to land and improvement costs
- a relationship to scale of the site, the neighborhood, and the geographic area

High densities are to be avoided because the problems of crowding are self-evident. However, the importance of density has to be assessed on a site-by-site basis. The orientation and relationship of buildings in a low-density environment can be a problem. Conversely, a high-density environment can be livable when the buildings are placed appropriately in relation to the human activities.

Three-Generation Housing

It is difficult for extended families to live in close proximity in public housing environments. Young families may have to move across town to another site to find an apartment. As the young family grows in number of children, it is common for them to have to move several times to find more bedroom space. Over time the same families need less space as older children leave the home. There is a new concept of three-generation housing that is actually a rebirth of the pre-World War II practice of providing room for boarders within the existing house design.

Three-generation housing concepts include the planning of architectural options to modify existing structures to increase apartment size or to provide for rental opportunities within one structure. That is, the apartment is designed to be broken into two apartments of various sizes. Conversely, an apartment could be designed to provide for an attic or attached efficiency that could be used for short-term rentals by college students or single tenants who can provide the adult presence needed for the support of a lone parent. Public housing applications will vary only to the extent of who serves as the landlord.

Three-generation planning for public housing provides architectural options that make it possible for extended families to stay close. Apartments may be modified or originally designed to allow for either up-sizing or down-sizing the number of bedrooms in apartments. One-bedroom flats may be joined or separated as families change. Two kitchens in one large apartment may be useful in promoting harmony among an extended family. This apartment could be split when the large family moves. Such flexibility allows the apartment to undergo many changes over the years to accommodate the needs of families.

The value of three-generation housing is potentially enormous. The alone parent will benefit from the potential support of other adults within the home. Child supervision will improve, which may result in less delinquency and vandalism. Higher achievement levels in school may result from improved attendance and study habits that will be influenced by increased parenting and supervision. Finally, it should be expected that quality-of-life issues will be affected in positive ways, thus making the housing community more popular for working families.

CPTED PLANNING AND DESIGN REVIEW

Planning

One of the first priorities for implementing CPTED is to place it in the planning process of the organization or jurisdiction. School districts, housing authorities, transportation systems, and local government all have fundamental responsibilities for public safety. It is necessary that a formal relationship between crime prevention and planning be established. Private companies and public utilities control extensive properties and huge labor forces. Each has a process for making decisions about new development and investment. The CPTED concept and process must be incorporated into these ongoing processes.

For communities and organizations, the CPTED process relates to and must be part of the following functions:

- *Comprehensive plans.* These determine the future patterns of land use and development. Comprehensive plans present the values of a community and a vision of what it will look like in the future. These plans establish goals and objectives for up to 50-year time periods. Crime prevention elements are clearly necessary in a community's comprehensive plan. Day-to-day decisions about problems and needs are improved by ensuring that they are consistent with comprehensive plans.
- *Zoning ordinances.* These are established to promote the health, safety, and welfare of the people by formally identifying the locations of land uses to ensure that activities are compatible and mutually supportive. Zoning regulations affect land uses, development densities, yard setbacks, open space, building height, location and amount of parking, and maintenance poilicies. These, in turn, will affect activities and routines that concern exposure to crime, surveillance opportunities, and the definition of space for territorial control.
- *Subdivision regulation.* This includes lot size and dimension, street and right-of-way locations, sidewalks, amenities, and location of utilities. These elements directly influence access to neighborhoods, reduction of pedestrian and vehicle conflict, street lighting, and connections with other parts of the community.
- *Landscape ordinances.* These govern the placement of fences, signs, and plant materials. They may be used to improve spatial definition, surveillance, access control, and way-finding. Hostile landscaping can make unwanted access to parking lots and private property less desirable. Landscape planting materials may also help to reduce graffiti by making large areas of walls inaccessible. Good horticulture improves the quality of life and helps to reduce exposure to crime.

- *Architectural design guidelines.* These guidelines specify goals and objectives for site and building performance. They will affect the location of activities and the definition of public and private space. The site decisions and plans for a building will directly affect opportunities for natural surveillance, pedestrian and vehicle access, way-finding, and links to adjacent neighborhoods or land uses.
- *Access for physically and mentally challenged persons.* These requirements generally improve accessibility and way-finding, but rarely consider the risk of victimization that may be created by the use of out-of-the way doors, hallways, or elevators.

Review Process

The work of builders, designers, and planners have long been affected by codes that govern nearly every aspect of a structure, except for security. Historically, a few jurisdictions enacted security ordinances, but most of these related to windows, doors, and locking devices. It is now becoming more common to find a local law or procedure calling for a full security or crime prevention review of plans before they are finalized. Nevertheless, it is still generally true that more attention is placed on aesthetics, drainage, fire safety, curb cuts, and parking access than on gaining an understanding of how a building or structure will affect the area in terms of security. A CPTED design review process must be established within communities and organizations to ensure that good planning is being conducted.

The manner in which physical space is designed or used has a direct bearing on crime or security incidents. The clear relationship between the physical environment and crime is now understood to be a cross-cultural phenomenon, as recent international conferences on CPTED have disclosed the universal nature of human/environment relations. That is, despite political and cultural differences, people basically respond the same way to what they see and experience in the environment. Some places make people feel safe and secure, while others make people feel vulnerable. Criminals or other undesirables pick-up on the same cues. They look at the environmental setting and at how people are behaving. This tells them whether they can control the situation or run the risk of being controlled themselves.

Someone has to question design, development, and event planning decisions. Do you think that anyone from the police department, or fire department for that matter, asked the builder of a major hotel in Kansas City whether they had extra steel reinforcing rods leftover when they built the cross bridge that fell and resulted in many deaths and injuries? Did anyone ask the planners what effect the downtown pedestrian malls would have when the fad swept the country in the early seventies? No! Major planning mistakes were made then and now because no one is asking the hard questions.

The real tragedy is that when we make a design or planning decision, it will stay with us for many years. The Internal Revenue Service generally sets depreciation schedules for buildings at 67 years. It takes a long time to undo our mistakes. Commenting on design and development plans relevant to crime prevention is a crucial step that must be taken by police agencies. Each building plan must be viewed as a potential legacy for the community. Traffic flow and routing decisions must be done in the context of preserving private neighborhoods. These decisions will be made in every community, whether or not a crime prevention survey is conducted.

It is a question now for communities to try to have a positive impact through an interagency design review process. It requires law enforcement and crime prevention specialists to learn about the building and design trades and professions to enhance their ability to communicate CPTED ideas. It also requires a primary commitment from the top executives of every agency. The chief of police must take this seriously. The days of attempting to blindly lead the police function while clinging to a badge, a gun, and a bible are past. The CPTED design review process is the key to effective community development and management.

Are there any compelling reasons for communities and organizations to get involved in a CPTED design review process, other than pure logic? Litigation and money are two big ones. Many lawsuits are being decided not on whether a guard or alarm system was present, but on design and management decisions. Questions are being raised about the foreseeability of problems and the reasonableness and adequacy of design and management responses. Perhaps the greatest emphasis in the future of security and security-related lawsuits will be on natural security. The courts' understanding of security is expanding beyond organized or mechanical methods to include the natural approaches that are inherent to managing human and physical resources. CPTED could be viewed as a major escape route for the beleaguered property manager. And that includes just about everyone. City parks, public buildings, schools, shopping centers, small businesses, industrial plants, and hospitals are all fair game when it comes to lawsuit.

But what if logic and law suits do not get the attention of community and corporate leaders? How about money? The better one manages human and physical resources, the greater the profit and productivity and the lower the security problems. It is axiomatic that problems emanate from sloppy or bad business management. CPTED concepts in their basic form are oriented primarily around natural approaches to making things work better. A well-run school or office building requires less space and operating cost, and has less security or crime problems. There is a direct link between good management, profit, and crime prevention. They contribute to each other.

Liability

The recent case law in general and premises liability has increased the responsibilities of property and business owners. Liability has been extended to architects, engineers, lending companies, and security contractors in wrongful injury or death suits. Parking lots have been found by courts to be *inherently dangerous*, which means that an owner or operator is liable even when there have been no prior incidents. Likewise, the isolation of restrooms by location and by design has been determined to be inherently dangerous.

The standard by which a property owner or operator is judged is based upon proof of *due diligence* or having done *all things reasonable* to prevent injury. Schools bear an additional duty — *in loco parentis*, literally, serving in the place of the parents — which places a burden of responsibility for the protection of students from *portal to portal*, a seemingly impossible task. The focus of this responsibility, however, is the actual school campus.

Employee, student, and parent convenience is perhaps the greatest obstacle to maintaining safety and security. More accidents and victimizations are caused by the defeat of good security practices due to the interest in convenience than any other hazard. It is worse to have procedures that are not followed than to have none at all.

New properties and operations are held to a different standard than existing ones. The designer, planner, and owner of a new property or operation will be held accountable for *conscious decisions* that affect the propensity for subsequent injury. Accordingly, a final decision about the design and use plan for a property must be *defensible*. The opinions of a recognized expert in the substantive area of the loss, peril, and hazard establish *proximate cause*, which then implicates foreseeability.

The so-called test of reasonableness that is the backbone of civil liability allows for the support of many factors in making conscious decisions. Aesthetics, educational mission, life safety, accessibility, feasibility, and environmental factors are weighed in the final determination of the adequacy of a school's duty and responsibility in the care and protection of students and staff. This is why CPTED has become so important to the civil law, because it allows for the blending of good aesthetics, profitability, and safety.

The willingness to compromise is an admirable trait, one that is essential in any human endeavor. But compromise in making decisions about the design and use of a physical structure must not be arbitrary or carelessly thought out merely for the sake of achieving harmony. A recent tragic accident involving a rear-end collision of a vehicle with a fire truck provides a chilling example of compromising decisions. The local fire department waited to replace its only truck with one that provided safe jump seats for the firefighters, despite the fact that this violated national safety standards. This saved a $200,000 expenditure, although it was one that would have to be made sooner or later. Unfortunately, two firefighters died and two were critically injured in the accident. It is estimated that the settlement on the wrongful death suits will be approximately $6 to $7 million, and the wrongful injury suits will be higher. A new truck that meets safety standards will also have to be purchased.

A western city experienced the worst nightmare of any community in 1993. The vehicle drop-off zone for an elementary school was located on a public street. It was a common practice for parents to pull up to a specific location to let off their child. A teacher routinely waved the parent ahead after the child exited the vehicle and slammed the door. This helped decrease congestion on the public street. It apparently, and tragically, became too routine: a fifth-grade girl jumped out of her mother's car and the teacher waved the mother on after hearing the car door slam. But the little girl's coat was caught in the car door and she was dragged to death by the unknowing mother. Would the cost of a proprietary drop-off lane have ever amounted to this one loss?

Is the preceding example merely an isolated, freak accident? Or does it have the potential to be repeated elsewhere? Does the cost of prevention, or at least doing all that is reasonable, offset the potential loss?

Four elements are involved in the determination of liability. These are:

1.   duty
2.   breach of duty
3.   injury
4.   causal link

These are the factors the court will use in assessing a school system's obligation in the event of a tragic accident like the one above. For its part, the basic requirements any school system must meet to establish a reasonable attempt to provide for safety and security are the following:

- Conduct a threat or problem analysis.
- Adopt a formal plan for safety and security.
- Prove that the plan was/is implemented.
- Document efforts to evaluate the plan.

The greatest protection for liability, crime prevention, and *peace of mind* is the presence of a plan of action that meets these criteria.

ACHIEVING THE RIGHT PERSPECTIVE

One mistake made by persons who attempt to use CPTED concepts is getting the objective wrong. They attempt to apply CPTED concepts solely for security reasons. It does not take them long to find out that no one is interested in listening to them, particularly business persons who justifiably have to concern themselves with profit and loss.

For instance, a crime prevention officer from Bossier City, Louisiana, conducted a security survey of a luxury clothing store. He recommended that the owner move the display of furs within the line of sight of one cashier, to keep the patrons from stealing them. The owner was not interested and refused on the basis of concern about insulting his special customers. The officer returned to the store after attending a CPTED course and made the same recommendation. This time, the purpose of the recommendation was primarily to enhance sales by improving the ability of clerks to make immediate sales pitches to customers whom they observed entering the display area. By switching furs with a lingerie display that was in direct view of the clerk, the store enhanced sales while reducing the potential for losses.

The underlying objective of CPTED is to help the various disciplines do a better job of achieving their primary objectives, with the added byproduct of improved security and loss prevention. The CPTED planner must ask the questions: What are you trying to do? How can we help you do it better? A successful use of these concepts will always result in this sequence of events:

1. careful design and use of physical space
2. resulting human decisions and behavior
3. improved productivity and profit and
4. byproduct of loss prevention or loss reduction

There are many examples of the tendency for people to overlook obvious solutions to problems. We have all heard someone who is having difficulty finding an object that turns out to be right in front of him say, "If it had been a snake, it would have bitten me!" CPTED concepts help us to look at the environment in a different light to take advantage of solutions that are often inherent in what we are doing anyway. Consider the following somewhat far-fetched, but true, example:

A school principal told the story that during the early part of the 1980s, when the rock group KISS was popular, with big red lips on the album, young ladies in school began to smear on red lipstick and put the imprint on the mirror of the restroom. When a janitor complained, the principal said, "Don't worry. It's a fad and will go away."

But it didn't. Soon the kiss imprints were on the walls and doors, despite repeated warnings. Some young men, walking down hallways, would feel a pressure on the shoulder or back and find they had been given a big red kiss.

Morale among teachers suffered. It was open warfare between young ladies and boys and teachers. Then a woman who had worked for 30 years as a janitor knocked on the principal's door and said she had an answer. She explained it, and the principal agreed it was worth a try.

What was the solution? The next morning she arrived in the girls' restroom with a bucket. She made a point of filling it with water from the toilets and she used that water to clean the mirrors. She was seen doing this all day, using toilet water to wipe the mirrors and doors. The problems ceased.

Although the final solution to the problem may have been extreme, it shows how the use of physical space and the environment has a direct impact on the perceptions of people, and thus on security.

4

Historical Precedents of CPTED: Early Settlement and Growth of Communities

THE BEGINNING

The weary travelers paddled furiously toward the riverbank and heard the ominous roar of the rapids ahead. They collapsed in exhaustion as their canoe ground into the riverbank. The woman and man had narrowly missed being swept down the rapids to a certain death. After what seemed an interminable amount of time, they finally pulled their craft ashore and sluggishly set up a tent to provide shelter for what they knew would be a cold night. Thus was sown the seed of a community that one day would be the home of thousands of people. Nature's accidental interaction with man — the rapids in a major river — had produced the inauspicious beginnings of a city.

The young couple decided to stay a while where they had landed. Eventually, others stopped at the same place to avoid the rapids. The original couple sold food and helped others to portage their boats and equipment to the lower river. Their tent, which had later become a lean-to, soon was filled with supplies. Hungry travelers depended on the young couple, now entrepreneurs, for temporary lodging and assistance as they made their way down the major river to new locations. The original couple had no choice but to move out of their lean-to so that they could expand it for their business purposes. They used the tent until another structure could be constructed for their personal use.

Each time their business expanded or another family settled near them, the founders of the little community had to dedicate their residential unit to commerce and move out further to undeveloped land. This began the pattern that affected the growth and development of cities and towns elsewhere. Residential uses naturally gave way to the higher priority of business and commerce, which provided jobs and the only source of sustenance for the burgeoning community. Housing could always await the establishment of work.

Early settlers followed trails that had been developed by native Americans, explorers, or even animals who established "traces" or paths. Some settler would eventually stop along one of these trails or paths, thus sowing the seed of a community. Their decision to stop was nearly always associated with some geological or geographical characteristic that conveyed the perception of safety and security.

It is easy to identify the oldest section of any American city by merely looking at a car rental agency map. The traditional downtown is squeezed into a central core that is surrounded by grid-pattern (square) streets that become gradually less crowded as they expand toward the suburbs. Historians have studied the pattern of city growth. Jane Jacobs, an urban planner, traced the development of downtowns in her 1961 book *Death and Life of Great American Cities*. She demonstrated how the central core was established by the growth of commercial activities, which gradually extended residential land uses outward. Ms. Jacobs used the analogy of concentric circles, wherein the commercial land uses dominated the center city or town. Each year a new layer of commercial growth replaced an older layer of residential use. The residential use pattern simply grew outward as it was displaced from the center.

The first step in the turnover of a neighborhood was the approval of a small professional business in what had been a residential dwelling. An aspiring architect, a real estate seller, or a chiropractor moved in with minor modifications to the facade of the property. Once the imaginary seal of that block was broken, it was easier to approve the next land-use change, and then another. There did not seem to be anything wrong with this pattern of development.

Most Americans today have been taught to accept urban growth as progress, as something that is good for all. Commerce is considered to be the anchor or magnet for community development. Residents even use forms of psychological repression to justify the undesirable byproducts of business. For instance, residents of Perry, Florida, refer to the abominable smell of a local paper mill as "the smell of money." The obnoxious smell of the major meat packing house and yard in Louisville, Kentucky, reminds the immediate neighborhood of their primary source of employment. As a child in Florida, I was taught to believe that the little city of St. Cloud was better off every time any business opened. It was believed that the residents owed it to the businesses to keep them in operation. Many young people learned a lot about the value of loyalty from these early childhood experiences.

We are proud of our communities and we often boast about the sizes of our malls and other commercial centers. Whenever an out-of-town visitor is shown around, what do they see? They see the downtown, that is if it is still habitable. Otherwise, they get an apology and they are taken to the river, or the mountain, or the brand new shopping center, to let them appreciate the success and potential largess of the community. Somewhere during the tour our visitors have to see our transitional neighborhoods. Many of our impromptu tour guides are compelled to point out that these apparently degenerating residential areas will soon be the upscale areas, boasting restored row homes and a variety of boutiques and professional offices.

THE GROWTH OF TRAFFIC PROBLEMS

All cities and towns experience the same traffic problems. Wagons congested New York City in the 1770s. New York City was the first to establish elevated walkways, in 1814, to overcome the pedestrian/vehicular conflict that was choking city streets. Omnibuses and trolleys appeared as an efficient means of mass transit. People lived in tenements and crowded accommodations to facilitate the ease of commuting to work. Cities and towns grew as the opportunity for work shifted from rural to urban settings. Laws were established to protect the pedestrian. Dodge City, Kansas, police were writing speeding tickets in the 1860s.

The economic boom of post World War I and the technological improvements associated with war time development created an unprecedented demand for automobiles. Large numbers of reasonably inexpensive automobiles rolled off the new assembly lines. Housing shortages that were caused by wartime controls were overcome through massive developments of near suburbs. Public policy efforts, such as Adolph Hitler's Volkswagen (people's car) propaganda, touched off a demand for autos and a desire for mobility that was unprecedented.

In 1927, the city of Knoxville, Tennessee, hired a consulting firm from St. Louis to conduct a study of the city government and the street system. The firm concluded that traffic was the major threat to continued economic growth. A number of recommendations were provided, especially a radical reorganization of the police department to include, among other things, a new motorized division, so that the police could become omnipresent. The conclusion was that the major problem was vehicles and, therefore, the police needed to become mobilized to respond effectively. The new motorized traffic division was expected to prevent more crime than the foot patrols, because of their omnipresence.

World War II produced the same cutback on housing and automobile development that had occurred during World War I. Added to this was the post-Depression mentality that held little faith in banks and the economy. Automobile production had been halted in 1941 in the interest of military requirements. From 1941 to 1945, American industry produced 350 thousand aircraft and another 10 million vehicles of all types. But the war ended and the United States was faced with the reversion to a pre-war economy, or the conversion of a massive production capability to post-war levels that were predicated upon war-time output.

Hitler's Volkswagen, or "people's car", concept became the dominant force in post-war development. It was argued that everyone, particularly veterans, deserved to own a car and a place to drive it to! Suburbia had to be created to provide a reason for autos. The single-family home was advanced as more desirable than apartment living. Affordable, matchbox style housing was created in and beyond the near suburbs. Curvilinear streets replaced the old grid-patterned design. Housing styles, as well as automobile design, had to emphasize affordability to appeal to the market.

Suburbia was spawned. Expressways were required. Banks discovered that their customers lived far away, so they had to create branch banks. Downtown shopping areas began to die, but traffic levels were even higher with the growing number of commuters. Something had to be done to recover from the congestion of traffic in inner cities, the associated effects of gridlock, and the damaging effects of the congestion on downtown businesses. The solution was to hire the engineers, who had so successfully created the atom bomb and modern technology, to resolve the problem.

The engineers came along and accomplished what was expected of them. Expressways, limited access ways, and interstate highways were created. Off-street parking (parking garages) and one-way streets were installed. Shrunken pedestrian spaces (narrowed sidewalks) allowed engineers to increase vehicle capacity on inner city streets. Synchronous signalization of traffic lights was implemented to the relief of many commuters and shoppers alike. There is, perhaps, no one alive who has not welcomed the convenience of coasting through a series of traffic lights without stopping. Nor is there anyone who has not experienced the frustration of encountering a series of traffic lights that has not been synchronized. Curb lanes were now for fast movement of vehicles, so the pedestrian beware!

What did it cost us, over the long run, to implement these so-called improvements? It may have cost us the very downtowns that we were trying to improve.

Consider the number of times that you as a user of space have attempted to find a difficult address within an area of a city that you were unaccustomed to negotiating. What do the locals and the commuters do as they encounter your uneven speed and driving pattern? Do they slow down and allow you to meander throughout their streets, or do they let you know what they think about your presumptuousness in acting like a tourist in their space? What do you do when some driver with an out-of-state license plate speeds up and slows down in front of you as you are trying to get from point A to point B?

It is common for traffic engineers to allow up to 5% of commuter and rush hour traffic to bleed through neighborhood street systems. Of course, this tolerance for through traffic is only as good as the day that it is imposed. For instance, a rough estimate of through traffic on a curbless, residential street in Honolulu, Hawaii, in June of 1989 revealed that about 20,000 to 30,000 automobiles per day use this low capacity residential street for access to a major expressway. A high capacity, seldom used street is only one block away, but it is not used. The result of the high traffic is a street that does not resemble its original nature. Cars are bumper to bumper and the residential use has regressed to transient housing, with very little observable concern for what happens. Was this high level of traffic originally planned, or did it happen over time once the trend was started?

Some contemporary planners and critics of downtown programs complain about the over-engineering of downtown streets. What was once considered to be the sacred cow of transportation planning, the one-way street system, is now coming under severe criticism. The engineers' solutions to downtown vehicular congestion were so successful in moving the automobile that the small, pedestrian-oriented businesses suffered. Pedestrians were inadvertently pinched into small pathways that were uncomfortable with high speed traffic immediately next to them. The presence of street people and other undesirable conditions made the now narrowed pedestrian zone a gauntlet of fear-producing encounters that could more easily be avoided altogether by going to a suburban mall or shopping center.

Did the solution become part of the problem? How many people have witnessed the acceleration of downtown decay once street capacities were increased to cure that very problem? It may be that cities and towns got caught up in the trend to implement what appeared to be improved street systems. Federal funding for transportation may have contributed to this malaise of the downtown, due to the trendy and innovative effects of what many feel is the low risk use of federal dollars for experiments. Whatever the cause, the damage has been done to many communities. Core areas that developed historically to serve business and commercial needs have declined. Business and other commercial or service activities have fled to the suburbs in search of customers, thus undoing the original purpose and value of allowing downtown cores to grow.

THE GROWTH OF PLANNING PROBLEMS

The first planning and zoning laws were adopted in New York City in 1916. Up to that time, growth and development followed investment trends and speculation, or patterns of development followed the original interests of surveyors or initial site developers. Midwestern communities were surveyed long before towns were built, so it was common for small sections of property to be dedicated for public use, such as schools and parks. But it was natural for communities to follow the concentric circle path of development that saw residential land uses give way gradually to commercial core growth. This seemed to be okay until center cities reached a size where they stopped functioning well for business.

Jane Jacobs' book *Death and Life of Great American Cities* traced the growth of American cities. She found that commercial cores grew to a point where they became, in her words, "a no-man's land," inhabited at night and on weekends by undesirable users of space. Core areas became unsightly and, thus, were perceived by non-residents to be unsafe. Jacobs surmised that a general principle of downtown planning should be that growth must be planned so that people generally could live near where they work and where they shop. She proposed that a mixed land use plan would provide literally for "eyes on the street" twenty-four hours a day, in the place of eight hours of activity, five days per week, with the remaining sixteen hours in chaos.

Jacobs' book ignited an interest in land use planning and development that emphasized planned growth based on a concept of self-sustaining villages that would be interconnected to controlled industrial and large retail areas. Each village would have a central commercial area with the capability to sustain the everyday shopping needs of the residents. A grocery store, library, and professional office for doctors and dentists were to serve as the core, or magnet, with succeedingly less dense forms of housing expanding outward in concentric circles.

A number of new communities were built with Jacobs' ideas in mind. Reston, Virginia, a suburb of Washington, D.C., and Columbia, Maryland, a suburb of Baltimore, were built from scratch using the interconnecting village concept. Reston was developed around the natural topographical features of the land, resulting in a reasonably dense mixture of multi-family and single-family homes nestled around small village clusters. Columbia followed the same design pattern as Reston, but altered the topographical features more to suit the new land use. Accordingly, Reston is composed of a somewhat confusing curvilinear street plan, whereas Columbia is more accessible. Coral Springs, Florida, was designed by Westinghouse Corporation about the same time. All three are large, thriving communities, with powerful homeowners' associations that strictly enforce a complex array of deed covenants that are designed to preserve the community.

One feature common to all of these projects is the allocation of green space and dedicated buffer zones that separate housing types and areas. The concept of green areas, otherwise publicly dedicated, was trendy when the master plans of Reston, Columbia, and Coral Springs were submitted. Planners conceived of living areas in which every resident could have access to an open, perpetually dedicated green area that was for communal enjoyment. These areas serve as buffers to buildings and private property. Deed restrictions were written so tightly that a resident could not even remove a twig that had fallen. Wildlife was protected and vehicles of all sorts were prohibited, until it became apparent that emergency and maintenance vehicles may be desired. It sounded like a good idea, but security problems ensued in many places because these green areas became "invisible" to the local resident who was prohibited from attaching any sense of ownership to the area.

Urban planning evolved from an emphasis on the logic of planned growth using zoning and building regulations and became a social science. Early planners were required to administer and implement public policy about land use that was set by the public through its elected representatives and appointed planning boards. The social sciences crept into the process and social engineering took off through the planning process. Many admirable and solid-sounding codes were enacted to govern housing, transportation, and landscaping. Urban planners gained credibility as legislation and litigation effects created an environment where community values had to supercede developers' profit motives. An increasing awareness of environmental hazards and conditions also had an impact on the public policy that guided planners.

A shift to suburbia on a scale greater than ever before occurred after World War II. Retooled auto makers began to turn out inexpensive cars that were sleek in shape (compared to pre-war vehicles) to save on materials. But, the sleek design looked good too! Likewise, hemlines went up during World War II to save clothing material. The public responded with support for the new look in cars and clothes. After all, the new look made things more affordable. But the designers could not resist the temptation to be extravagant. European dress designers reintroduced the long look once fabrics became plentiful again. Auto makers could not be outdone as the world, especially the United States, entered a period of prosperity.

Many people remember with nostalgia the 1949 and 1950 Ford that became famous in *Thunder Road*. Car designs were simple and sleek. The 1952–53 Chevrolet models were virtually indestructible. Many World War II veterans aspired to own a house, albeit small, and a Chevrolet. So everyone bought one, of course! But the designers had to create not only a new market but a recurring market. Styles had to change rapidly. Obsolescence was planned so that cars would wear out quicker. As a result, fins, battering rams, and wild designs appeared on American cars. Engines became monoliths that consumed gasoline like water. Automobiles became ugly and distasteful at a time when everything else in life had gotten out of hand, at least from a design standpoint.

No wonder planners decided that cars were ugly and asphalt was uglier. The urban "street-scape" became littered with automobiles and unattractive asphalt parking lots. During the day, the lots looked like the proverbial tourist with finned sunglasses. After work and at night the parking lots were covered with oil spots and litter. Readers may remember that it was natural to dump one's litter anywhere but in one's car!

The horror stories produced by the press and the planners were used to lobby for strict regulations on parking lots and landscaping. For the first time, municipalities began to require that businesses, and even parking lots, adhere to style requirements. Cars had to be hidden behind buildings or in parking garages that hid the vehicle from view by using steel-reinforced concrete retaining walls. Designers accepted these requirements and found that it was better to go with the flow. This possibly subtle sentiment was reinforced by the gradual acknowledgment that the tougher codes increased the price of construction, which increased fees. One had to be careful, but a skillful entrepreneur could make more money going with the flow. Moreover, the smart designer knew that the new dominance of planners, who had become socially driven, would contribute to the potential for flexibility in design.

The trends resulted in the general adoption of landscape and building codes that hide the automobile behind buildings and obscure the vehicle from any natural view of the public. Landscape ordinances require the obscuring of vehicles by bushes, when all they have to do is psychologically screen the autos from the general sight patterns of the passerby. Ordinances have minimum height standards when they really ought to have maximum height standards, so that the landscape does not obstruct natural surveillance.

The urban and general societal unrest in the 1960s allowed the planners to experiment with a wider variety of social theories. This is not to say that anyone had any better idea at the time. In the absence of any better direction, planners advanced the general proposition that water and amenities are good. The reasoning is that people reject society and urban space because it is undifferentiated and cold. Accordingly, people need open space to enjoy fountains and to sit on benches while they commune with nature, perhaps enjoying a sandwich that they brought from home for lunch. This time outside may then help people to cope with the inside pressures of a dull job, with nowhere to go, or of an equally dull existence in a marriage or neighborhood that offers little promise for improvement.

It did not take long for the social thinking of planners to go from supposition to practice. William H. Whyte's book *City* describes in detail the process that was undertaken to induce developers and architects to add open spaces to their projects. Height limitations on buildings were waived on a ratio of planned open space to additional floors. Was there a scientific basis for this ratio? No, it was based simply upon what seemed to be a good idea at the time. This is not to say that open space is bad, or undesirable, but merely to demonstrate the somewhat capricious nature of public policy decisions. Many open spaces are tremendous successes, because the resident user makes them work. Quite a few open spaces are disasters, because the desired user population never took control and made these places work according to plan. Somebody else beat them to it!

Pedestrian malls have been uniquely susceptible to failure. For instance, Oxnard, California, Kansas City, Kansas, and Louisville, Kentucky, installed pedestrian malls in downtown areas to revitalize business, only to further destroy what little they had left. Each of these projects so emphasized the use of amenities and landscaping that little useful open space remained for festivals and seasonal commercial activities (e.g., car and boat shows, art exhibits). The planners also failed to allow for the magnetic effect their amenities and landscaping would have on the indigenous populations of these areas. These run-down areas were inhabited by vagrants and drunks during the daytime and were the scenes of prostitution and drug sales at night. Thus, the areas acquired a bad reputation, despite evidence that few crimes occurred.

The criticism here is of the assumption that what works in one place will work elsewhere. This is referred to in management experience as the "canned goods" and "instant grits" syndrome. Why bother to match the functional requirements of a given space with a unique design and use plan, when all you have to do is go get what someone else has done? Then all you have to do is put the concept in and presto, "instant grits." Another criticism is the tendency to accept blindly the idea that socially desirable amenities and landscaping are always good. In the face of repeated failures, the planner would be better advised to consider amenities and landscaping as options rather than requirements.

The standard to adopt is the process of determining what will make a site plan work, in the place of what it should look like. Even though this approach leaves room for manipulation and avoidance by developers, it allows for more creative thinking and for adaptation of the spirit of the local codes to the immediate situation. For instance, I recommended to the Portland, Oregon, convention center planners that the fountain project intended for the front of the center be delayed, but not deleted, to give the desired users of the site time to take control. The indigenous population was composed of vagrants who had dominated the area for so long that they had become part of the scenery. Portland needed time to make the project work, to displace the dominance of the vagrants with the desired businesses and customer groups. Otherwise, the fountain would serve as a magnet for vagrant grooming and other body functions, thereby presenting a highly visible security and maintenance problem. In another place, where the desired users were already entrenched, the fountain would be a good idea at the outset.

THE GROWTH OF HOUSING PROBLEMS

Public housing and publicly supported housing are relatively new concepts on the American scene. Public housing in America is also atypical of housing throughout the rest of the world in that the United States provides publicly supported housing for only about 5% to 7% of the population. This accounts for only about 4 to 5 million units of an estimated 80 million total housing units in the United States. Great Britain provides about 40% publicly supported housing and modern Asian countries are the same.

Nineteenth century housing in the United States for low-income families was predominantly located in the industrialized urban areas in tenements. One of the oldest designs for tenements, after the age of the simple walk-up apartment building, was the dumbbell style complex, so called because it was a long, rectangular building, with a "T" on each end. This was an attempt to provide a large number of apartments within a small land area within a city. Many of these apartments were poorly ventilated, without windows in the bedrooms. The larger the number of dwelling units required, the more difficult it was to include the normal amenities expected in even the most basic housing. Cold water taps and primitive plumbing were the order of the day.

The First World War created a housing shortage, due to the lack of materials that were diverted to the war effort. This was followed by a housing boom that was short-circuited by the Depression. The Second World War forestalled the growth of housing, which, by the end of the war, was at a critical point in terms of need. Once World War II was over, the housing industry boomed again. War-related industry had to be fed at a level unprecedented by pre-war standards. Moreover, a major shift occurred in public and private policy about housing. The returning veterans were assured that a thankful public would guarantee that each family could afford a single family home. The small, affordable tract house style was developed and suburbia flourished.

Transportation changed the course of history of the public and private housing industry. The Volkswagen concept developed by the pre-war German propaganda machine took hold in the United States where a war industry was attempting to recover from an economic base that had built and sold over 1 million vehicles in four years. Lower and middle class housing moved to the newly expanded suburbs. This provided an excuse for the idea that all people (e.g., those who could afford it) deserved a car and a house. There had to be a place to drive the car, so suburbia was created. Interstate highways followed, in the place of mass transit, so the country was committed to a transportation-driven housing economy and public policy.

Lower class and publicly supported housing was developed near public transportation routes, as close as possible to sources of employment. Post-war, publicly supported housing projects, incredibly, forgot the automobile and turned their back, architecturally, on the car. Many post-war housing projects were designed without the automobile in mind. They focused inwardly on gardens and undifferentiated space, which was conceived as a great way to emulate middle class concepts. The result was the creation of large, unmanageable housing projects that failed because they had no defensible or identifiable territorial space. Moreover, public housing policy emphasized the elimination and reduction of dependence on public housing, so there was no official desire or intention that the residents would identify with and control their space.

Public housing has undergone a change from a policy that originally dictated large, high-rise projects, to the complete reverse, with the idea of scattered housing. A compelling, socially based theory of the late 1950s placed emphasis on placing the underprivileged family into a socially desirable, middle class definition of housing—the high-rise project that thrust the housing unit high into the air so that the occupants could enjoy the view (which was mostly of other buildings, railroad tracks, slums, or swamps). Of course, this policy failed.

Research confirmed the suspicion that the large projects were prone to failure. The dispersion of housing to small, manageable projects made sense. Evaluative research confirmed the fact that the problems (e.g., crime, low occupancy) associated with the large projects were not displaced to the dispersed locations. The research associated with Oscar Newman's book *Defensible Space* demonstrated clearly that large projects could not work. Accordingly, large projects fell off the drawing boards of government and a policy of dispersion of housing ensued.

Federal funding for public housing has been diminishing. The heyday of funding for both construction and social service programs has passed in the relatively short time since the Department of Housing and Urban Development (HUD) was established at the federal level in 1965. HUD's budget has declined from 7% of the federal budget in 1980 to less than 1% in 1988. Communities are now faced with the following legacy:

- large projects that were designed with their backs to the surrounding neighborhoods, making them inaccessible and undesirable
- declining occupancy rates
- changing emphasis of public and private investment to the scattered housing concept
- deteriorated and unsightly areas that serve as magnets to outsiders who deal in drugs and stolen property
- dispersed housing that is prone to attract transients who are associated with serious crime and family problems, thus undermining the continuity of existing neighborhoods
- housing stock that is aging and in need of massive renovation or replacement

Local government now, more than ever, is left holding the bag. The cost of demolition of useless buildings and the relocation of families to suitable housing is a local responsibility.

The large public housing projects of the 1960s are off the drawing boards. Likewise, the high-rise tower projects will no longer be built, because they were proven disasters in perpetuating crime problems. This led to low occupancy rates and failure of the projects. Current policy is directed toward small projects that, theoretically, can blend into the neighborhoods, rather than stand out as a sore thumb. The residents of the older public housing projects were the primary victims of crime. Thus, it is hoped that the scattering of the large volume of housing into small parcels will reduce resident victimization and ameliorate the negative impact on the contiguous neighborhoods.

It is clearly understood from research that the large, high-rise public housing projects are not desirable. Crime analysis units in police departments have found consistently that public or subsidized housing units have a disproportionate number of habitual offenders per capita than other types of housing. Moreover, there is a lot of evidence that much of the perceived problem with public or subsidized housing projects is created by adults and young persons who do not live there, but who use the project as a place of business. Another unfortunate finding is that public projects are magnets for outsiders who are looking for sources of drugs, prostitution, and fencing opportunities.

Many large public and subsidized housing projects have become anonymous entities within neighborhoods or sections of communities. Some have been referred to as "islands of despair" because of their problems. Despite the evidence that the residents themselves are largely the victims and not the major source of the problem, the projects have taken on a bad image. Accordingly, the neighborhoods in which projects are located have turned their backs to the projects as a compensatory reaction.

The move toward a large number of small, scattered, publicly supported housing units presents a problem for the tracking and control of habitual offenders. The centralized projects, which have identifiable boundaries, are now becoming dispersed throughout the community. This may appear to be good for the residents, but there is the possibility that a number of major, unintended outcomes may occur:

- *Rejection*. The project becomes a wedge in what was viewed as a traditional neighborhood or block. Resident, block, and neighborhood use patterns change in a manner that freezes out the project. Everyone loses.
- *Substandard sites*. It is common for sites to be selected based on low land cost. It goes against popular belief, but it is common for public and subsidized housing sites to be located in land areas that have little, if any, redeeming value. Sites are often selected because they have no other useful purpose. Areas enclosed by swamps, railroad yards, industrial areas, and other natural barriers prevail.
- *Displacement*. There is concern that the problems of a large complex will move to the smaller and more dispersed units. Research in the 1960s has shown that this does not occur on a grand scale. But it is clear that demand for services will increase with the change in housing types and the resultant increase in population in the new areas. There is a fear that community values and cultural differences will affect the existing structure of the new host neighborhood. The result may be that the new neighborhood may turn its back on the project, thereby hurting both parties.

- *Land use degeneration.* Blockbusting in its truest sense is occurring rapidly throughout many communities where there is an avid attempt to develop alternatives to large public housing projects. Many bona fide attempts to provide low income or affordable housing result in the squeeze. The squeeze is where every socially desirable condition exists, but the injection of small multi-family housing units into a block with traditional single family housing stock alters the composition sufficiently to begin the process of turnover and conversion of the surrounding housing units. Land and building values drop accordingly. It is common for these small units of eight to twelve apartments to house transients, instead of local needy families. This transient housing is highly correlated with the dwelling locations of habitual offenders.

Major shifts in public housing policy will produce changes in the patterns and activities of criminality.

THE GROWTH OF COMMERCIAL AND RETAIL PROBLEMS

The rapid change of communities after World War II had a dramatic effect on the business world. Television helped to revolutionize advertisement, and traditional values in shopping and marketing were reoriented to a much more mobile society. Downtown banks were faced with massive shifts of population to the new suburbs. Grocery stores began to lose their clientele to distance and mobility. Fast food began to rapidly replace the home-style restaurant. Drive-in and drive-through hamburger joints became the rage of the young and the adult sets.

Many retail businesses were oriented around the pedestrian customer, who was often a repeat patron. But the congestion and lack of parking opportunities in downtowns led to the migration of businesses to strip shopping centers, and then to malls. Standardization of products became important to a media-conscious public who had become extremely mobile. Radical new designs for attracting customers were implemented. The "Googie" style restaurant was created in California to tout the value of standardized family food menus. This fad spread throughout the country. The fast food industry exploded in popular appeal, attended by architectural styles that involved massive parabolic arches and caricatures of boys delivering hamburgers.

The banking industry was in a real fix. Still suffering from the loss of confidence during the Depression years, the banking industry was facing a dilemma. Customers were moving out to suburbs, but their money was still being held in large, secure, fortress style buildings that were located in the center city. Branch banks were required to make banking services more accessible, but many bankers feared the public would perceive small branch banking facilities as insecure. After all, how could one's life savings be kept secure in a dinky little building? It did not matter that a person's money was really not kept at a branch facility. It was the image that mattered, so, with little forethought, bank architects set out to design minifortresses that conveyed the sense of security.

No one really criticized the fortress concept of branch banks. With the advent of the drive-in teller concept, banks sought after corner lots so that vehicular access could circulate from one street through to another. Planners liked this since the cars and ugly parking lots were obscured from public view. Traffic engineers like the concept, not because they cared about screening the public from ugly cars, but because it reduced traffic hazards from people who slow down as they look for a parking spot before they exit the main street or highway. The planners and engineers agreed for once, but for different reasons.

Security specialists were concerned about the circulation plan for branch banks since most customers came by auto. They had to park on the side or back of the bank and then walk to the front to get in. This increased the exposure of the customer to robbery, or just to fear of robbery. The bank seemed to be safe, but the customer was not. Finally, by 1985, the Bank Administration Institute published some new guidelines, based upon its own funded research, that called for a complete reversal of branch bank design. The research showed that robbers actually preferred the enclosed fortress design because they felt that it protected them from drive-by surveillance while they committed their robberies. The robbers even preferred a limited number of entrances, since it made their job easier in controlling access and escape during their robberies. A number of other internal design conflicts were discovered as well.

The advent of the automatic teller machine (ATM) signaled the change in the way of thinking about branch banks. The first ATMs were placed in the walls of the building so that they could be serviced from the secure teller area inside. But where was the secure teller area? In the back, of course, since the layout was oriented to vehicular traffic that would flow to the side and back of the building. This placed the early ATM machines in untenable locations, out of the view of any natural surveillance during the times they would most likely be in use—nights and weekends.

The traditional grocery store was made obsolete by the post-war expansion of transportation. As a child, I remember going once a week to a grocery store that was near my dad's plant. Every Friday, the paycheck was cashed, and food was purchased immediately. This was a dramatic improvement in convenience over the pre- and post-war practice of having groceries delivered, which really put a limitation on the ability of the shopper to compare prices. But even the original supermarket concept fell prey to distance. Paychecks could be mailed to branch banks. New shopping centers were built closer to where people lived, instead of close to where they worked. Everybody had a checkbook. Finally, the convenience industry was conceived as a remake of the old "Mom and Pop" store.

The commitment to the automobile as the primary source of transportation, in all but the most urban settings, continued the rapid change of environmental effects on behavior and safety. People had to have a place to drive the car, so expressways and interstate highways were created. People who traveled along these highways had to have a place to eat and sleep, so the roadside stops were created. Residential housing moved near access points to interstate highways to take advantage of the ease of commuting. Local businesses moved out to interstate highway corridors to chase the residential users. Interstate or expressway interchanges became hot properties for development. Service stations, convenience stores, fast food restaurants, and branch banks took up the best locations. Of course, crime followed in the wake of this development activity, because transportation made criminal opportunities more convenient. Thus was created the ultimate paradox. The very conveniences that attracted the urban dweller to the suburbs had the same effect on the criminal. Who says that humans do not respond to the environment?

The expansion of roads and superhighways to accommodate the needs of a more mobile society may have had a more profound effect on the commercial and retail environment than any other in its history. Who goes to a main bank office anymore? What happened to the typical "Mom and Pop" grocery store? Have you noticed the decline of the traditional supermarkets? Now the grocery industry has had to go to the "hyper store," where you can do everything from shop for groceries, get your prescriptions, buy lunch, order your eyeglasses, conduct your banking, and have your car serviced — all at the same place.

What does this have to do with crime prevention? First, these changes to the environment have shifted the patterns of criminal activity and have created new levels and types of crimes and losses. Second, most of these environmental changes and conditions occurred without input or advice from security and law enforcement personnel.

The easiest way to avoid a problem, to most cynical persons, is to do nothing. This mentality has not only dominated the security and law enforcement profession, but it has become the stereotypical image of these professions that has affected public policymakers and developers alike. This book is a refutation of the concept that security thinking cannot contribute to the achievement of human objectives.

Pedestrian malls, shopping centers, branch banks, fast food restaurants, and convenience stores have taken over the commercial and retail activities of communities. According to the National Association of Convenience Food Stores annual report for 1987, the average sales per member store were $1.1 million. A recent article in the *Louisville Courier Journal* revealed that the typical McDonalds restaurant has sales of $1.05 million per year, while the typical Kentucky Fried Chicken restaurant may have gross sales of $.95 million per year. Another newspaper article revealed that as much as

80% of all Bandaid bandages were sold in convenience stores. Finally, it is common for an ATM machine to contain a range of as much as $70,000 to $100,000 dollars on a daily basis.

The level of robberies and customer victimization at all of these properties is high. Moreover, the level of customer and general public fear is higher, which has an immeasurable effect on the sales and viability of these businesses. Can these industries use the environment to improve profit and reduce fear and concern? The answer is yes! Many are already doing it!

5

Behavioral Precedents of CPTED: From Caves to Fast Food

CAVES

Cave dwellers did what we do now when we move into new housing or offices. Cave dwellers cleared areas in front of their caves. They stacked rocks along the periphery of the area that they claimed. They painted the entrances and the interiors to reflect ballads or stories about their past. Why did they do this? Obviously, to mark their space. They did not have alarms, fences, or other home security devices. They had to ensure that a passerby would observe that the forest or jungle was, somehow, differentiated from surrounding space, thus indicating ownership. The intruder, who had learned territorial behavior from her antecedents, knew that this was controlled space. If she were going to violate it, she had better do it quickly.

How does this relate to contemporary society? Why is it that the home team has an advantage over visiting teams in any sport? Is it just because the fans cheer louder, or is it because they are defending their turf? It is common for teams to be excused for their road losses, because everyone knows how tough it is to win on the road. Moreover, it is becoming clear that employees are more likely to take care of property that is assigned to them personally, than that which is generally available.

The first thing most people do when they move into a new apartment or office is to personalize it. One's belongings have to be unpacked and personal items put out for the new occupant of space to be comfortable. Everyone is different in this regard. Some people move into an office and reorient their work station toward the window. Others are wall facers. Still more are door facers. Some don't like to face anything directly, so they place their desk on a diagonal line. The open space office designers really missed this point during the early 1970s when they put everyone in the open with the same desk, the same colors, and facing the same direction.

Border definition and symbolic barriers were important to early humans. Sticks with skulls atop were strategically placed to signify entrance to controlled space. Drums were beat constantly to define closed space by the distance to which the sound would travel. Accordingly, contemporary humans feel the need to identify with space, both permanently and semipermanently. Later chapters will deal with territorial behavior, but it is important to note here that the fundamental territorial nature of human beings has changed little in the last 5,000 years, and remains a powerful factor in behavioral control.

GREEK TEMPLES

During the early period of the Greek empire, nearly 2,700 years ago, the designers of temples used environmental concepts to affect and control behavior. Greek temples built in Sicily, which was the largest Greek colony at the time, were constructed of stone dug from quarries that were below sea level, and as near as possible to the sea. Designers found that this stone contained high levels of phosphorous, from thousands of years of the decay of sea animals. When this stone was used to form columns, it reflected light in such a manner as to appear golden immediately after dawn and preceding dusk.

These designers were using the environment to affect human behavior. They knew that people would notice and be impressed by the golden spectrum of the temple as they approached it for services — which were naturally scheduled at dawn and dusk. This golden effect elicited a psychological effect, reinforcing the powers of the faith and of the priests, who clearly must have turned the temple to gold just for the services.

The designers also knew that people would focus on the golden aura emanating from the columns, which would have a physiological effect on the eye. Even though the ambient light level was reasonably low at dawn and dusk, the reflected light from the columns would cause the worshipers eyes to react. The pupils of the eyes would contract as a response to the intensely focused light, thus robbing the worshiper of his night or low-light vision. Guess what happened when they entered the temple? It was the same effect as entering a movie theater on a hot summer afternoon. You can't even see your feet, let alone a priest who has been strategically stationed to literally scare the daylights out of you.

Light is important to human beings. Sunlight is a source of vitamin D. Light is used psychologically and physically as a therapy. We refer to smart people as being bright. We have bright ideas. We shed light on problems. We tell people to sleep on problems, because things are better in the morning—when it is light. We tell people to lighten up when they are in dark moods. Ernest Hemingway described light as a remedy for depression in his short story, *A Clean, Well-Lighted Place.*

Humans are so oriented to light that it is significant in the "fight versus flight" protective response, which we all possess. A person's reaction to being pinched surreptitiously in the dark will be radically different from the same event occurring in broad daylight. Don't we keep people in the dark, when we want to keep them guessing?

MEDIEVAL CITIES

Height was used as a defense throughout early history. Normal people went to bed when the sun went down, and they got up when the sun came up. Only abnormal people went out at night, so natural barriers were used for personal defense. The ground floors of dwellings were designed only for daytime activities. Ladders were used to go to upper floors, so that they could be pulled up at night, denying vertical access to sleeping and high value areas. Stairs were only used to connect the upper floors.

Height has always been used on the macro scale to protect whole communities. Any tourist who has scaled the many steps to cities and castles in medieval Europe can relate to this. The tiny country of San Marino, located in northeast Italy, is a classic example. It is less than a square mile, but it is perched on top of a mountain. Accordingly, it has never been conquered.

How is height used in contemporary society? Church steeples and the ministers' pulpits are high. Judges in courtrooms and desk sergeants in police departments have traditionally sat on high benches. The convenience industry has discovered an advantage to elevating the position of cashiers, so that they not only can see well, but command respect and attention throughout the store.

Height is important socially. Kings did not allow anyone to rise beyond the level of their heads, so people had to kneel to demonstrate subservience. A common expression is that some people "look down on others," as a means of demonstrating their perceived superiority. Lifeguards at swimming pools sit up high and so do judges at professional tennis matches (possibly for their own safety).

It is certain that height, in many situations, is used to facilitate visibility. But do not overlook its value in terms of symbolic power and superiority. A security guard who is standing on a platform or looking down from a gallery onto a parking lot has a lot more power than one who may be standing in the midst of the autos. A prison guard may control many more prisoners from her perch in a tower than when she stands on the ground. Is this only because she can see more people, or does it have something to do with advantage? Which rooms cost the most in hotels?

Height is used symbolically in building design and urban planning. The height standard for buildings in Washington, D.C., is the Capitol. It would be against local standards, mostly unwritten ones, to build a structure higher; but, realistically, it would probably sink anyway in the swampy geological make-up characteristic of the D.C. area. After all, it had no real land value, so they made it into the nation's capital.

Height is used symbolically to denote authority and position. Kids are moved to the head or top of their class. Executives move to the top of the organizational chart. People who are successful generally move up in life. They move up the ladder of life. Other people get down on their luck.

BAROQUE MANNERISM

Artists and philosophers were no different hundreds of years ago than they are now. It is impossible for one human being not to compete with another. During the period between the Renaissance and the development of baroque styles of architecture, art, and classics (1500 to 1700 A.D.), a few artists said, "The heck with this balance stuff!" They broke conventional rules of style and balance by leaving things in disarray, or imbalance. Musical compositions always ended on a consonant chord. Stories were supposed to end happily ever after. Plays were supposed to have some redeeming value. Paintings were supposed to be two-dimensional depictions of the subject, which was usually religious.

But the mannerists established their own personal styles, or they simply went beyond convention. The more radical sought to achieve dissonance where there was once consonance. Paintings and frescoes (painting in wet plaster) were designed to create anxiety, as a message or pedagogical device, to convey a new attitude or philosophy. Modern psychologists refer to similar effects as "cognitive dissonance," which are attempts to disrupt balance in cognitive perceptions as a basic step in attitude reformation.

Machiavelli was a famous writer and political adviser to the king of the city state of Florence. An old story that was told in Florence was related by Dr. Frederic Licht, who happened to be my professor during his stay in Italy in 1968. He told of a situation wherein the famous Machiavelli assisted the king in handling a serious problem. Apparently, the king had to give up some voting power to the local merchant guild because they controlled the money that he needed to run the little country. Se he went to Machiavelli with his political problems. He said, "Mach, I am in deep trouble. I had to give the vote to those merchants."

Machiavelli was not to be outdone by a group of merchants. After all, he had achieved great fame as a behind-the-scenes expert in political maneuvering. So he recommended two strategies to the king. One was to use rules of order. This gets everyone, because everyone seems to lose equally, so they are happier. The second strategy was to design meeting chambers that created so much stress that people came in, voted fast, and got out quick. How did he do it? He hid the standard ceiling support columns behind false walls and installed narrow fake columns. This made the walls appear to be weak. He then installed additional beams in the ceiling to make it appear heavy. He added to this additional statuary and violent frescoes painted into the ceiling to convey the impression of heaviness. Hence the person sitting in a meeting was bound to become anxious. Vote quickly and get out before the ceiling falls on your head!

This set a design standard that is commonly used in church sanctuaries, courtrooms, public meeting facilities, legislative chambers, and hotel ballrooms. Many of the contemporary designers of these facilities are vague about the origin of this design practice. They just do it because that is the way it has always been done. This could present a problem in current design if the architect used a heavy ceiling design over a location intended for relaxation and contemplative activity. A poorly used place is costly, nonproductive, and prone to security problems.

Dissonance in music has been used in contemporary society to affect public attitudes. The anti-war period in the late 1960s produced dissident music that was intended to upset the listeners, not to please them. Screeching sounds were combined with lyrics that threatened traditional standards and beliefs. Dissonance in art was used since before World War II to upset and to scare. Nazi Germans were depicted as craven monsters. The Japanese were portrayed as bloodthirsty animals. German posters presented the American as an oversized degenerate who enjoyed torturing prisoners. Posters during the Vietnam War period contained strange and foreboding caricatures of the Uncle Sam image and the U.S. flag.

The artist, sculptor, musician, and architect consciously use their media to achieve the psychological and behavioral effects that they desire. Others copy these patterns without consciously acknowledging the original purpose or intended effect. People react positively or negatively to these designs without consciously questioning their purpose. A state police academy in the northeast United States was constructed using the most up-to-date concepts for training. The interior designers purposely used a high-stress-producing color on the accent walls behind the instructors. The students facing these walls were kept awake and more attentive. But the desire for uniformity in decoration overpowered the thought process of the interior designer, so the same color was used as the accent wall in each instructor's office. Yet the behavioral requirements of these offices were the exact opposite of the classroom. Instructors' offices were for contemplative work, principally in developing lesson materials, so a color scheme was needed that allowed the worker to pass time more effectively and work calmly.

It did not take long for the staff of the academy to know that something was wrong. No one was ever in his office when you needed him. Eventually, it became clear that if you wanted to find anyone, you had to look in the cafeteria or the library. People who had to complete any major project ended up going to these places.

LOUIS XIV

Louis XIV was the king of France (1643–1715). Louis introduced what would later be called "urban renewal" to the streets of Paris. He installed broad boulevards and extensive landscaping. Louis was proud of his beautification efforts, until he found them defaced by vandals during his morning rides. So he embarked on a massive security program that culminated in the installation of nearly 7,000 street lamps from 1700 to 1701.

This was the first wide scale use of outdoor lighting in history. But this lighting was installed primarily to protect property. Normal people got up when the sun came up and went to bed when the sun went down. People were afraid of night air, thinking that this air carried more diseases. They closed up their homes at night, even in hot weather. It is interesting that a Johns Hopkins University study in the mid-1980s confirmed the suspicion that night airs carry more viruses.

Contemporary outdoor lighting is viewed popularly as a fundamental device for protecting people. Louis XIV's lighting initiative may have changed the course of human history, because he introduced outdoor lighting as a means of protecting property, since normal people did not go out at night. The widespread credibility and confidence in the technology of outdoor lighting must have planted the seed of change that has irreversibly affected the quality of life.

People now go out at night. They go to church and to school at night. They go to athletic events at night and they play golf at driving ranges that are open all night. People jog at night for convenience and comfort. People prefer nighttime for many outdoor functions. Technology and the willingness to use it, even for a somewhat selfish and costly reason by Louis XIV, has significantly changed the course of human history.

Yet most people take the presence of light for granted. Lighting engineers have learned a lot about the effects of light on human behavior. Indoor lighting was designed traditionally to provide a balance of natural and man-made lighting at the floor level. Lighting sources were placed in hallways and foyers at the center of ceilings, so that the cones of light would cover the floor. But people's eyes are not on the floor; their feet are there.

New experiments have demonstrated that traditional interior lighting may not have taken advantage of its potential effects on human behavior. Hallways and foyers were centrally lit, so that the cones of light would cover the floor. People stand and see at a range of 4'8" to 6'0". Accordingly, it has been noticed that people will walk near the middle of centrally lighted corridors. They will stand near the middle of centrally lighted foyers. The closer they are to people the more likely they are to exhibit avoidance behaviors, out of politeness and discomfort.

When the light source is oriented toward the walls in hallways and foyers, people will walk, or stand, closer to the wall. They are more likely to establish eye contact because of the increased distance. They are more likely to feel comfortable and safer. Recent research has demonstrated that there is a 30% reduction of noise in these well-lighted hallways and foyers.

Lighting clearly has an impact on people's perception of space. People need distance to feel safe from potential threats. The perception of distance is important, perhaps more important than the reality. Lighting can easily affect the perception of distance.

The easiest way to fully understand these concepts is to spend part of a day in an elevator. The fewer the people, the further apart they will stand. But they are more likely to establish eye contact. As the elevator becomes more crowded, people will give each other social distance by practicing avoidance behaviors. They will look up or down, but avoid eye contact, even though they are touching others due to crowding. Touching is legitimate and nonthreatening when there is a crowd. However, watch what happens as the crowd departs the elevator: continued touching will be perceived as a threat, to the point that it becomes fear-producing enough to be considered an assault.

Lighting experts are thinking more than ever about how to use lighting to achieve behavioral affects.

NAPOLEON III

Napoleon III (1808–1873) introduced concepts that were later adopted by Hitler, Mussolini, and Roosevelt. Napoleon learned, as he ascended to power in 1853, that governments in financial crisis, fearing social unrest, spend money and build buildings. After all, only the government has money when there is a financial panic.

Napoleon III built roads and buildings. He proclaimed that cities needed broad boulevards so that people could enjoy the environment and commune with nature. His underlying purposes were to keep people busy thinking that all was well, and to improve the military's ability to control the masses. In this latter regard, Napoleon had learned that a small number of people could barricade a narrow street, effectively neutralizing a large number of soldiers who could not outflank the blockage. Broad boulevards were harder to barricade and more amenable to flanking maneuvers of troops. So, under the guise of urban renewal, Napoleon attempted to control the public by implementing a plan of street improvements.

Napoleon III did something else, which were it not for his perverse intent, would be the major objective for CPTED specialists. He authorized his chiefs of police to raze or demolish any building or habitat known to be the hideout of criminals. Baron Haussmann, the chief of police in Paris, wrote in his memoirs that he delighted in his newfound authority to get rid of any building or structure that was unsightly, merely by saying that criminals used it. Baron Haussmann was apparently very discriminating when it came to architecture, which must have been unsettling to many Parisians.

Hitler and Mussolini spent massive sums of money that were needed desperately by their constituents to prove that all was well within their governments. Following Napoleon's example, Mussolini and Hitler erected buildings and committed government funds to projects that would not have been supported by the private sector. Hitler initiated the Volkswagen campaign to draw attention away from the excessive expenditures on the military that deprived consumers. Mussolini constructed buildings, including the ugly memorial to King Victorio Emmanuele in Rome, which appears to be, and therefore is called, the "marble cake." Mussolini was effective in wiping out organized crime in Sicily by assigning the army to eliminate anyone who was connected remotely to the Mafia.

President Franklin D. Roosevelt had to adopt some of the same techniques, out of necessity. Works Progress Administration (WPA) and Civilian Conservation Corps (CCC) employees built buildings all over the mall in Washington, D.C., as well throughout the United States. These programs supplemented major public housing assistance projects that were supported under several domestic funding activities. Many large military family housing projects were funded as an indirect source of affordable housing, as well as an incentive to join the armed services.

Some of the projects were, clearly, make-work in their orientation. There is still the shell of a bridge left in northeast Florida that was built by a CCC gang. Unfortunately, there is no water nearby, nor any reason for the bridge, except for the future potential of a cross-state barge canal.

One thing leads to another in this world. Roads have to be used and buildings have to be inhabited. Bridges need traffic and ships have to be filled. Why? Because we have them! History has produced legacies for the present population that must not be taken for granted. Everything must be questioned because, many times, what we are doing is justified for one purpose, when the original reason was something different.

The issue here is to learn from real history, not from habit. Moreover, it is imperative to cut through the surface of official justifications for doing things, to understand the real reasons.

CONTEMPORARY

Everyone who is in a competitive situation, especially those who are successful, uses any opportunity to his advantage. The people who play and manage major league baseball are not rocket scientists, but they record and map every pitch and every swing. Why? They want to know the tendencies of every player. It doesn't work every time for them, but it helps to prove that random response is less valuable. Any edge is important.

The fast food industry may be the most oriented to using the environment to control behavior. One major chain, which may be credited with the introduction of standard food products, has pioneered most strategies in environmental manipulation. This corporation made the drive-through lane famous. It introduced the talking sign that has created stage fright and embarrassment for many a customer, although it increases impulse buying. The same chain introduced the two-window system, where you give up your money at one window and get your food at another. Customer participation is the implicit message in all of this chain's procedures.

This fast food chain invites customers to place special orders, then when you get to the second window, they tell you that you have to go sit in the "idiot" lane until your food is done. Had you ordered it "their way," you would have gotten your food immediately. Why do they put the "idiot" lane immediately in front of the second window? Is that to make it easier for the store employee to bring out your special order when it is finished cooking? Or is it possible that they want the people behind you to notice that you had to wait? Could it be that they want the person behind you to have to make a radical turn to get around you, so that they will be reminded that it is the people with the special orders who mess everything up? Have you ever tried to balance your cold drink and your hamburger in one hand as you negotiated your way around some "idiot" who clearly must have placed a special order?

Most of the fast food industry depends on customer participation to create at least the illusion of efficiency, which is supposed to contribute to low prices. Customers usually do not mind handing over their money first before getting their bag of food, which clearly prevents an unscrupulous customer from ruining things for everyone by running off without paying. The industry has found that customers are less likely to complain if a bag is placed next to the cash register while the money is being taken. The bag may even be empty as long as the customer believes that it is her bag.

Most parents teach their children to pick up after themselves. So does the fast food industry. In the spirit of customer participation, it is expected that people will dispose of their leftovers and trash. Try leaving your tray next time and see how the other customers react. It will probably be the first time anyone looked at you or established eye contact. The industry has discovered that customers will generally avoid contact with others, unless something unusual happens, whereas they are prone to stare and smile at others in traditional restaurants. Why? Because few people dress up to go out for fast food. Nor are they apt to use their best table manners, so they really want to avoid being seen or seeing others, particularly whom they may know. The last thing anyone wants is to be seen wearing curlers while pigging out on a sloppy hamburger.

One major corporation recently hit upon a brilliant strategy. They hire senior citizens to work in the customer areas, which is largely a cleaning and straightening job. Young people had traditionally performed these functions and were largely invisible to customers. But who can miss grandma or grandpa puttering around cleaning up? Grandma and grandpa may even be a bit grumpy with someone who is messy or with a small group that is noisy, or that leaves belongings in the aisles. People are less likely to be offended by an older person, so they will not lose face by submitting to her control.

Most fast food chains use a total environmental management concept that emphasizes stress. Active colors are combined with cut tempo music. Employees are influenced to do everything quickly. Orders are repeated loudly, as if the food will really be custom made. Furnishings are designed for appearance and ease of cleaning, not for comfort. Trash receptacles are placed prominently to reinforce customer participation. The environment is designed to create the impression, if not the reality, that you got fed fast.

Employees wear matching uniforms. Some chains dress their new employees in different uniforms identifying them as trainees. This seems to elicit greater tolerance for their delays or mistakes. A customer would have to be a real jerk to complain about the service.

Food is generally well packaged, even if it is to be eaten on the property. This helps to preserve the freshness, but it also keeps the customer from examining his purchase at the counter. The customer is less apt to complain about a mistake when he will have to get in line again, or submit to the disapproval of other customers for butting in at the head of the line.

Food that is prepared already is arrayed in color-coded packages so that the customer can see what is immediately available. Once again the customer is participating in the process that delivers fast food by being obliged to order what is ready. Customers also find themselves rushing to fast food restaurants at odd hours, to beat the crowd. Have you ever been in a discussion with fellow workers about where to go for lunch, when one states that it is only 11:30 A.M. and you just have time to get to McDonalds? Why should we be in a hurry to get to a fast food place? Because we know that we will get fed fast if we come at times other than breakfast, lunch, or dinner.

Finally, why do some of the chains refuse to use cueing lanes that are common in airports or banks? Why don't they use two outdoor signs so that you have time to organize your order before you get to the sign that talks? Why do the clerks call out for your order over the head of the customer in front of you who is trying to gather her stuff and get out of your way? Why do customers frantically scan the posted menus, when everyone knows what a fast food restaurant serves? The answer is stress. Customers under stress are more manageable and they are more likely to impulse buy.

Anyone who is in a competitive business will use any appropriate angle to get ahead. The environment is used to direct and control customer behavior for the sake of the business's objective, to deliver a quality service and make money. Other contemporary industries use the environment to their advantage. The convenience industry is experimenting with new store designs and procedures. Gas stations have changed dramatically. The new kiosk gas station has several islands of pumps, convenient food item sales, and a carwash. All of this is placed under a sea of light that is more welcoming and safer than the outside of traditional service stations.

6

Using the Environment to Affect Behavior

HUMAN/ENVIRONMENT RELATIONSHIPS

Perhaps it was easier for ancient human beings to appreciate and respect their dependence on the environment. The environment provided sustenance and it provided challenges to survival. Humans had to adjust to their environment, for they were limited in the type and amount of changes they could make to it. Adaptation was the rule. Trial and error methods produced knowledge about clothing, fire, and the preservation of foods. When early humans learned that foods could be grown as well as found, the first step in using the environment to human advantage was made.

Humans eventually discovered that the environment could yield elements that were useful, but they had to be put in new combinations that were not inherent or endemic to nature. They learned to extract medicines and spices from plants, and to extract and process metals for tools and for ornamentation. Somewhere along the line, early humans learned how to combine ingredients to cause chemical reactions that produced alcohol. The final step for primitive human beings in the process of learning to control their environment was the harnessing of nature through water power and gravity. The wheel revolutionized human existence. Moreover, the discovery of their intellectual mastery over animals gave humans greater power to manipulate the environment.

Most of contemporary human responses to the environment are involuntary. They are either metabolic responses that are inborn or they are learned responses that seem to come naturally. Most responses are so automatic that they occur in our subconscious states. We don't have to think about most stimuli analytically to react to them. Our responses to the environment are similar from a pure survival standpoint, but our responses to other stimuli vary with our socialization and training.

An earlier chapter referred to the tendency for police to subconsciously scan openings — doors and windows. Illumination consultants scan ceilings.

Wallpaper advisors only look at walls. And floor specialists are always looking down. An engineer looks at structural cues. The architect looks at the appearance and functionality of a building. The fire chief looks at access. The normal user of a building only looks at where she is going, after the first encounter. It is clear that we orient ourselves socially and vocationally to a range of subconscious and conscious responses to environmental cues.

Figure 6–1 presents a simple model of human/environment interactions that divides the basic reactional elements of humans into three categories: metabolic, perceptual, and skeletal/muscular systems. The model identifies six elements of the environment that impinge upon human beings: temperature, pressure, humidity, light, sound, and gravity.

Human metabolic mechanisms are mainly those that are biological. People are born with these mechanisms that scan the near environment. The near environment may be defined as that which we are touching, or that which may be within reaching distance.

Temperature is a significant variable in affecting metabolic mechanisms. A controlled experiment would show that in a room full of people in which the temperature was changed radically in only half of the room, overall body temperature would not change significantly. Why? It's called "homeostasis"! The body automatically responds to a rise in temperature by opening the pores to emit moisture, which evaporates to create a cooling sensation of the skin. The veins expand and move closer to the surface of the skin to emit core heat. The mind automatically slows down

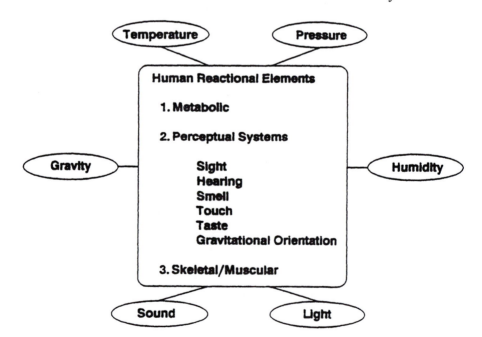

Figure 6–1: Human/environment relationships.

certain body functions. The legs become uncrossed and the arms become unfolded.

This explains the paradox that occurs when there is a boat accident. The strong swimmer attempts to go for help. The weak, or nonswimmer, stays with the boat. Who survives? It's always the nonswimmer who automatically stays in a fetal position awaiting rescue. This natural reaction preserves core heat and allows the nonswimmer to survive. The swimmer turns up the internal motor and increases core heat: the body gets confused, the veins swell, the pores open, and the swimmer dies of hypothermia.

How may temperature be used to affect behavior? It is done all the time. Time and space relationships are important. A warm classroom is just about the worst possible environment for maintaining attention immediately after lunch. Once food reaches the stomach, the body transfers blood to the thoracic region to provide fuel for the muscular gyrations involved in digestion. Some of this blood comes from brain supplies, so the shortage of blood in the brain induces drowsiness and lack of concentration.

A hot room induces stress and anxiety. People will complete their business and leave for more comfortable surroundings. A cold room will also induce stress, but in different ways. The use of temperature to control behavior is indisputable, but it must be used based on the uniqueness of the situation.

A police chief told the following story about the kitchen that had been placed in the new public safety building. Once the building had been opened, what had been planned as an employee convenience became a hangout area. The chief of police would occasionally walk in and clear the area of employees who alleged that they were merely on break. The chief became the heavy in a growing management and labor conflict. With the advice of a CPTED specialist, the chief secretly arranged for a special damper to be placed in the air conditioning ducts. The temperature rose 12 degrees and no amount of tinkering with the thermostat helped. Eventually the kitchen was written off as a permanent problem, an aberration of the architectural design. The chief of police reports that now there are never more than three people in the kitchen, and there is usually only one person sitting. Where do you think that this chief of police and I met with one of his recalcitrant lieutenants who is in charge of a special project? You're right, the kitchen! Once the lieutenant had broken out into a sweat, the chief and I laid on the results of the evaluation of the lieutenant's project. It was amazing how quickly he responded positively to the proposed improvements.

Heat, light, temperature, pressure, sound, humidity, and gravitational effects may all be used to affect behavior. Each of these elements has already directed and channeled human reactions and growth in the natural environment. The question then becomes how to use these elements to enhance the achievement of human objectives.

Perceptual systems include the senses of sight, hearing, smell, touch, taste, and gravitational orientation. These are the human traits that are used to scan the middle and far environment. Most humans believe that the sense of sight is the strongest, but we actually rely on all of our senses. Nearly everyone has observed the uncanny perceptual capabilities of a person who is either visually- or hearing-impaired. One wonders how he is able to develop such instincts. But all humans, often without realizing it, very subtly use all their instincts continually.

One example that is used in CPTED training is to blindfold all of the class and drive them around town in a bus or van with the windows open. The students are asked if they think they can identify the area in which they have driven. Most state initially that they do not think they could do so. But it doesn't take long for them to begin to pick things out as they concentrate on sorting their perceptions and bring recognizable cues to the conscious state. The odor of bus exhausts and refracted sounds of traffic will suggest that they are downtown. The odors of dumpsters and cooking mingle with the voices of kids playing and balls bouncing to lead the class to the conclusion that they are in a housing area. The class finds that they are more likely to notice music and cooking aromas that are different from their own experience.

Some Russian research in the early 1980s found that newborn children have the same intellectual capacity as a mature adult. The difference is that they do not have the years of learning and the millions of bits of information that are compiled through life experiences that the adult uses to analyze environmental cues. The intellectual power is there, but its use has to await programming. A person raised in the country may have difficulty distinguishing among the sounds and smells of the inner city. Moreover, a nonresident is more likely to identify these cues than a resident, who has had time to become inured to her environmental condition. An understanding of these observations about behavior is important to the CPTED planner.

The visual sense collects information about what may be seen in the environment. This information is processed initially by the subconscious to determine its value. Everything that occurs physically within the line of sight of any human is captured visually, but it may not rise to the level of consciousness unless there is something significant enough about it that it stands out.

Each person's socialization and vocational training has established a set of variables that dictates the evaluation of visual scanning. Police officers notice things that other people fail to recognize. Customers and users of space respond to environmental cues and variables that may not be recognized by local residents or business people who have become accustomed to that particular location. A builder or engineer may notice things that escape the conscious recognition of a property owner or security guard. Each person is attuned to a different visual perspective of the environment.

The auditory sense, hearing, is more powerful than most people imagine. Sounds are recorded by the ear and transferred to the brain for evaluation. Pressure changes are recorded by the ear and transferred as well.

The ears collect data about the environment that is processed by the subconscious. Significant data is passed upward to the level of conscious awareness for action. Other data is erased or stored in the subconscious. People are more likely to consciously "hear" music or other noise that is foreign to them and to be annoyed by it. The companies that specialize in background music purposely compose or recompose music so that it may be recognized. Why? So that it will stay in the subconscious or subliminal state. Otherwise it would be noticeable and distracting, rather than useful for suppressing extraneous or unwanted noise.

The olfactory sense, the ability to smell, is as powerful as the other senses. Smell is linked to taste, which is also linked to the visual sense. That is why chefs are so careful about the visual presentation of food, as well as its taste and smell. Some of the smarter public housing designers have learned to use flowers and blossoming trees to serve as visual delimiters and to provide masking of unpleasant odors.

Because smell defines many human functions, it may be important to maintain certain smells. Can you imagine a fish market that doesn't smell of fish? Can you imagine a popcorn vendor who sells canned popcorn? No way, because the interaction between sight, sound, and smell is critical to affecting behavior. A downtown mall in Louisville has problems leasing business locations that are near the exits. Why? Restrooms are located near the entrances. The principle users of these restrooms are vagrants. The restroom entrances are near public telephones, which legitimize vagrant activities. The smell of urine is overpowering.

Real estate sales persons know the tricks of smell. Some homes or apartments have odors that are associated with water problems or animals. Mildew and backed-up drains really make a place seem less desirable. Pets can create a lot of problems through uncontrolled elimination of wastes and through the chemical excretions associated with territorial behavior. What does the wise realtor do with a "stinker"? The solution is to mask the odor or eliminate it. The latter costs too much, so masking is the normal response. Using freshly baked bread is an excellent strategy. The aroma not only masks other odors, it evokes powerful nesting responses.

A potential buyer may look at a house or apartment that has serious cosmetic problems. He will certainly be turned off and will comment that the place is in lousy condition. Add the smell of freshly baked bread and the prospective customer may say that the home really looks lived in. He still may not want to buy it, but his overall impression will be different. He may appreciate the certain quality of the dwelling that caused the previous family to spend a lot of time there.

The smell of freshly baked bread could enhance the attractiveness of a renovated pedestrian mall or a strip shopping center, particularly where heavy pedestrian activity is expected. The developer or management company may wish to offer lease incentives, or loan guarantees, to get bakeries to come into a project. It would also be desirable for the baker to be influenced to bake during business hours or early evening, instead of the traditional middle of the night. Bakeries could be located temporarily to serve as inducements for pedestrian activity that in turn would increase other business prospects.

The tactile sense, touch, is more than what may be felt by the fingers. It is linked to the metabolic mechanisms as well as to the perceptual senses. Touch involves a complex set of sensors in the skin and muscles that give us the ability to perceive temperature, humidity, pressure, shape, texture, and weight of objects. Few persons think of the sense that allows the individual to feel pressure, which may be something as slight as a breeze or a person walking behind them. The sensing of texture helps us to discern the difference between yogurt and the side of a brick. It helps us to distinguish a slippery surface from one that has more traction.

Everyone has seen how people change their walking style when they encounter smooth, wet-appearing surfaces. They look down and take short, tentative steps. This would not be good for enhancing feelings of safety, nor for encouraging people to establish eye contact. However, people can be kept from congregating in an area by making it appear slippery. A slippery or uneven surface may be used to direct the user's attention away from a private workspace or sensitive operation. Finally, have you ever noticed that the streets are always wet in automobile ads? It makes the car appear to move, or to go faster. Besides, it looks better than dull pavement.

Texture may have other important effects on behavior. The author recently surveyed a large high school. The walls in many of the high-capacity hallways, including the side walls of the auditorium, were cast in rough form concrete. The forms created extremely sharp ridges that were uniform throughout. The designer may have considered this to be aesthetically appealing and easier to construct. It may have been intended to reduce opportunities for vandalism, but it guaranteed avoidance of any proximity to the walls. The hallways were congested because everyone walked in the center. Fear of injury was intensified. All someone had to do to get hurt was to slip or be shoved against one of these walls.

Touch extends to interpersonal relationships, where it is also culturally defined. Anthropologists know that there are minimum and maximum spatial dimensions that are required for all human activities and relationships. Each function has its own set of needs. Distance between people tends to increase as the relationship becomes less personal. The men in certain Middle Eastern and Asian cultures hold hands when they walk or talk. The men in some other cultures place their arms around each other when they discuss business. South American men will sit very close together for discussions. But don't mimic these behaviors with a North American male!

Touching is legitimate during certain times and places. Otherwise, it can be fear producing and result in avoidance behavior. Try observing behavior in elevators. Two people alone in an elevator will stand against opposite walls. They may nod politely and exchange pleasantries. As others enter at different floors, there is less eye contact and social exchange. By the time the elevator is full, everyone is either looking up or down to avoid eye contact, even though they are being touched on all sides. Friends will even drop their voices or stop talking altogether as the elevator becomes more crowded.

Interaction between the sexes on the elevator is even more interesting. A man and a woman who are strangers would not dare touch if they were alone. It would be fear producing and impolite. Yet, as the elevator fills up, it is socially legitimate for the man and woman to be pressed together, with little concern. They will move apart immediately as people exit. The same thing occurs on airplanes, buses, and in private cars. Think about it as you jam into your next car or elevator.

The gustatory sense, taste, is also important to our reaction to the environment. It is linked to smell. Remember when you couldn't taste anything the last time you had a cold. Taste is more complex than allowing us to differentiate among foods. We taste exhaust fumes as well as smell them. Our sense of taste contributes to metabolic mechanisms. The ability to sense temperature and humidity is supported by taste. Taste and touch are linked in the human perception of texture.

A human being's orientation to gravity, the proprioceptive sense, is linked to touching. This sense is the ability of the body to assess and interpret internal changes. The change or shift of muscle tension in various body parts indicates changing motion or elevation. Of course, this movement or shift of muscle tension is a direct response to gravitational changes. The human body is constantly monitoring and responding to space.

People do not like to stand on elevations. The human body is able to discern as little as one or two degrees of elevation change. How many times have you stood on someone's kitchen floor or back porch and felt depressions or low spots? Some instructors will report finding high spots in the front of lecture halls and standing on them throughout their presentations. Why? It is obviously a subconscious attempt to reinforce the student's attention. Humans prefer a steep staircase to a flight of stairs in which the risers are uneven. Many people are uncomfortable on heights. Do you remember when you were terrified to stand on an extended balcony, but had no fear of one that was recessed?

Sympathetic reactions are good examples of how our other senses translate to our proprioceptive sense. Has your leg ever moved when you watched a high jumper or pole vaulter? Have you ever gotten dizzy or nauseated while watching a stunt film? Have you experienced a weird sensation of movement when a car next to yours backs up slowly at a stop light? Why does this not occur elsewhere? Answer: it is not legitimate to back up at stop lights, so your sense of movement is thrown off. Watch an audience at a circus when the tightrope walker loses her balance. The audience will sway with the walker.

Designers have used knowledge of these reactions to gravity to their advantage. Slight elevations have been planned in movement areas to prevent congestion and loitering. Elevated galleries may be used to raise the pedestrian height along the sides of a fortress-type convention center, to increase perceived visibility and reduce gathering behavior. Moving objects and uneven surfaces may deter lingering. The rough walls of the high school mentioned earlier may be desirable in park or other outdoor area to discourage the use of the wall for leaning or sleeping. It certainly discourages graffitti and ball playing. The trick is to know what kind of behavior you desire and what type you want to suppress.

In conclusion, humans constantly react to the environment, both consciously and subconsciously. It is the task of the CPTED planner to always be mindful of these human/environment interactions and to practice bringing them to the level of conscious awareness. In this way they are an integral part of the application of CPTED concepts.

USE OF LIGHT AND COLOR

The visual sense is the most comprehensive means of collecting information about the environment. It has been estimated that about 90% of all our information about the external world comes as a result of visual perceptions. However, our visual sense is so linked to the other senses that it is difficult to differentiate among them. For instance, when we say, "It looks like a carrot," or "It looks like sand," or "It looks OK to me," we are restating in visual terms what resulted from information that may have been captured by other senses. Smelling, touching, weighing, and tasting may have been involved in the data gathering process.

Light and color are essential components of the environment. Light enables plants to grow. There would be no air to breath or food to eat without light. Plants give off oxygen. The food we eat comes from plants or animals that eat plants. Light was essential in the development of natural fuels. Light from the sun heats the earth and illuminates human activities.

Humans have learned how to manufacture light for use at night or in places where there is no sunlight. Light is used as a therapy for depression. Light is used to produce biological changes. For instance, lights are left on in chicken coops to make the chickens think that it is daytime and lay more eggs. Correctional researchers are now exploring the use of different lighting levels and colors on behavior in prisons.

Humans generally have a directional orientation to light. Its source is commonly from above. We are "cast in the most favorable light" when its source is above. We look awful when the source is from below. We use a flashlight pointing up into our faces from the neck level to scare children at Halloween. Horror films and tragedies use lighting from low sources to enhance the sense of fear or foreboding. Conversely, comedies and upbeat musicals use highly placed light sources. We highlight our accomplishments and take a dim view of failures.

Light is a form of energy that can travel freely through space. The energy of light is referred to as *radiant energy*, which also includes infrared rays, ultraviolet rays, X rays, and radio waves. Light is composed of colors that range from red to violet. These are the visible colors of light, whereas ultraviolet and infrared are invisible.

Light actually consists of energy that is emitted from excited (heated or phosphorescent) atoms. Excited atoms release and absorb energy in tiny bundles called *photons*. Light consists of streams of these photons. The different colors of light are made by photons with different energy levels. White light consists of a combination of all levels of photon energy. This is easily demonstrated by the use of a common prism, which disperses white light into all of the different colors.

As shown in Figure 6–2, the visible spectrum of light is composed of the basic colors of red, orange, yellow, green, blue, and violet. Each has a different wavelength. The longest wavelength is red and the shortest is violet. Infrared has a longer wavelength than red. Ultraviolet has a shorter wavelength than violet. Both are invisible to the human eye.

Light affects human functions. Industry research has demonstrated that lighting levels have an impact on productivity and on the rate of accidents. Lighting levels must increase directly with the complexity of the job. Hence the expression, "Let's shed some light on the subject." Bright lights can have an adverse effect on less critical human activities. An expensive restaurant geared to the patron's desire for long, lingering meals would go under if

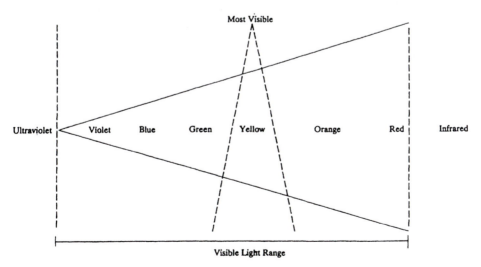

Psychophysiological activity is stimulated by colors in the widest wavelengths and by intensity of light.

Figure 6–2: Visible light and color spectrum.

lighting levels were intense. Accordingly, they place the ceiling in shadow and use table lighting sources (e.g., candles).

Acute depressions, which are suffered by most people at one time or another, are generally affected by light. Have you ever been depressed about a personal problem at work or home, possibly a medical concern, and found it hard to go to sleep? Many depressed people just want to go to bed and forget about their problems. But as soon as they get there, no matter how tired they are, sleep will not come. The person begins to shift positions. The more this is done, the higher the stress level goes. One's spouse or cohabitant gets grumpy about the disruptions, so the person attempts to lie still. Then the anxiety level hits the ceiling. Sleep eventually comes, but it is disturbed. Events are played out in dreams, repeatedly, in grotesque manners. The same speech or the same fouled-up athletic play is recycled over and over. Finally, as the clock approaches 4:30 to 5:30 A.M., the victim falls into deeper sleep, only to be awakened by the alarm at 6:30 A.M. One hint about the average range of time in which the individual falls asleep, 4:30 to 5:30 A.M., is that it is dependent on where the person lives within a given time zone. What begins to happen around 4:00 to 5:00 A.M.? The ambient light level begins to increase. The sun is coming up — it's a new day. Things always look better in the morning. Isn't it common for people to say, "Why don't you go home and sleep on the problem, because things will be better in the morning?"

It is an irony of human nature that when a person falls asleep watching the television in the family room, someone will eventually wake the sleeper to inform him that he can't sleep there — it's time to go to bed. What was wrong with sleeping there? The problem is that by the time he complies with the urgent demands to come immediately to bed, he is wide awake and can't sleep! The underlying explanation for the behavior of the family room sleepers is that for certain people it is easier to fall asleep with the television and lights on. It may be that they are lazy, or that they are prone to fall asleep in relaxing circumstances. It may be a subconscious method of dealing with stress and depression. The presence of light seems to be the key.

The next time you feel a little depressed and cannot go to sleep, go to the living room or den, turn on the television (a light source), and sit or lie in a comfortable position. Do not forget to warn your spouse or cohabitant, because she may come and mistakenly interrupt one of the best sleeps you've ever had. This is not a remedy for chronic or extremely acute depressions, but it may help you go to sleep. Hemingway's short story *A Clean, Well-Lighted Place*, was the writer's way of describing the need for light that is experienced by chronically depressed individuals. They will close the bar down and then sit in a well-lighted room awaiting dawn, and the sleep that comes with it.

It is clear that light affects human behavior. Light may be used to attract people. The convenience industry has discovered that high lighting levels in stores, combined with more open space, increases sales. Too much or too little light will have different effects. It is now generally accepted that performance improves and fatigue levels drop in direct proportion to increasing levels of light, but this relates to the work or play environment. The important thing to remember is that each human function has an optimum lighting level. It becomes a question of defining the human function and matching the level of light that is required to achieve optimum effects.

Color fills our world with beauty. Colors may be arranged in consonance to sooth and calm. Colors may be arranged in dissonance to produce stress and discomfort. Colors are used to describe moods. Some persons are said to be "in a blue mood." Others are "in the pink." Colors are associated with traditions. The Irish wear green on St. Patrick's Day for good luck. People in mourning for the death of loved ones wear black.

Colors also serve more functional purposes. Color serves as a form of communication. Red lights mean stop. Green lights mean go. Athletic teams wear opposing colors. Referees carry the dreadful yellow flags that signify penalties. The colors of some kinds of plant blossoms attract insects. Colorful fruits attract certain fruit-eating animals whose subsequent droppings spread fruit seeds for further growth.

Color is used as protection by many animals. Arctic hares turn white in winter to serve as camouflage. Similarly, fawns have white spots for protection. Chameleons change colors to match the background in which they are hiding. Female birds develop mixed plumage of earth tones to protect their nests during the birthing season. The males retain their bright colors to serve as distractions for predators.

We do not really see colors. Our eyes merely pick up different wavelengths of electromagnetic energy, which is within the visible light spectrum. Color televisions produce thousands of tiny dots that glow in the primary colors of red, green, and blue. We see these dots in combinations that are interpreted as different colors. The combination of blue, green, and red produces white light, which allows the television to show black and white pictures.

Colors can produce surprising effects. We have become so accustomed to these effects that we recognize them at the subconscious level. Cover half a sheet of white paper with another sheet of brightly colored paper. Stare at it for 30 seconds, then remove the sheet of colored paper. What happens? If you just conducted this demonstration, you will note that the half that was covered previously with the colored paper will appear lighter than the other half.

The eyes will produce an afterimage if we stare at a colored image for 30 seconds and then look at a white surface. This afterimage has the same shape, but a different color. The afterimage of red will be green. The afterimage of green will be red. Blue areas become yellow and yellow areas become blue. Black reverses with white. One common trick is to show an American flag with a yellow field and green stripes. What happens when you look at a white surface after staring at this yellow and green flag for 30 seconds?

Phantom colors also appear in areas that are really black and white. A flashing black and white pattern similar to the rolling of a television picture (in black and white) will produce phantom colors. Other colors appear lighter when displayed on a black background. Background colors will affect the perception of primary central color.

Colors affect behavior. Some behavioral responses are learned, such as responses to red lights and green lights. Blue police uniforms cause socialized responses that we tend to associate with authority. Some seem to be more natural, although one may become used to a color over time, thereby muting the effect. Red lights produce more activity within groups. People pass the time less well in red light. Red leads to an increase in blood pressure, respiration, and the frequency of eye blink. Blue has the opposite effect. It seems to suppress activity. Time passes better. Blood pressure, respiration, and eye blinks are lowered. Of course, there are mitigating factors.

There is a general principle that says that the physical and psychological effects of light increase with wavelength and intensity. Thus, the "red light district" of town effectively uses light as a communicator and as a behavioral stimulator. Red has the largest wavelength and violet has the smallest. It is interesting to note that visual perception is highest in the middle of the spectrum of visible light (color). The spectrum ranges from red to orange, yellow, green, blue, and violet. The middle, or yellow-green, bands have the most visibility. The reds and violets have the least.

So why aren't all police cars, ambulances, and fire trucks green-yellow? Some are, but many fire departments and police departments are staying with the traditional colors because of their communication value. We are taught to identify with red fire trucks and red lights. Many police departments have switched to a combination of red and blue emergency lights. Each of these colors has different recognition levels depending on whether it is night or day. This also helps to differentiate between a police car and fire vehicle. Traditional or cultural values will generally prevail over the predicted effect. However, this applies to a small number of situations.

Lighting has two purposes within the CPTED conceptual model: one is for the illumination of human activities and the other is for security. It is important for the CPTED planner, before spending extra money on security lighting, to think about using the behavioral effects of already existing lighting that is required for illuminating human activities to promote crime and loss prevention.

Lighting does make people feel safer, but most outdoor lighting has been installed with a confused set of objectives. Many street lights are so high that they light only the street, but not the sidewalk. Cars have lights; people do not! Lighting in many public, off-street garages is placed over the vehicle lanes, not where people are when they emerge from or attempt to get into their cars.

Illumination consultants emphasize planning for lighting to enhance natural opportunities for light that comes through windows. Lighting has to be planned for nighttime use as well. The primary measure or objective of planning for lighting is to place light fixtures in numbers and locations sufficient to provide complete coverage of the floor within a minimum number of footcandles or lumens of strength.

My own office has a centrally located bank of fluorescent lights. The cone of light does reach the total square footage of the floor, but I stand over six feet and sit at 54 inches. The illumination is fine for normal desk work, but it leaves the walls and bookshelves in shadow. This makes the office appear to be small and cramped to visitors, who are reacting to the office as it really appears. What psychological effect would occur if track lighting were installed to illuminate the walls? Would it matter as much to me as it may to the visitor, in terms of comfort and perception?

The answer to these questions is that a change of the lighting to better match the objectives of the space would be effective. Lighted walls or ones that reflect light, such as mirrored walls, make a room seem bigger. Pictures of certain types take the place of windows. Pictures give insight into imaginary places. However, the lighting strategy has to match the behavioral objectives of space. No lighting engineer or consultant can design the ultimate lighting effects without explicit knowledge of the desired behavioral effects or objectives.

Foyers and hallways have been traditionally lighted from the center of the ceiling. It was logical to assume that a centrally placed light would provide a cone width that would cover the floor. Some research that was conducted in Louisville, Kentucky, found that persons who assembled in elevator waiting areas that were centrally lighted tended to stand in the center and avoid eye contact. When they were interviewed later, they felt that the lobby was uncomfortable and unsafe. The lighting in the same lobby was redesigned to illuminate the walls and leave the center of the room in shadow. People stood nearer to the walls and established eye contact. They felt that the room was very comfortable and safe. They even thought that the room was larger than its actual dimensions.

Hallways that are illuminated from the center of the ceiling are most likely to be perceived as crowded. People will walk toward the center and avoid eye contact. Once the illumination is diverted to the walls, people will walk closer to the wall and will be more likely to make eye contact with one another. They will walk faster, feel safer, and think that the hallways are wider. A fringe benefit is that there is a 30% reduction in noise, even though people are walking faster. A number of factors are associated with this latter result, but it is clear that the walls help to absorb some of the normal noise that is associated with people in motion.

Airports do a good job of promoting desirable behavioral effects through design. The tube-like pedestrian corridors that are used to move people from the landside to the airside terminals are generally enclosed, but the corridors above ground use a lot of glazing to increase visibility and natural lighting. In the walkways that are below ground or totally enclosed, the walls are covered with rented advertising space. These advertisements are generally required to be brightly colored and well lighted, not only to attract attention but to diminish the "dead" effect of the walls. Of course, a behaviorist will note that people walk closer to the walls, feel less cramped, walk faster, and feel safer.

The designers of the remodeled United Airlines terminal at Chicago's O'Hare Airport have gone a major step beyond other designers of underground pedestrian access ways. They have installed a sequential neon light system that appears to move with the pedestrian. The speed of the sequence is geared to a fast pace. The overall effect is enhanced by the use of background music that sounds like electronic wind chimes. The music seems to be synchronized with the moving light system. Subliminally below the effect of the light and sound is a woman's voice that continuously repeats the phrase, "Keep walking, keep walking." The walls use an intricate pattern of panels that are connected to matching overhangs. The panels seem to undulate along the passageway with the tempo of the light and music. One's first encounter is curiously, but appreciatively, bewildering. You are sure to tell others about it. However, some veteran travelers mock the subliminal message, "Keep walking, keep walking," as they sprint through the tube.

Private security directors and police detectives have long known the value of environmental effects on interrogations. The use of lighting, desk size, chair height, clothing color, and pregnant pauses have proven to be beneficial in eliciting information from uncooperative individuals. Psychologists use many techniques in the interviewing and counseling process. Police are now trained to use such diagnostic as opposed to interrogatory interviewing techniques when dealing with victims of crisis or abuse.

One of the most vexing uses of the environment is to position the visitor to one's office in direct or refracted sunlight. As an eyeglass wearer, I am made personally uncomfortable as a visitor to someone's office when I have to remove my glasses to see beyond the glare, only to find the host still sitting in an aura of light. My revenge is to move my chair to a more comfortable position, without asking for permission. By invading the host's space, possibly moving beyond the side of the desk to the area behind it, out of the glare, the host is annoyed to have this little bit of gamesmanship exposed.

The following examples are just a sample of the kind of knowledge that is being gained through studies of the effects of color and light:

- Blue-green in operating rooms eliminates glare and helps the physicians focus on the red and pink colors of the body. Yellow-green should be avoided, as the reflection on human flesh makes it appear sickly.

Color variation is important to the frame of mind in both patients and staff.[1]
- Using black colors makes you look thinner and feel better.[2]
- Exposure to bright light helps to overcome jet lag and reset circadian rhythms.[3]
- The deeper the density of the color the more it inspires consumer trust. Bright orange and lime green should be avoided because they have negative connotations. Primary colors like red, blue, yellow, and green are generally well received by consumers.[4]
- Light may be used to cure winter depressions and the general blahs. Light has direct effects on learning and on treating affective disorders.[5]

These references to research on the use of light and color on human behavior are just the tip of the iceberg. A reference librarian at any public library can introduce the reader to an overwhelming volume of literature on the subject. Moreover, practically all libraries will offer an incredible array of literature on the use of architectural design and space management techniques to influence and manipulate behavior.

The problem is that researchers all have different standards for what they consider to be acceptable and pertinent research findings. The various professions tend to limit their reading and research to the topic areas that contain the name of their subject. A criminal justice specialist or academic criminologist will probably stick to that profession's journals, and will look for the words crime or crime prevention in any list of references. The traffic engineer, on the other hand, will not be interested in a title with crime prevention in it. Likewise, the planner, developer, and architect look to the title for the determination of their interest. Paradoxically, there is a wealth of information that has been developed over the years by experimental and industrial psychologists that could be used immediately in practical situations.

FENG SHUI

Feng Shui is a centuries-old Chinese art of promoting harmony by manipulating the spatial environment. It has some mystical elements but also many practical, commonsensical theories and observations about how people

---

[1] Birren, F. "Color and Psychotherapy." *Journal of Interior Design*, December 1983, 166.
[2] Malkin, N. "Nobody's Perfect." *Harper's Bazaar*, January 1989, 90.
[3] Pool, R. "Illuminating Jet Lag." *Science*, June 1989, 1256; Czeisler, A. "Bright Light Induction of Strong Type or Resetting of Circadian Rhythm." *Science*, June 1989, 1238; Fackelmann, K. "A Light Touch Changes the Biological Clock." *Science News*, June 1989, 374.
[4] Tucker, J. "Psychology of Color." *Target Marketing*, June 1989, 40.
[5] Zimmer, D. "Light Fantastic." *World Press*, April 1987, 55; Graves, B. "Facility Planning: Shedding Light on Learning." *American School and University*, March 1985, 88; Pechter, K. "Heal Yourself with Light." *Prevention*, May 1984.

respond to space management and design. The mystical elements have over time served to develop a belief system about the importance of a harmonious spatial environment that is near religious in nature. But each of these elements is expressed in fundamental concepts of environmental psychology in modern applications.

Feng Shui is pronounced differently depending on the dialect of Chinese being spoken. The common English pronunciation is "fongue schway." There is a growing interest in Feng Shui in North America and in Europe that parallels the interest in CPTED. Moreover, studies of how people respond to space management and design are abundant in modern marketing research.

Over 150 books and manuals on the practice of Feng Shui have been produced over many centuries. While there are some differences in definitions and the use of terms, the fundamental concept of Feng Shui remains the same: the desire to promote spatial harmony by emphasizing positive forces and minimizing or eliminating negative forces. Positive forces are often expressed as *ch'i* and negative forces as *sha*, or negative ch'i. Ch'i is the force that links humans with nature. Sha is misaligned or bad currents of energy that disrupt the environment.

Wind, water, light, and color are important elements in Feng Shui. They are observed by Feng Shui experts, who are called "geomancers," in existing space to determine their effect individually and in combinations on behavior. Environmental cues are established by how space is designed and used. These cues affect behavior in positive and negative ways. CPTED and Feng Shui are similar in observing that negative cues produce fear and avoidance behaviors on the part of normal or desired users of space. Positive cues produce desired responses and behaviors; they reinforce proprietary concern for space and territorial behavior.

Following are some of the many examples of Feng Shui and CPTED applications:

- weaving pathways or roads are preferred because they divert negative arrows of energy (sha) and they promote a wider field of vision for observation because of the need to maneuver
- offset glass-lined store entrances in malls and shopping centers deflect sha and increase visual access to identify the store and observe activities
- bay-type windows increase visual access to and from sidewalks and streets, promoting visual ease and harmony and increasing the perception of natural surveillance
- continuous sheer walls that serve as noise barriers along expressways tend to reflect negative energy and dominate the field of vision of drivers, thus producing tunnel vision and safety hazards
- sitting with one's back immediately in front of a window facilitates the absorption of negative energy, thus promoting discomfort and

avoidance behavior of these spaces; it reduces the perception of natural surveillance

- a teacher or boss whose desk or workstation faces the students or workers reflects sha and creates conflict through the apparent inaccessibility and superior message; revealing one's side to the student, worker, or client produces ch'i, or positive energy, and a better team environment, which increases proprietary concern for space and territorial behaviors
- theater, meeting room, or classroom doors that open outward allow sha to escape from these spaces and also promote easier egress for safety reasons
- sharp edges on buildings and corners in hallways project sha, thereby increasing anxiety and discomfort; round or curving edges produce chi, resulting in increased comfort, wider fields of vision, and increased perception of surveillance
- a bedroom door that opens immediately onto the head of the bed produces negative sha that increases anxiety, thereby interrupting sleep; it also reduces the time required for a person to identify and respond to an attacker
- landscaping that obscures windows and the pedestrian approaches to buildings creates confusion and anxiety (sha); it also reduces natural surveillance
- enclosed elevators trap sha or negative energy that creates anxiety and avoidance behavior; a glass-backed elevator or one with mirrors on the back wall deflects sha and improves comfort; it also allows the potential user to see if anyone is inside and increases natural surveillance
- grid-pattern streets facilitate the flow of sha, which in turn facilitates speeding and ease of access for unwanted persons, increasing anxiety and avoidance behavior for pedestrians and residents; streetscape improvements can deflect sha and increase ch'i, thus slowing speeds, increasing the field of vision of drivers, and enhancing the perception of safety

It is clear that Feng Shui provides another tool for helping CPTED planners to understand interaction between humans and their environments. It also provides a better means for the CPTED planner to articulate environmental and behavioral concepts to the designers and users of space.

7

Aesthetics, Environmental Cues, and Territorial Behavior: Implications for CPTED Planning

FORM VERSUS FUNCTION — THE BATTLE WITH AESTHETICS

Many people find it very difficult to resist the urge to mess with things. Nearly everyone has turned a screw one too many times and broken it off, or made an extra cut on a piece of cloth that ruined it. It seems that automobile manufacturers cannot resist the temptation to change body styles. Men's ties get wider each year until a point, and then they get more narrow. I have found it impossible to grow a mustache without ruining it in the trimming process, leaving me looking like Hitler.

It is fundamental to human nature to go through cycles that start with an emphasis on function (e.g., getting the job done) and eventually end up focusing on form (e.g., how things appear). The form of things, or the aesthetic quality, tends to drive the thinking of consumers and designers alike. Once humans learn how to build something new, or do something different, the initial attention to merely reaching the objective shifts with the confidence that comes with experience.

The history of the Ford Mustang automobile is a good example of the natural continuum in which function gives way to form, or aesthetics. Ford introduced a sleek, efficiently designed car in the second half of the 1964 model year. It was an instant success and trend setter over the monstrous tail-finned vehicles of the late 1950s and early 1960s. What had happened to the automobile after World War II? The retooled auto industry had to go to mass production of inexpensive cars to recover from the loss of the demand for war material. Once the economy picked up, competition caused the auto designers to add fins to the tails of cars and battering rams to the fronts. So much emphasis was placed on form by 1962 that function had been sacrificed. Planned obsolescence reduced many autos to failure within two to three years. But even Ford could not resist the temptation to change its design for the Mustang. The Mustang failed as a product line in 1974 because of a number of changes that were made to the design. The 1974 Ford Mustang barely resembled its 1964 predecessor.

Human activities seem to follow the continuum from an early emphasis on function to later preoccupation with form. Function becomes overlooked, which generally results in catastrophic failure of the human activity. The "long hairs" of the sixties have become the "short hairs" of the eighties and nineties. The "crew cut" crowd of the sixties now wears their hair long. The movie *Butterfield Eight* was met with outright indignation by my hometown preacher when it was released in 1960. After years of waiting to see the movie, I was sorely disappointed in the content. Yet, soap operas in 1999 now offer more explicit sexual and sensitive material than anything that could have been imagined even as late as the early nineties.

It must be that the changing world requires that people become gradually accustomed to change. Whatever the explanation, it is clear that nothing will ever remain the same except the predictability of change and human nature. Accordingly, it must be assumed that form, or aesthetics, will always outweigh function in any human endeavor.

CPTED concepts require the user to question everything. CPTED concepts require the user to relate design and use decisions to the objectives of space. But the CPTED planner must seek to achieve a balance between the necessity to meet the requirements of human functions and the need to fulfill the aesthetic demands. Otherwise, the human function may not meet its objectives.

Figure 7–1 contains a model of the conflict between function and form. The model presents form and function in reverse relationship. As the requirement for functionality increases, as in the military base, the tolerance for aesthetics or emphasis on form decreases. But at the other end of the spectrum, a tomb or mortuary has very little functional demand, so form is not only tolerated, it is demanded. Monuments and military bases, as human activities, have clearly defined functional requirements, but the functional requirements of most human activities are not so obvious.

Most human activities fall within a few degrees plus or minus of the center of the continuum. As their functional requirements become less clear, it is likely that form may win over function in the final design. The schools, houses, offices, shops, and major commercial centers are susceptible to the error of leaning too far toward aesthetics in design. It does not become a problem until the aesthetic demands alter the human function. Designers in Louisville, Kentucky, forgot their objective of creating a pedestrian street when they installed cobblestones in the place of paver tile or asphalt. People cannot walk easily on cobblestones. Jacksonville, Florida, designers

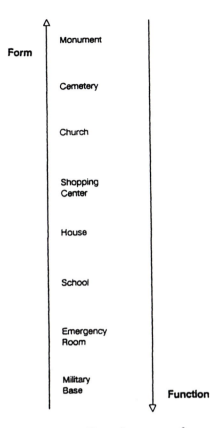

Figure 7–1:   Function versus form.

forgot that 51% of our population wear high-heeled shoes at night when they specified that the new "River Walk" boardwalk site would use lumber strips that were separated to allow the pedestrian to see the water below. Downtown planners, nearly everywhere, forget to determine how the desired user of space will get to a location. Many buildings are designed to appeal to the pedestrian, when the ultimate user group has to arrive by car, park behind the building, and walk around to the front.

Perhaps the greatest service that a CPTED planner may provide is to question everything. It has been demonstrated that the CPTED approach works best when the planner is guided by the desire to make the human function work as the primary objective. This is not to say, however, that the CPTED approach is against aesthetics. Aesthetics are critical to human existence. Even the person who is most unmoved by aesthetics will not be indifferent to that aspect of design when it comes to marriages, christenings, bar mitzvahs, parades, burials, and other special events.

The best way for a person to use the CPTED approach is to (1) share the concepts and (2) ask questions. The most important thing is to ask "What are you trying to do here and how can we help you do it better?" The emphasis has to be on attaining the objectives of the human function, whatever it may be, instead of merely avoiding security problems. Human functions that work well have fewer security problems. Human functions that are failing experience more security and loss problems, which exacerbate their demise.

ENVIRONMENTAL CUES

Environmental cues have important effects upon both normal and abnormal users of space. The cues that tell a normal user that she may be unsafe will usually have the opposite effect on the abnormal user, who will perceive the same cues as indications that she is at low risk of detection, thereby safe. Conversely, cues that tell a normal user of space that he is safe will increase the perception of risk for the abnormal user. He will feel unsafe.

Perhaps the only environmental cue that has the same effect on both normal and abnormal users of space is distance. The farther an individual is from a potential threat, the easier it is to manage. For instance, a person who has to encounter a drunk or a group of boys on a downtown sidewalk has very little space in which to squeeze by on the typical shrunken pedestrian space in a high capacity street. Cars are whizzing by in high numbers and at high speeds. The net result is avoidance behavior. One either refuses to come to that street, or if required to be there, one chooses to divert eye contact and hurry by the potential threat.

Distance is often a safety cue for the potential offender. The farther an offender or abnormal user is from a threat — in this case a police officer or a determined landowner — the lower the value or impact of the threat. Distance is directly related to the magnitude of the number of excuses for improper behavior. For instance, "Coach, I didn't hear you yelling at me!" "Officer, I thought you were waving Hi to me!" "I thought you were chasing someone else, or you were after another car," is a typical excuse. Direct and close exposure to people in control of environments is anathema to the abnormal user.

Strategies may be planned to affect only the normal users of space, since they may be the primary objective of the human function. A shopping center or mall is a good example of human space that is oriented around the attraction of large numbers of desired users (normal users). An athletic facility or ocean beach is the same. Some other environments may influence the CPTED planner to emphasize behavioral affects on the abnormal user (undesired). A public park may be oriented to attract normal users (desired) during daytime, but strive to keep away abnormal users (undesired) at night. Strategies may be entirely oriented around the abnormal user because of the uniqueness of the area. For instance, a reservoir or protected game area may need to eliminate all human usage. A warehouse, industrial zone, or riverfront docking area may specifically desire to exclude the vagrant from using the location for any purpose.

It is easy to observe the various effects that the environment has on behavior. The design of the environment exhibits cues that affect behavior. The management, or how the environment is being used, has direct effects on behavior. How the users react to the environment also sets off cues that affect other's perceptions of space. A shopping center or mall is a great place to observe these human/environment interactions, especially late in the day or at night. People try to park next to other cars. They try to park within line of sight of their desired entrance. Once they exit their vehicle they scurry toward the mall entrance, almost as if it were freezing cold. Their shoulders are rolled forward and they avoid eye contact with others by looking down at their feet. Anyone who converges on their path is given a wide berth and is viewed suspiciously.

The overt behavior pattern changes once the person reaches the entrance to the mall or shopping center. The shoulders roll back and the walking pattern changes from scurrying to strolling. Eye contact is established with others who are encountered closely. Staring is permissible. People even report that they enjoy watching others, to see what they are wearing and how they act. Try doing that in the parking lot and see the reaction it gets! These controlling or challenging cues say to others that someone is watching who feels safe, and who will not tolerate any improper activity, but the avoidance behavior (cues) in the parking lot tends to reinforce the abnormal users' perception of safety, or low risk.

Environmental cues in a residential area are important. Clean gutters and staring behavior tell outsiders that they have been noticed. Holiday decorations make a clear statement that the residents are house proud and competitive. Many euphemisms are used to describe this behavior, such as pride, cohesiveness, and community spirit. However, the underlying motivation is the basic nature of humans to be competitive, jealous, and envious — the real behavioral qualities that keep a neighborhood together.

Normal users of space feel safer when they enter a neighborhood where the residents stare at them, thus acknowledging the visitor's presence. Abnormal users feel more exposed, or at greater risk. Normal users feel unsafe in a neighborhood where people refuse to establish eye contact, where avoidance behavior is commonplace. Tightly curtained windows signify the withdrawal of concern by residents. Unkempt lawns and sidewalks indicate a retreat from the street. Conversely, the loosely curtained window and manicured, or at least cared for, sidewalk and adjacent planting strip convey a cue that says, "We own this."

Residents and nonresidents of space act differently and respond differently to environmental cues. Residents become inured to the gradually changing environment. Nonresidents see it as it is. A shabby restaurant or convenience store may be popular among residents, because they identify with the owners and have a proprietary concern for the continuity of the establishment. Resident customers or clients are loyal to their favorite store, even if the prices are not competitive. Why? Humans are social animals and need familiarity as comfort for the daily stresses and pressures. It is, therefore, easy to become accustomed to environmental conditions that may be repugnant to outsiders.

Nonresidents of space see places as they are. Environmental cues jump out at them as they enter an area. Accordingly, their attitudes are affected by the first impression. This differentiation of the resident from the nonresident is crucial to the CPTED planner. Environmental cues will either make or break a project that has failed to identify and define the target user group. Successful projects must also continuously assess their user group to ensure that design and space management procedures are consistent with the potentially changing behavioral patterns.

Environmental cues are observed continuously by all humans and they are reacted to in the decision making process that directly affects the productive use of space and the related quality of life in places that work, that are achieving the aims of the human function. Territorial behavior is linked directly to environmental cues because the cues are manifestations of proprietary concern and ownership.

TERRITORIAL BEHAVIOR

Cave dwellers cleared areas in front of their cave to mark their private space. Now the first thing a person does when moving into an office or apartment is to put their "stuff" up. Travelers always unpack their bags and hang up their clothes once they check into a hotel room, before they do anything else. This not only helps to hang out the wrinkles, it personalizes the room. Each traveler has her own habit in this regard. As a regular traveler, I have observed a wide range of idiosyncrasies among associates. Some will place all of their belongings in either the closet or the drawers, while others will stack everything in neat little piles on the spare bed. Most business travelers will leave as much as possible of their clothing in the suitcase, but will produce an elaborate display of business materials and working papers.

Territorial behavior is characteristic of all human, even all animal, existence. Humans establish hierarchies of territories, or turf, that range from private to semi-private to semi-public to public space. Humans, in particular, have a need to establish both temporary and permanent ownership of space. That a person's home is his castle is a universally recognized concept and legal tradition. Experts in crisis intervention know that even the most minor offense that involves an intrusion into one's abode is a major stress-producing event. Police are trained to be sensitive to an individual's concerns and resultant fears about minor burglaries. It is common knowledge that the most meek person is fiercely protective of the home front.

Humans and animals mark their turf. People put up signs of ownership, pictures in rooms and flowers or other landscaping outdoors. Animals allocate turf naturally based on the number of animals, the food supply, and the terrain. South American llamas establish territories in perfect squares. Common squirrels allocate yard space and fight whenever another squirrel ventures into an established space. Dogs defend their turf vigorously, even when they are outsized. Interestingly, other animals tend to acknowledge turf identities and respond accordingly. Human beings mark their turf using fences, signs, and plain border definition. The common law requires that turf or property be identified as a prerequisite to the defense of property rights.

Everyone encounters turf identity and recognition problems daily. A person goes through many transitional turf states from the time he or she arises and goes to work, until returning home. The homemaker encounters a daily interaction with turf issues. Child supervision and lawn maintenance are part of the process of turf. Admonitions to children such as, "Don't leave our yard," or "Don't walk through the neighbor's yard," reinforce turf identity. The hanging out of laundry is a simple reinforcement of turf that is generally taken for granted. Where the automobile is parked is a more direct establishment of turf. This is why the broad, undifferentiated parking areas in many apartment or public housing complexes are anathema to successful housing management. Accordingly, one of the better ways to establish harmony in a garden apartment complex is to arrange the parking areas as cul-de-sacs so that parking spaces seem to belong naturally to certain housing groups.

Turf identification, behavioral responses, and environmental cues are linked. For example, upon moving to Louisville, in 1985, I went to the downtown area to photograph the convention center, which had nearly destroyed the commercial activities around it even though it was originally intended to revitalize them. Parking on the east side of the center, I stepped across the street to take a panoramic shot of the building. However, as I attempted to step onto the sidewalk, I encountered three young men who were passing along in front of a series of porno shops. The youngsters wore orange and green hair, chains, leather jackets, and were prominently displaying (and playing) a boom box. Without stopping to think, I did an about-face and went back across the street to study the roof line of the building. Of course, I neatly concealed my expensive camera as well. What had I done?

I had actually not only conceded turf to these young men, but had also through my overt avoidance behavior reinforced their territorial behavior. What would have happened if these same young fellows had visited the NCPI campus and actually had the audacity to walk down one of the hallways when I was teaching a class? It is easy to surmise that the reaction would have been different. The young men would have been immediately challenged and the boom box would have been turned off. They would then have been assisted by the class members in finding the main entrance to the campus. Why would my reaction to the young men have been so radically different, just because of the difference in location? Obviously, I would feel safer with a classroom full of police and security officers. Moreover, I would be defending my own turf, and, therefore, would automatically put fight before flight, or challenging behavior before avoidance behavior in responding to the situation.

It would have been ludicrous for me to have challenged the young men on the downtown street. First, I had no ownership. Second, I would have been beaten up for my trouble. Any challenge would have been just too much of a threat to the macho identity of the youngsters. They would have been compelled to demonstrate their ownership or territorial prerogatives; otherwise they would have lost the stability or foundation for coping within their environment. This sense of retention or loss of fundamental control is crucial to the existence of users of space. Fear is a strong and dangerous motivator of human response mechanisms.

Territorial behavior is demonstrated through both design and use responses. Any area that is well defined by borders and signs says to the user that it is controlled, that it is owned. Permanent ownership of space is defined by law, by deed, by occupation, by acknowledgment, and by design. Temporary ownership of space, such as one's seat at a meeting, is defined by occupancy and by signs. Signs of temporary ownership include the marking of the space by leaving a personal item (e.g., briefcase, jacket, or notebook) to signify that the space has been claimed. A newspaper or magazine will not suffice in the claiming of temporary space, because these items are not personal in nature. Sometimes other forms of physical signs are appropriate. A chair that leans up against a banquet room table says that someone went to some effort to signify claim. The chair just did not get there by itself.

The physical definition of ownership sets the stage for the user's enforcement of territorial prerogatives. For example, if someone moved your jacket and briefcase from a seat at a meeting while you were off to get a cup of coffee, you would be totally within your rights to challenge the individual actively upon your return. An active challenge would be something like this: "Excuse me, but I think that you took my seat." The language is polite, but the message is clear that the person violated another's space. A more direct and challenging approach might be: "Obviously you knew that someone had already claimed this seat when you moved my stuff!" Both of these challenges are formally polite, but are clearly stated as an indictment.

Consider the opposite situation wherein an individual approaches another who is already sitting in a desired spot. "Excuse me, but would you mind terribly doing me this awfully important favor, by letting me have your seat?" First of all, how can someone mind terribly doing an awful favor? Certainly, this is a phrase or expression, but it also says that one has to "mind" a lot to refuse the "awful" inconvenience of moving to a less desirable spot, especially after going to the trouble of getting there early to claim a choice seat. Of course, the person who already owns the seat is put on the spot by having to refuse the request. However, anyone who is involved in marketing knows that guilt is the strongest tool in making sales. People are affected by their perception that they owe something to the sales person who took the time to help them look at or try out a product. Accordingly, a passive challenge may be as powerful as an active challenge. It depends on the situation.

Users of space respond to challenges based on their perception of the situation. Environmental cues that indicate extended or intensive territorial concern convey the sense of safety for the normal user and risk for the abnormal user. Challenging behavior on the part of the normal or desired users of space enhance design features that signify ownership. These behaviors reinforce territorial markers. I have experimented with this phenomenon in a variety of neighborhoods.

Once while driving through a residential area in Minneapolis, I stopped along the curb in an older neighborhood. The gutter was clean and the homes were well-maintained. Flowers and little fences were prominent on the edges of lawns. Some residents had even placed flowers in the planting strip between the curb and sidewalk. As I emerged from my auto, an elderly man who was watering his lawn began to demonstrate staring behavior by edging over toward the car and moving his head about in exaggerated motions, with a perplexed expression on his face. What was he communicating? Why couldn't he simply have waited until I approached him to let him know what I was doing before he challenged me? The answer is that he felt very secure on this street and naturally exhibited intense proprietary concern for what was happening on his street.

As I jumped about to avoid being doused by the spray of water from the hose that the man was holding, I responded to the man's question about my intended business by asking for the correct house of a person who he knew lived four doors down the block. The older man pointed this out and then repeated it in very emphatic terms as I began to walk down the street. "I said, young man, that the Smiths live down there!" What was he trying to communicate? Clearly, he was indicating that if I was going to the Smiths that I had better move my car in front of their house, and not leave it parked in his gutter in front of his house.

In another neighborhood, which was clearly run-down and poorly maintained, I was neither challenged nor stared at, even as I began taking photos. The few persons who were outside disappeared. There were no flowers in the planting strips and there was very little border definition of individual yards. Front porches were largely bare of any furnishings. Many of the homes had fenced in back yards that obscured visual access. What was the message emanating from the design and use behavior in this neighborhood? Had these people turned their backs to the street? Had they surrendered their territorial imperatives? What reaction would this have from an abnormal or undesired user? Would this person feel safe, at low risk of challenge?

While conducting a CPTED training program in Trenton, New Jersey, I assigned a 10-block section of a residential area to one of the class teams for their site assessment project. The area was composed of small, tightly packed row homes that came all the way to the sidewalk. It was easy to see major differences in territorial concern as one walked along the street. On one end it was observed that the windows on each house were tightly curtained. There were no flower boxes hanging below the windows and the front stoops were not upgraded. They were also poorly maintained. No chairs or benches were in front of the homes and the sidewalk was uneven and considerably littered and dirty.

Farther down the street awnings placed over front doors and windows became more numerous. Windows were loosely curtained. Stoops were upgraded. The farther one went the more the street changed. Flower boxes were hung beneath windows and placed next to the sidewalks. Chairs and benches were prominently placed in front of homes. At the very end of this section of homes, flower boxes had been placed along the curb and the sidewalk had been replaced in many areas with decorative brick.

What were these environmental cues saying to both the normal and abnormal users of this street? Had the folks at one end turned their backs to the street? Had they surrendered their sidewalk? What were the residents at the other end saying to the passerby? The team that was assigned to conduct a site assessment found out very quickly. Some boys attempted to sell them drugs at one end of the street and the Trenton Police stopped them at the other end in response to a neighbor's call about some suspicious acting people who were walking around looking at houses. Is it hard to guess which end was which?

Temporary custody of space is nearly as important as permanent ownership. The next time you are in a check-out line at a drugstore or supermarket, watch the territorial behavior that goes on. Airplane ticket lines, fast food restaurants, and banks share the same phenomena. What happens when someone steps out of line to look at a display or to pick up another product? There is a tendency for the people behind to move forward, to assume the other person's space. They are very reluctant to step back when the person returns, as if this is their way of indicating their displeasure.

Drivers are even worse about the moving custody of space. I watched a driver actually speed up, nearly causing a collision, when an oncoming driver made a turn across the path of the other driver. What was in the mind of the aggrieved driver? Was he trying to punish the other one for preempting his space and creating a dangerous situation? Wasn't he making the situation worse? Yet this happens every day on the street. My study of assaults in Fairfax County, Virginia, found that more than 10% of all reported assaults occurred as a direct result of disputes between drivers. It is very common for drivers to aim their vehicle at an oncoming car that is going the wrong direction down a one-way street. How many times have you waited until an oncoming car at night was right upon you to switch on your high beams to let them know that they had failed to switch theirs off. This must be the natural way to scold another who endangered one's safety through their lack of attention, by increasing the danger to both.

Temporary custody of space has some interesting, if not funny, implications. For years, I have routinely moved people's stuff during the first break of a CPTED lecture or presentation. It is simply a great way to involve the audience in understanding territorial behavior. This practice ended in a near calamitous situation when I was giving a presentation of safe neighborhoods to a group of senior citizens.

I called a break to let the folks get a cup of coffee or tea. I immediately, without thinking, moved a few purses and jackets. Within minutes there were a number of groups arguing openly until I shouted for quiet to admit, rather smartly, that it was all a joke to show them about territorial behavior. Most people laughed until the crowd parted to reveal an elderly gentleman who was shaking his finger in my direction, shouting that it was no joke, that he had already called another old guy a jerk for moving his stuff. The man was really upset.

Proprietary regard for space has proven throughout history to be a motivating force. The convenience industry is finding that the employee who is busy throughout the store is more likely to protect it than the one who spends most of his time behind the counter. When the industry converted to lower shelves and wider aisles, the employees complained that they would have to restock more often. They wanted to put everything out as it was delivered, instead of storing some products first until the smaller shelf systems were depleted. After all, why stack things twice when you can put it all out on high shelves in the beginning. Yet employees are busier, time passes more quickly, and losses are lower in the new stores. This is a powerful example of the impact of management of space on increasing and extending proprietary concern, which then affects profit and losses. The employee who regularly services and stocks an area of a store is going to notice more things and act more protective than one who only occasionally goes to that area.

Oldham and Fried's article, "Employee Reactions to Workspace Characteristics,"[1] reported that employees were most likely to withdraw from offices and experience dissatisfaction when the following conditions were present:

- The work space was rated as dark.
- Few enclosures surrounded employee work areas.
- Employees were seated close to each other.
- Many employees occupied the work area.

It seems to be axiomatic that people will take care of space and assets in which they have a proprietary concern. Perhaps there is a lesson here for

---

[1] Oldham, L., and Fried, G. *Journal of Applied Statistics*, February 1987, 176.

increasing productivity and reducing loss. Common experience is replete with examples. For instance, take-home police cars cost less to operate than pool cars. Carpenters and machinists have always been required to buy their own tools. They take better care of them that way. Likewise, a homeowner who physically participates in the care of common areas is more apt to pay attention to what transpires there.

The better a place is defined regarding ownership, the more likely a nonresident or visitor is to be conspicuous. Another near standard that is emerging from CPTED experience is the objective of minimizing unassigned space. Multiple purpose space may best be assigned to the most prevalent user group, with the provision that others use it when necessary. Hallways, foyers, and stair systems are generally unassigned, despite the fact that the interior spaces that they adjoin are claimed. It is common for interior decorators to recommend that uniform color and furnishings be used in these areas, which further detaches them from any perceived ownership.

It is a given that humans behave territorially. All humans move transitionally each day from private to semi-private to semi-public to public space, and back again. It is an inexorable process that will never change. The CPTED planner needs only to bring these observations to the conscious level in order to share these behavioral concepts with people who are making decisions about human space, and to ask the questions that no one thought to ask.

VISUAL BUBBLES, LANDSCAPE, AND ART

Human beings are born with natural responses to certain environmental stimuli. Others responses are learned within the context of culture, education, training, and experience. Tests with newborn humans and animals reveal that they inherit natural responses to visual stimuli. For instance, when the newborns are shown a film from the perspective of someone approaching the edge of a cliff, the subjects will automatically react when they think they are going over the side. Visual stimuli are some of the most important to humans, but by no means are they mutually exclusive of other forms of perception.

Perhaps the best means of understanding the impact of visual space is to use a camera as an analogy. Cameras are designed to simulate functions of the human eye. The lens admits light that is reflected from objects. The light energy has been altered by objects which allows the images to be represented on the film. Similarly, the retina or back of the eye absorbs the light energy and interprets the various wavelengths into three-dimensional shapes. This is where the similarity ends, because the field or width of vision and depth or distance of vision of a camera may be adjusted. Conversely, the human eye records the environment with a fixed field of vision and depth perception.

Humans establish *visual bubbles* that vary in depth, height, and width according to territorial definition and geography. A visual bubble may be defined as that space in which a person consciously recognizes things within the environment. Most environmental cues are dealt with subconsciously outside of the visual bubble, unless something unusual happens to bring one of these elements to the level of consciousness. For instance, an opaque fence in a person's back yard will establish the outer limit of a visual bubble. Symbolic fences may create the same effect of psychologically obscuring what is happening on the other side, or outside of the visual bubble. Thus, an offender who thinks that a solid fence provides concealment unknowingly has the added benefit of the fact that neighbors or passersby are probably not looking anyway.

Why is this important to a study of CPTED? The answer is that the visual sense scans the middle and far environment to collect information for immediate survival and protection. Environmental cues are assessed by all the human perceptual senses. But the visual sense provides information about hazards, finding one's way, identity of objects in the environment, and what attracts the perceiver. There is a whole field of study dedicated to the perception of art, sculpture, advertising, fashion, landscape design, and safety. For instance, highway safety is almost totally linked to visual perception. Traffic engineers know that certain locations have a high volume of accidents. Other locations seem to induce excessive speeds. Noise attenuation barriers along the side of expressways are known to create tunnel vision in drivers that leads to accidents.

Following are some examples of the importance of planning for visual space in CPTED:

- Downtown pedestrian malls and regional retail malls quite often use landscape elements and sitting areas to push customers closer to businesses on the theory that they will be more likely to make a purchase if they are within the zone of influence of the business. But the customers' field of vision is dominated by individual elements of the store and is prevented from identifying the store itself. This results in hostility and avoidance behavior that can lower sales and create the perception of lack of safety, particularly when the customer has a limited number of choices for maneuvering.
- One-way streets with off-street parking and synchronized traffic signals surely speed up the flow of vehicles and diminish the disruption of continuous speeds. But this ease actually reduces the drivers' field of vision to a narrow visual bubble, which results in higher speeds, more hazards, and little notice or surveillance of surrounding land uses and activities.
- The height of ceilings in hallways and meeting rooms has a direct relationship to attentiveness and movement; low ceilings suppress behavior and high ceilings tend to stimulate activity and attention.

- Transitional landscaping on curving portions of walking and bike trails increase the depth of vision and provide the user of this space with more information and choices regarding safety hazards or criminal threats.
- Wider porches in front of convenience stores help to give the customer more choices to avoid potential contact with nuisance persons, thus increasing sales to adult customers who would avoid the store if they had to encounter juveniles.
- Towers and spires on buildings located on corners or intersections help people find their way and relieve anxiety about distances and identification of places.
- Noise barriers along expressways can contribute to an increase in accidents by creating tunnel vision for drivers when the barriers are constructed of sheer walls and opaque materials.
- Opaque enclosures of trash receptacles and loading docks will dominate the field of vision of a passerby; conversely, transparent fencing material used in screening of trash receptacles and loading docks will cause these areas to fall into the visual background, which is precisely what the designer intends.
- Hostile landscaping can reduce maintenance costs and prevent graffiti and unwanted entry to properties.
- Landscaping helps to identify borders between public and private space; it also helps to reinforce the definition of desired behaviors by defining movement areas.
- Art and sculpture are powerful tools in promoting territorial behavior and proprietary concern for space. They attract attention to spaces and help people find their way. One of the greatest values of street art is how it contributes to *triangulation*, which helps people to psychologically connect places, thus increasing perceptions of territoriality and control.

8

Examples of CPTED Strategies and Applications

CPTED STRATEGIES

CPTED strategies have emerged from history and from contemporary crime prevention experiments. Most of the strategies are self-evident. That is, the reader will probably think, "I knew that!" The strategies and examples contained in this chapter are basic. Their applications are unlimited.

CPTED concepts have been and are being used in public housing projects. Schools and university properties are using CPTED applications that were initially pioneered in the Broward County, Florida, school CPTED program that was funded by the federal government. (Appendix A contains a matrix summary of these concepts.) The list of potential CPTED applications is practically endless. It would be difficult to find any human function that is not amenable to the use of CPTED concepts. It is merely a matter of looking at the environment from a different perspective, questioning everything, and learning the language of the various professions involved in making decisions about our communities. Learning the language means being able to communicate with others and to understand their objectives. This is the principal reason why CPTED planners are trained to share concepts and ask questions that no one would have thought to ask.

CPTED planners are trained to re-program their thinking from focusing solely on security and crime prevention to emphasizing the objectives of the agency or organization that they are trying to help. It is important to remember a CPTED motto, "What are you trying to do here, and how can we help you do it better?" If you are meeting your objectives, the potential for crime and loss will be reduced. It is an axiom that human functions that are achieving their objectives will experience fewer crimes and losses. Crime and loss is a by-product of human functions that are not working.

Following are the nine major CPTED strategies that may be used in any number of combinations:

1. *Provide clear border definition of controlled space.* It is a common-law requirement that space must be defined to preserve property rights. Boundaries may be identified physically or symbolically. Fences, shrubbery or signs are acceptable border definition. The underlying principal is that a "reasonable individual" must be able to recognize that he is transitioning from public to private space. The arrangements of furniture and color definition are means of identifying interior spaces. Plaques and pictures on walls in hallways help to define ownership and are powerful environmental cues that affect the behavior and predispositions of owners, normal users, and abnormal users, alike.

2. *Provide clearly marked transititional zones.* It is important to provide clearly marked transitional zones moving from public to semi-public to semi-private to private space. As transitional definition increases, the range of excuses for improper behavior is reduced. The user must be made to acknowledge movement into controlled space.

3. *Relocation of gathering areas.* It is appropriate to formally designate gathering or congregating areas in locations with good natural surveillance and access control. Gathering areas on campuses may be placed in positions that are out of the view of undesired users to decrease the magnetic effect, or attraction.

4. *Place safe activities in unsafe locations.* Within reason, this strategy may be used to overcome problems on school campuses, parks, offices, or institutional settings. Safe activities serve as magnets for normal users who exhibit challenging or controlling behaviors (e.g., staring) that tell other normal users that they are safe, and that tell abnormal users that they are at greater risk of scrutiny or intervention. Some caution must be used to assure that a safe activity is not being placed in an unreasonable position that it cannot defend.

5. *Place unsafe activities in safe locations.* The positioning of vulnerable activities near windows of occupied space, or within tightly controlled areas, will help to overcome risk and make the users of these areas feel safer.

6. *Redesignate the use of space to provide natural barriers.* Conflicting activities may be separated by distance, natural terrain, or by other functions to avoid fear-producing conflict. For instance, the sounds emanating from a basketball court may be disruptive and fear-producing for a senior citizen or toddler gathering/play area. The threat does not have to be real to create the perception of risk for the normal or desired user.

7. *Improve scheduling of space.* It has been found, generally, that the effective and productive use of spaces reduces risk and the perception of risk for normal users. Conversely, abnormal users feel at greater risk of surveillance and intervention in their activities. Well-thought-out temporal

and spatial relationships improve profit and productivity, while increasing the control of behavior.

8. *Redesign or revamp space to increase the perception of natural surveillance.* The perception of surveillance is more powerful than its reality. Hidden cameras do little to make normal users feel safer and, therefore, act safer when they are unaware of the presence of these devices. Likewise, abnormal users do not feel at greater risk of detection when they are oblivious to surveillance potentials. Windows, clear lines-of-sight, and other natural techniques are often as effective as the use of mechanical or organized (e.g., guards) methods.

9. *Overcome distance and isolation.* Improved communications and design efficiencies increase the perception of natural surveillance and control. School administrators have learned to carry portable radios to improve their productivity, as well as create the perception of immediate access to help. Restroom locations and entry designs may be planned to increase convenience and reduce the cost of construction and maintenance.

CPTED APPLICATIONS

There are many examples of CPTED applications. Those that follow are intended to stimulate the reader to think of adaptations to her own environmental setting. Each situation is unique, requiring its own individual application of CPTED concepts. No two environmental settings will be exactly the same, even though they serve the same function. Accordingly, the reader, now hopefully a CPTED user, will have to use the strategies that make the most sense within each different location.

OBJECTIVES FOR COMMERCIAL ENVIRONMENT

1. *Access controls.* Provide secure barriers to prevent unauthorized access to buildings grounds and/or restricted interior areas.
2. *Surveillance through physical design.* Improve opportunities for surveillance by physical design mechanisms that serve to increase the risk of detection for offenders, enable evasive actions by potential victims, and facilitate intervention by police.
3. *Mechanical surveillance devices.* Provide businesses with security devices to detect and signal illegal entry attempts.
4. *Design and construction.* Design, build, and/or repair buildings and building sites to enhance security and improve quality.
5. *Land use.* Establish policies to prevent ill-advised land and building uses that have negative impact.

6. *Owner/management action.* Encourage owners and management to implement safeguards to make businesses and commercial property less vulnerable to crime.

7. *User protection.* Implement safeguards to make shoppers less vulnerable to crime.

8. *Social interaction.* Encourage interaction among businessmen, users, and residents of commercial neighborhoods to foster social cohesion and control.

9. *Private security services.* Determine necessary and appropriate services to enhance commercial security.

10. *Police services.* Improve police services in order to efficiently and effectively respond to crime problems and to enhance citizen cooperation in reporting crime.

11. *Police/community relations.* Improve police/community relations to involve citizens in cooperative efforts with police to prevent and report crime.

12. *Community awareness.* Create community crime prevention awareness to aid in combating crime in commercial areas.

13. *Territorial identity.* Differentiate private areas from public spaces to discourage trespass by potential offenders.

14. *Neighborhood image.* Develop positive image of commercial area to encourage user and investor confidence and increase the economic vitality of the area.

DOWNTOWN STREETS AND PEDESTRIAN AREAS

Downtown Streets

Poor Design and Use: Figures 8–1 and 8–2

A. The growing dominance of the vehicle over pedestrians resulted in off-street parking, one-way streets, synchronized traffic signals, and shrunken sidewalks to accommodate the auto.

B. Pedestrian-oriented businesses have failed or chased the buyer to the shopping centers and malls. As businesses moved, there was less pedestrian activity, which forced more businesses out.

C. Narrow pedestrian footpaths increased conflict and fear between vagrants and other abnormal users of space. Normal users avoided these streets, thereby reinforcing the decline of business and normal downtown activities.

D. Downtown streets became "no man's" land at nights and on weekends.

E. Pedestrian malls were created to replace the vehicle with people, but most failed because the designers lost track of their Three Ds. Aesthetics

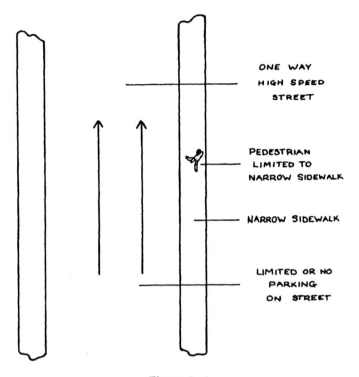

Figure 8-1.

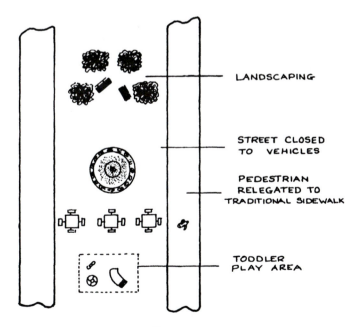

Figure 8-2.

outweigh function resulting in the replacement of the vehicle with cement objects, in the place of people.

F.   Many of the cement objects — amenities and landscaping — attracted abnormal users. Litter and bird droppings made outdoor sitting areas undesirable for normal users.

G.   Normal users feel threatened and unsafe in these areas. Abnormal users feel safe and at low risk of intervention. Authorities are obliged to surrender these areas to vagrants because of special interest group pressure and the lack of any consistent normal use of the area.

Good Design and Use: Figures 8–3 and 8–4

A.   One option is to purposely decrease the vehicle capacity of the street by reestablishing on-street parking, wide sidewalks, two-way streets, and nonsynchronous traffic signals. This should reroute commuter and other through traffic.

B.   Higher pedestrian capacity will limit vehicular access to those with terminal objectives on the block (e.g., residents or purposeful shoppers).

C.   Another option is to schedule the street for temporary closings on target shopping days and festival times. Portable amenities may be used and stored when not in use. Businesses may be granted variances of local codes to use vendor carts and other forms of extended business activities into the street.

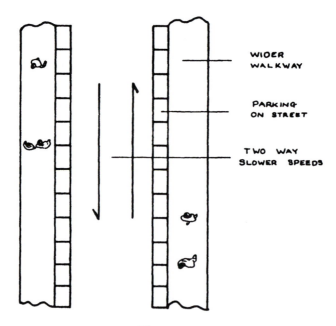

WIDER
WALKWAY

PARKING
ON STREET

TWO WAY
SLOWER SPEEDS

Figure 8–3.

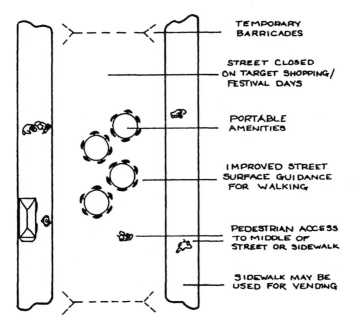

Figure 8-4.

D. The planned increase of normal users will make them feel safer and exhibit controlling and challenging behaviors much like they do in indoor shopping malls.

E. Abnormal users will feel at greater risk.

Barriers to Conflict

Poor Design: Figure 8-5

A. A toddler and/or senior recreation area is immediately contiguous to a conflicting activity of basketball.

B. Basketball activity involves aggressive behavior and noise, which is annoying and threatening to senior citizens and parents with small children.

C. The athletic activity may serve as a magnet for abnormal users of space.

D. The designated athletic activity may legitimize certain offensive behaviors, such as swearing and physical abuse, which threatens normal users and passersby.

Good Design: Figure 8-6

A. A natural barrier of distance, elevation, or the parking lot may be used to avoid conflict.

B. Any natural barrier will reduce the propensity for the undesirable or abnormal users to preempt the contiguous spaces.

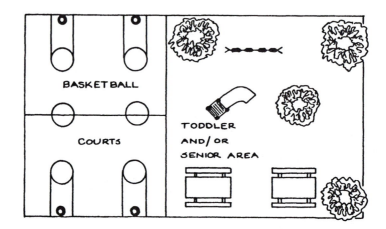

Figure 8–5.

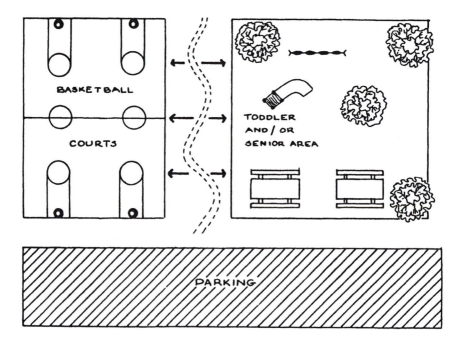

Figure 8–6.

C.   Abnormal users will feel at greater risk when there is a clear barrier through which they have to pass.

Outdoor Sitting Areas

Poor Design and Use: Figure 8–7

A.   Sitting walls have replaced the traditional benches and picnic tables in open spaces, but they are easy to hide behind and serve as a barrier to effective surveillance.
B.   Elevation drops and terraced sitting areas reduce perceived opportunities for natural surveillance, which makes abnormal users feel safer in colonizing or preempting these spaces.
C.   Tourists and office workers who may desire to eat lunch in these areas, or take an evening stroll, will be afraid to go there if vagrants are already there or have left signs of their regular use (e.g., litter, graffiti, human waste).

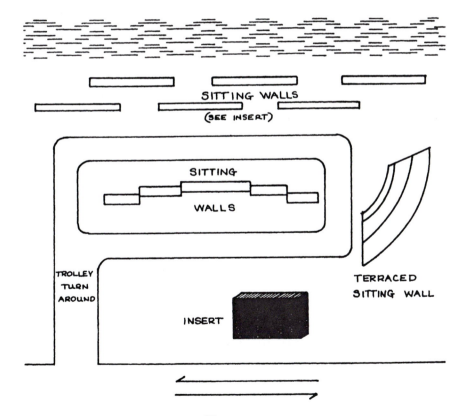

Figure 8–7.

D. Litter and waste present odor problems and may attract scavengers. If it looks and smells bad, it must be bad, which defeats the purpose.

Good Design and Use: Figure 8–8

A. Sitting rails may be used in the place of the more expensive walls. This will increase natural surveillance and prevent improper use, while still meeting the functional and aesthetic demands of the open space.
B. Terraced sitting or staging areas should be oriented so that they are clearly visible from the street.
C. Open spaces can be made to work with CPTED concepts, while reducing overall construction costs. Normal users will feel better about coming to these areas and they will displace abnormal users.

Plazas

Poor Design and Use: Figure 8–9

A. A typical plaza in a rehabilitated business area meets all the local code requirements for landscaping and aesthetics, but at the cost of reducing the usable square footage.

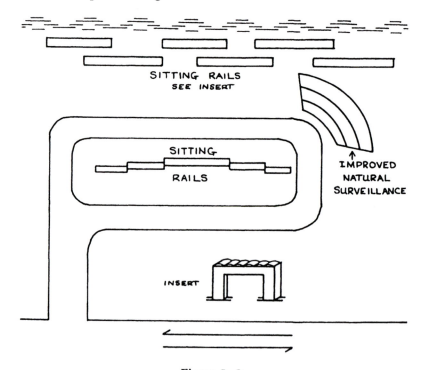

Figure 8–8.

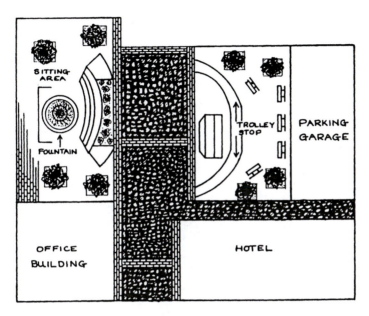

Figure 8–9.

B. Aesthetics or form outweighed function in the selection of cobblestones to use in replacing the street paving. These stones are difficult to walk on, especially for women in high-heeled shoes and the elderly.

C. Benches, tables, and the fountain area may easily be colonized by vagrants, or serve as bombing targets for pigeons.

D. Normal users will feel at risk and abnormal users will feel safe.

Good Design and Use: Figure 8–10

A. Compromises must be made between form and function. Paver tiles may be used in the place of cobblestones to make it easier for walking.

B. Portable amenities and landscaping may be substituted for permanent furnishings to increase flexibility in planning outdoor events.

C. Vehicles may be allowed limited and restricted access to facilitate a wide range of uses and to allow police patrols.

D. A well-used plaza will attract normal users and make people feel safe.

Pedestrian Mall

Poor Design and Use: Figure 8–11

A. The present design and traffic flow pattern reduce the parking opportunities.

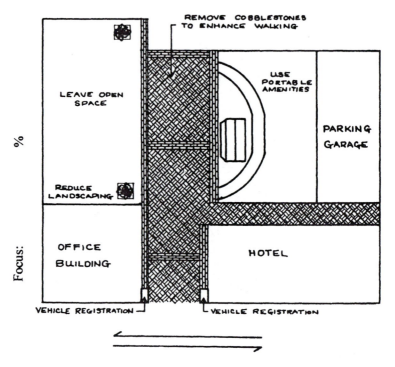

Figure 8–10.

PEDESTRIAN MALL

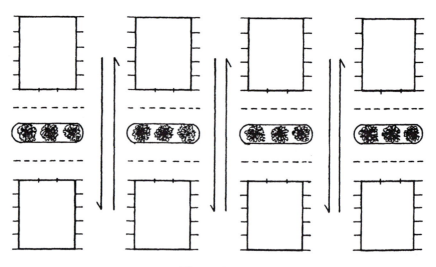

Figure 8–11.

B. The pedestrian area and upgraded median are excellent, but is all of this space needed everyday? Will it be used regularly or will it be used mostly on holidays and weekend shopping days?

C. This design plan would be a problem for senior citizen shoppers who may have to park some distance away. Parallel parking is also a problem for the senior citizen shopper.

Good Design and Use: Figure 8–12

A. Traffic flows may be controlled to allow for angle parking to recover needed parking that is close to shops.

B. Vehicular speed may be radically controlled to reduce pedestrian conflict.

C. Barricades may be used to close off vehicular access during certain periods of high pedestrian activity or low use periods. The design is flexible, allowing a variety of use patterns based upon commercial and promotional planning.

Good Design and Use: Figure 8–13

A. Traffic flows may be controlled to allow for angle parking to increase available spots and frontal access to business.

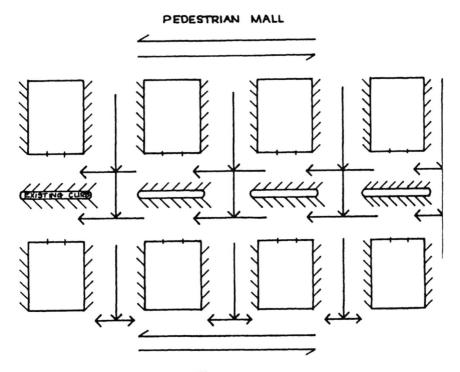

PEDESTRIAN MALL

Figure 8–12.

PEDESTRIAN MALL

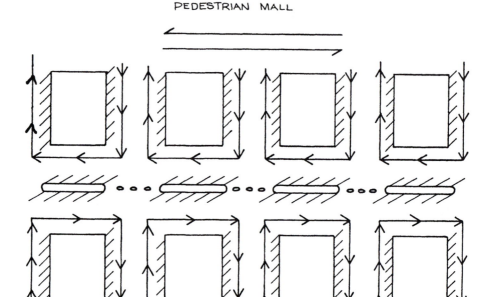

Figure 8–13.

B. Vehicular speed may be radically controlled to reduce pedestrian conflict.
C. Barricades may be used to close off vehicular access during certain periods of high pedestrian activity or low use periods.
D. Barricades may be used permanently or temporarily to control through access of vehicles.

PARKING LOTS AND STRUCTURES

Parking Lots

Poor Design and Use: Figure 8–14

A. A typical lot layout on the ground level or each level of an off-street garage. Late arrivals get the less desirable spots, which are generally located in unobserved places. Early arrivals take the best, most safe spots, but they are the first to leave, at the safest times when an attendant may still be there.

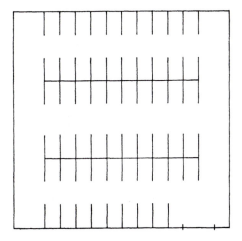

Figure 8–14.

B.   The last in are the last out, generally when the lot is deserted.
C.   This situation has been overlooked for years, with the assumption that the early arriver should naturally get the advantage. This is not a valid assumption where customers or employees are legitimately shopping later hours, or scheduled for late shifts. Fear, higher victimization, and liability problems arise.

Good Design and Use: Figure 8–15

A.   Barriers are used to divert parking activity to create safe locations for the late arrival.
B.   A variety of plans may be used depending on a parking needs assessment. Floors may be alternately closed. Aisles may be partially opened.

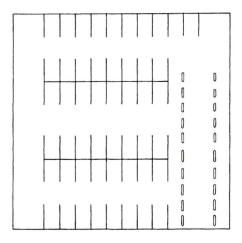

Figure 8–15.

C. Some balance between the legitimate needs of the early arrival and the late arrival should be met.
D. Physical barriers (e.g., cones or barricades) are less upsetting to users than attendants or guards who are directing flow past what are perceived as choice spots. However, guards or attendants are useful to serve in a rule enforcement or reinforcement function.

Parking Lot Access

Poor Design and Use: Figure 8–16

A. The parking attendant's location prevents this person from providing natural surveillance over the employee parking area.
B. Landscaping may serve as an additional barrier to natural surveillance.
C. Employees will feel less safe and abnormal users will perceive that there is a low risk of detection.
D. A guard would have to be employed to protect employees and their vehicles.

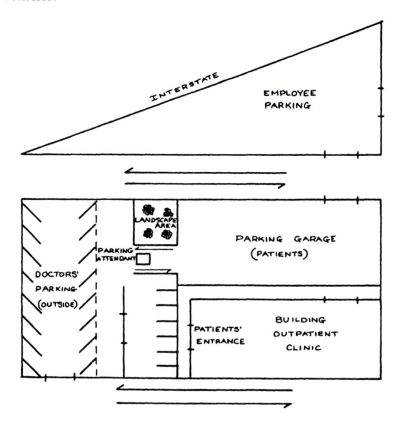

Figure 8–16.

Good Design and Use: Figure 8–17

A.   The parking attendant's location is naturally in a position to control all parking areas.
B.   Employees will feel safer and abnormal users will know that they will risk detection.
C.   This design would free the guard for patrolling activities elsewhere.

Parking Structures

Poor Design and Use: Figure 8–18

A.   Ground levels of parking garages are underused and create a fortress effect on the pedestrian, as well as on contiguous land uses.
B.   Reinforced concrete retaining walls are used commonly and reduce surveillance opportunities. This creates the perception of lack of safety for the normal user and low risk for abnormal users.

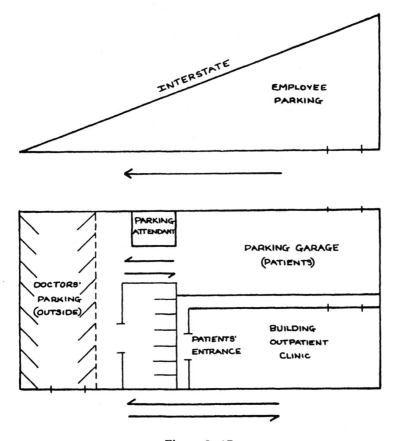

Figure 8–17.

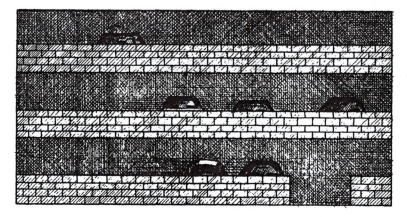

Figure 8–18.

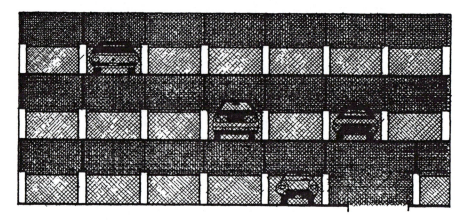

Figure 8–19.

C. Retaining walls do more to hide the automobile than to assure safety. Designers and local planners are often confused regarding the purpose of the walls.

D. Lighting inside is located generally over the driving lanes, instead of illuminating the parking spots where people are outside of their cars, and most vulnerable. Cars have their own lights; people do not!

Good Design and Use: Figure 8–19

A. Ground spaces should be dedicated to pedestrian oriented businesses and activities, leaving the airspace for the car. This will increase business revenues and enhance the perception of natural surveillance and access control for the garage and adjoining street space.

B. Retaining walls should be replaced with stretched cable of railings that allow for maximum surveillance and illumination. This will produce a considerable cost savings and improve perceptions of safety for normal users. Designers may even improve on the aesthetics over the concrete walls.

C. Reflective paint or materials should be used inside and all pedestrian areas should be illuminated to increase feelings of safety.

OFFICE AND INDUSTRIAL SYSTEMS

Office Access

Poor Design and Use: Figure 8–20

A. Elevators from below ground to working floors so that people would have access to all floors.
B. Main entrance from which people could go directly to elevators without registering.
C. Side entrance that allows no surveillance by receptionist or guard and that allows access to the elevators.
D. Guard/receptionist booth that is not centrally located, but is positioned so the person stationed there cannot see who enters or exits.

Good Design and Use: Figure 8–21

A. Elevators serving lobby and floors above.
B. Elevators serving lobby and floor below.
C. Rest rooms that are visible from the entrances.
D. Main entrance.
E. Main floor corridor that is visible from main entrance.
F. Controlled access/egress door.
G. Security/receptionist station to screen entrances.

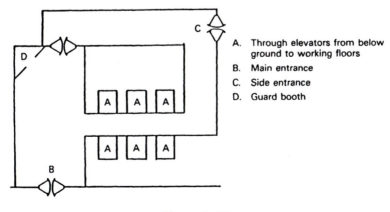

A. Through elevators from below ground to working floors
B. Main entrance
C. Side entrance
D. Guard booth

Figure 8–20.

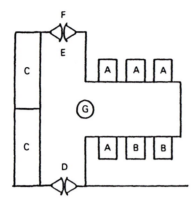

A. Elevators serving lobby and specified floors above
B. Elevators serving lobby and floors below
C. Rest rooms
D. Building main entrance
E. Main floor corridor
F. Controlled access/egress door
G. Receptionist/Security Guard station

Figure 8–21.

Office Building Site Plan and Parking

Poor Design and Use: Figure 8–22

A. Parking is undifferentiated by time of day and day of week.
B. Through access and night-time use are poorly defined and unclear.

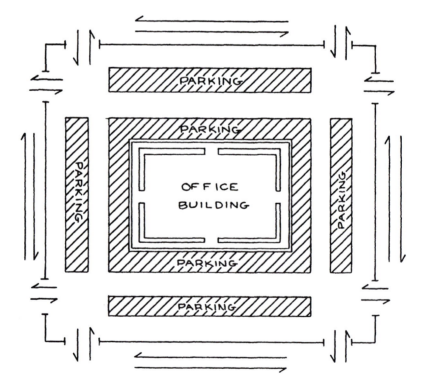

Figure 8–22.

C. Cars parked anywhere are not subject to scrutiny by security, law enforcement officials, or building management.

Good Design and Use: Figure 8–23

A. Parking is zoned and clearly identified by allowable spatial and temporal uses.
B. Improper parking is more subject to notice and scrutiny by local law enforcement officials and security officers.
C. Zones may be closed depending on need.

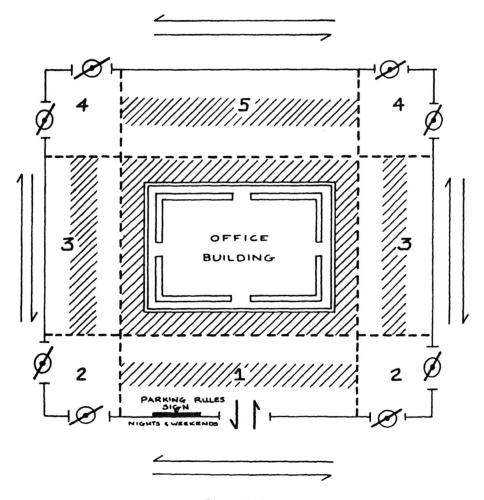

Figure 8–23.

Shipping and Receiving and Vehicle Access

Poor Design: Figure 8–24

A. Confused and deep internal access for external vehicles.
B. Easy mix of external vehicles with those of employees.
C. Multiple access from facilities to employees' vehicles.
D. Shipping and receiving in same location legitimizes people coming and going with boxes.
E. Guard or full-time monitor required to screen access and packages.
F. Wide range of excuses for improper behavior, thus increasing pressure on guards or shipping/receiving clerks.

Good Design: Figure 8–25

A. Parking segregated from external delivery or vendor vehicle access to property.
B. All employee/visitor parking clearly visible from buildings.
C. Shipping and receiving separated by distance, which reduces range of excuses.
D. Legitimate behavior narrowly defined by location.

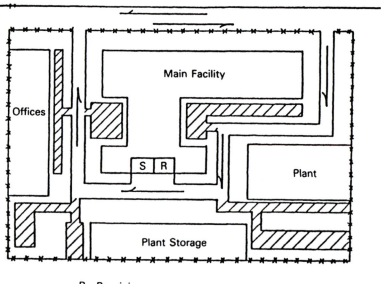

R - Receiving
S - Shipping

Figure 8–24.

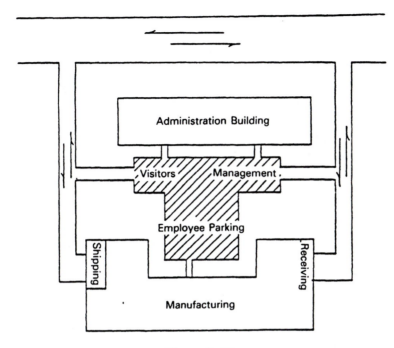

Figure 8–25.

E.   Transitional definition of movement is clear from opportunities for signage and rule enhancement in purchase/shipping orders and policies.

Plant Design

Poor Design: Figure 8–26

A.   Confusing vehicular internal access.
B.   Too much access for external vehicles to building entrances, which may easily promote collusion between employees and vendors or subcontractors.
C.   Shipping/receiving located in same site, which may encourage abuses.
D.   Extended locations of employee parking and strict access control through security negatively affects morale and subsequent labor negotiations.
E.   Receptionist position provides little natural access control and surveillance.
F.   Perimeter security fencing encloses a large area, which increases cost and vulnerability.

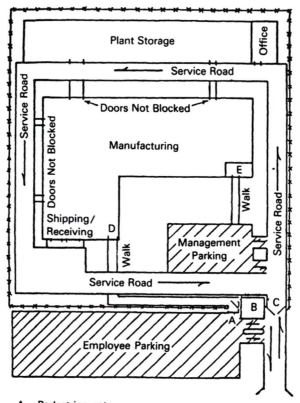

A. Pedestrian gate
B. Guard station
C. Vehicular gate
D. Employee entrance
E. Receptionist

Figure 8–26.

Good Design: Figure 8–27

A. Campus site plan that emphasizes openness and natural distance to increase an intruder's perception of risk of surveillance.

B. Convenient employee parking in front of building increases perception of surveillance of the employee from the building, while decreasing the negative effect of isolated parking on morale.

C. Segregated shipping/receiving may reduce opportunities for theft.

D. Guard post may be partially staffed or eliminated altogether, by replacing it with a receptionist or other natural (non-organized) function to provide the perception of natural access control and surveillance.

E. Reduced magnitude and cost of perimeter security.

F. Employee parking is protected by distance from public street access and by direct line of sight from the reception areas.

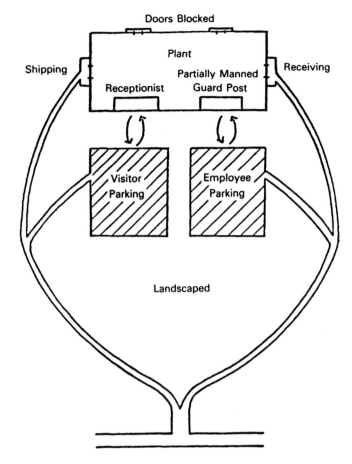

Figure 8–27.

G.   Site development and building costs should be reduced. Internal space footage requirements should also be reduced.

HALLWAYS AND RESTROOMS

Hallways

Poor Design and Use: Figure 8–28

A.   Most hallways in schools, hospitals, and offices are left undifferentiated. They do not identify what is on the other side of the wall, nor who owns it.

B.   Hallway uses become confused by the placement of lockers and furniture. Hallways are for movement, not for gathering behavior.

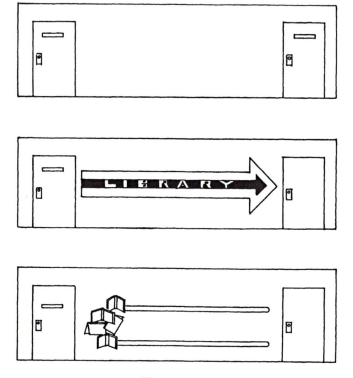

Figure 8–28.

C. Tenants or persons who are assigned internal spaces or work areas will actively control their spaces, but will assume little proprietary regard for the adjoining hallways or corridors.

D. Hallways usually carry the definition of extremely public space, even though extremely private space is only inches away.

E. Some new buildings prohibit any decoration or encroachment by tenants into hallway systems, as part of an interior decorating plan.

F. Multiple-purpose classrooms or meeting spaces suffer from lack of ownership.

G. Normal users demonstrate avoidance behavior in these undifferentiated spaces, which makes abnormal users feel safer and in control.

Good Design and Use

A. Hallways may be assigned to the tenant of the adjoining internal space. Users should be influenced to mark their turf to identify their boundaries.

B. Boundaries and turf cues should be extended to consume unassigned or undifferentiated spaces.

C. The legitimate uses of hallways and corridors need to be reinforced through policies and signs.

D.   Graphics may be used to promote movement and to indicate direction.
E.   Floor coverings and colors may be used to identify public versus private spaces.
F.   Normal users recognize and honor others' turf or ownership cues. Normal users feel safer in these areas and exhibit challenging and controlling behaviors. Abnormal users respond to these cues by avoiding these areas or with avoidance behaviors when they are in the vicinity.

Restroom Location and Entrance Design

Poor Design and Use: Figure 8–29

A.   Restrooms are traditionally isolated by location, as a cultural sensitivity and for economic reasons.

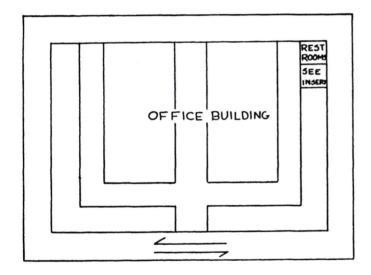

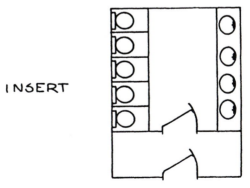

Figure 8–29.

B. Public restrooms are common sites for illegal and illicit activity.
C. Many children are afraid to use the restroom at school.
D. Malls and shopping centers have tended to hide the restroom, as a means of reducing demand for this nonrevenue bearing activity.
E. The lack of convenient and clean restrooms clearly reduces the average time per visit to most stores and businesses, thereby reducing sales.
F. Isolated locations and double door entry systems present unsafe cues to normal users and safe cues to abnormal users.
G. Double door entry systems produce a warning sound and transitional time that is an advantage to abnormal users.
H. A normal user or guard must move inside the second door swing to figure out what is going on in a restroom.

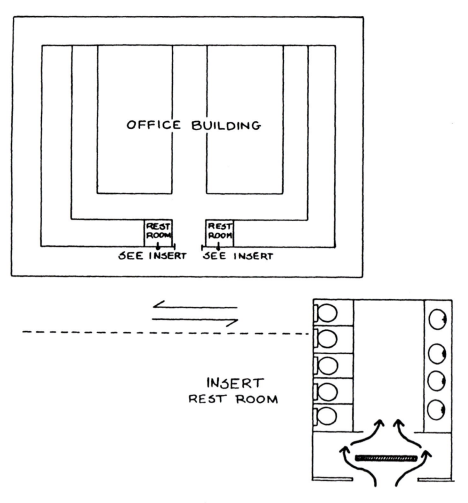

Figure 8–30.

Good Design and Use: Figure 8–30

A.   Restrooms should be located in the most convenient and accessible location to increase use, which increases the perception of safety.
B.   A maze-type entry system or doors placed in a locked open position will increase convenience and safety.
C.   Normal users may determine who is in the restroom by glancing around the privacy screen or wall.
D.   Abnormal users will feel at greater risk of detection.
E.   Customer (or student) convenience and safety should contribute to the attainment of the objectives of the space.

Informal Gathering Areas

Poor Design: Figure 8–31

A.   Hallways and corners in schools, office buildings, malls, and apartments attract small groups of abnormal users who preempt this space and promote conflict.

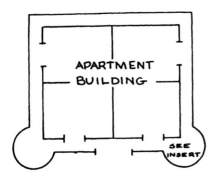

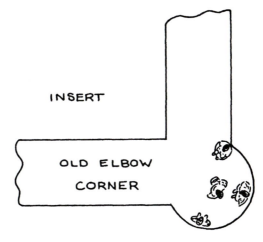

Figure 8–31.

B.   Normal users avoid these areas, which reinforces the perception of risk.
C.   Congestion is often created elsewhere because of the avoidance behavior
     of normal users.
D.   The avoidance behavior reinforces the perception of safety and turf
     ownership of the abnormal users.

Good Design: Figure 8–32

A.   A safe activity may be located in the poorly used space to displace the
     unsafe use.
B.   A safe activity will serve as a magnet for normal users who will be
     attracted to the area.
C.   The safe activity and normal user behavior will create and intensify the
     perception of risk for the abnormal user.
D.   Space utilization and productivity will go up in most cases.

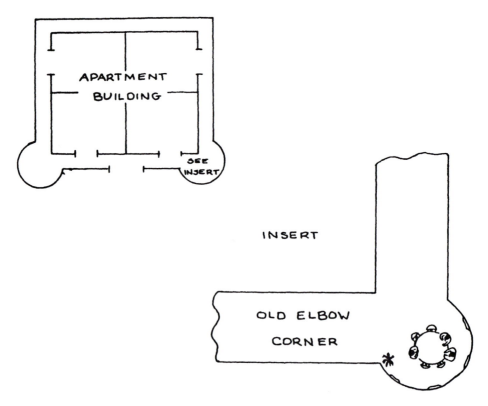

Figure 8–32.

MALLS AND SHOPPING CENTERS

Shopping Mall Parking

Poor Design: Figure 8–33

A. Parking is 360-degree and undifferentiated.
B. Safety hazards persist because of uncontrolled access to all lanes.
C. Undesirable night-time activities occur.
D. Transition from public to private space is undefined.

Good Design: Figure 8–34

A. Parking is enclaved in relation to business entrances.
B. Lateral access by vehicles is severely restricted.

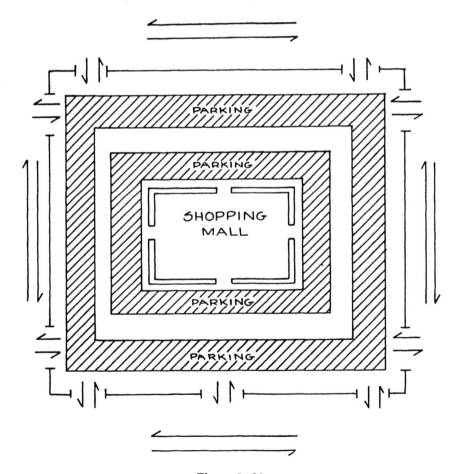

Figure 8–33.

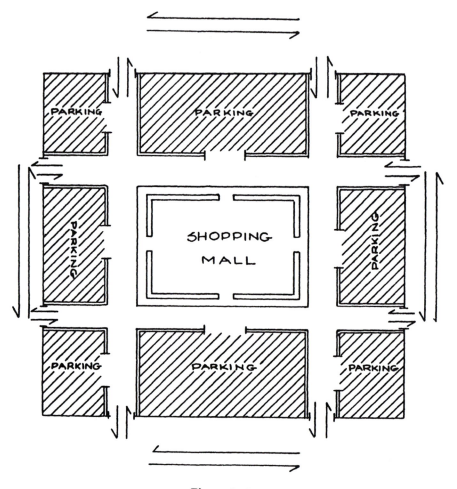

Figure 8–34.

C. Aesthetic design opportunities are enhanced to screen ugly parking lots.

D. Extreme transitional definition exists, thereby reducing escape opportunities.

E. Parking areas may be closed with barricades at different times of the day.

Mall Design

Poor Design and Use: Figure 8–35

A. Malls have traditionally been designed in a fortress style, which turns it back on the parking areas.

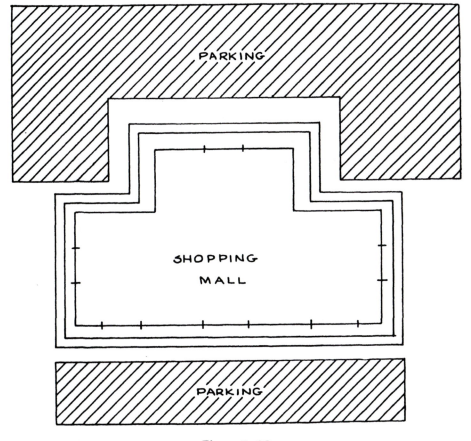

Figure 8–35.

B.   Many dead walls on the least used sides, or backsides, of malls prevent opportunities for advertising and limit natural surveillance.

C.   Designers tend to reflect their perceptions of an area in their designs. Buildings in isolated areas will end up fortress-like in form. The dead walls serve as a barrier to surveillance from or to the building, despite the fact that many people are inside the building, separated by a 16-inch wall from the parking area.

Good Design and Use: Figure 8–36

A.   Display cases may be attached to dead walls to market products and to reduce the negative effect of the fortress designs.

B.   Active displays with lighting and mannequins will attract attention and create the impression of natural surveillance.

C.   False windows and lighting panels may also break up the monotony of the fortress designs and reinforce the impression of natural surveillance.

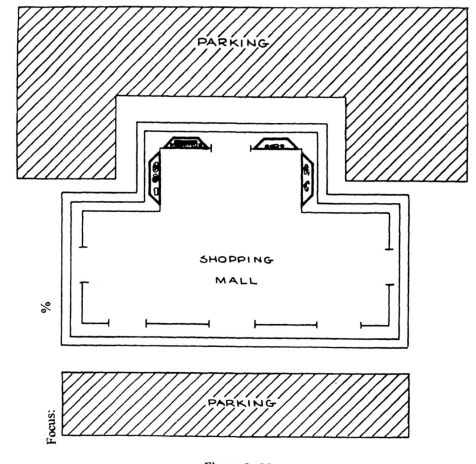

Figure 8–36.

Barriers to Conflict

Poor Design: Figure 8–37

A.   Shopping center parking is contiguous to a major conflicting activity of a play area.
B.   The location of the basketball hoops legitimizes the presence of young persons in and near the parking area, to chase balls and for informal gathering.
C.   Normal users feel that their property and their persons are at greater risk.
D.   Abnormal users feel safer.
E.   Even legitimate use of the play area is perceived negatively by others.

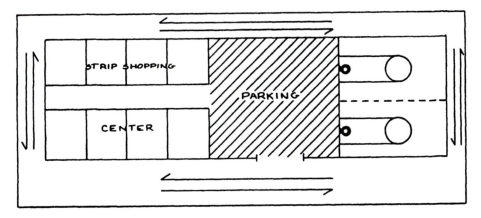

Figure 8–37.

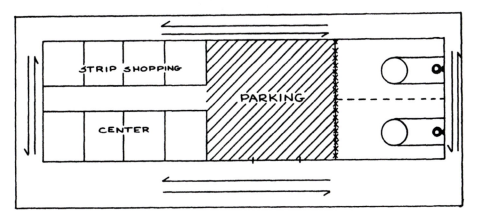

Figure 8–38.

Good Design: Figure 8–38

A.   Distance may be used as a natural barrier to conflicting activities.
B.   The natural barrier of distance reduces the range of excuses for being in the wrong place.
C.   Abnormal users will feel at greater risk of scrutiny and detection.

CONVENIENCE STORES AND BRANCH BANKS

Convenience Stores: Traditional Design

Poor Design and Use: Figure 8–39

A.   Gas pumps were installed after original site planning, so most were placed wherever there was an open area. This often resulted in a

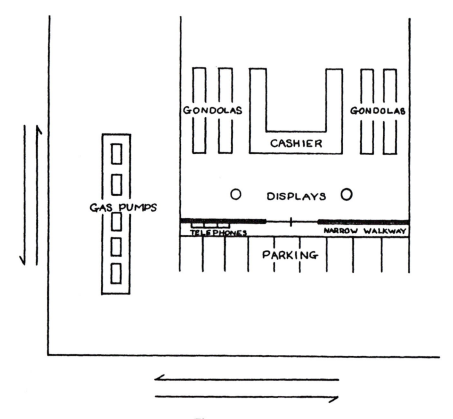

Figure 8–39.

site placement that is not surveillable from the cashier location in the building. Some stores have installed windows that affect cashier location and surveillance.

B.   Parking is traditionally in front, but walkways are generally too narrow for customers to avoid close contact with young people or construction workers who legitimately hang out in these areas.

C.   Telephones are often placed too close to the store entrance. Young people hang out in these areas, as well as some undesirables, which turns off normal adult customers. Robbers like to stand at a pay phone as a cover for casing the store.

D.   Although the research is conflicting, the centrally located cashier station does result in the cashier having her back to customers when only one clerk is on duty. A frontal or rear location of a central cashier station would be preferable.

E.   It is common for stores to obscure the front windows with signage and to orient gondolas and shelves perpendicular to the front of the store. Signage prevents customers and police from looking into or out of the store. Improper gondola and shelf orientation prevents clerks from observing customers. Likewise, abnormal users feel safer in stores where gondolas and shelf systems eliminate natural surveillance.

Good Design and Use: Figure 8–40

A.   Parking in front is always more convenient and safer.
B.   Most stores use ample amounts of glazing in the front, which improves both natural and perceived surveillance.

Convenience Stores: Locations Near Dense Commercial or Housing Sites

A.   Convenience stores located in these sites experience robberies associated with access from the rear of the store to the front. Escape is easy around the back of the store into dense commercial building or housing sites.
B.   Customers are afraid to use these stores because of hanging-out activity by local residents, and by undesirable users, such as drug dealers and unruly young people.

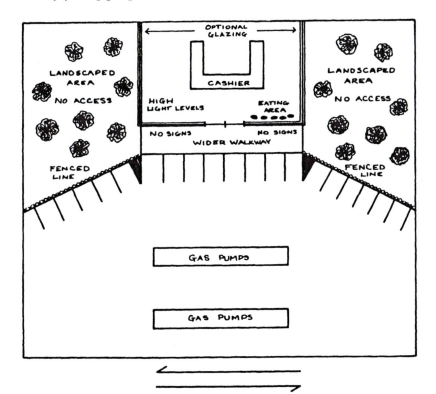

Figure 8–40.

C. The standard modus operandi is for the perpetrator to come from behind the building to the front and rob the cashier. Escape is so easy that stake-out teams of police may not catch the robber that they observe committing the offense, because the person may easily melt into the buildings that are contiguous to and behind the convenience store.

D. A fenced line that takes the corner of the building diagonally to the property line will reduce or eliminate the robberies that come from behind the store. The fence increases the offender's perception of exposure, even though the fence does not provide a continuous enclosure of the property.

Convenience Stores: Hexagon Shaped

Poor Design and Use

A. Double entry systems make customer control difficult.
B. Eating areas may attract people who hang out.
C. The design will work only on corner lots.

Good Design and Use: Figure 8–41

A. Telephone location and interior management may reduce customer conflict between juveniles and construction workers, and adult buyers.
B. Well-lighted gasoline areas will serve as a sea of light, attracting customers.
C. Eating areas in the front of the store will attract adult customers who may find it inconvenient to eat hot foods in their automobiles. Small seat and table designs will keep people from lingering or hanging out.
D. Marketing studies have demonstrated that impulse customers prefer a store that has other customers, which means that they have to see them to be attracted.
E. Segregation of customer groups is achieved by the hexagonal design, which makes these groups less threatening to each other.

Convenience Stores: Fan Shaped

Poor Design and Use

A. Some stores do not have continuous glazing across the front.
B. Fan designs are ineffective when they are in mid-block locations.

Good Design and Use: Figure 8–42

A. Clear view for cashier of all parking and gas pump areas.
B. Corner locations allow for effective vehicle access and excellent surveillance and control.

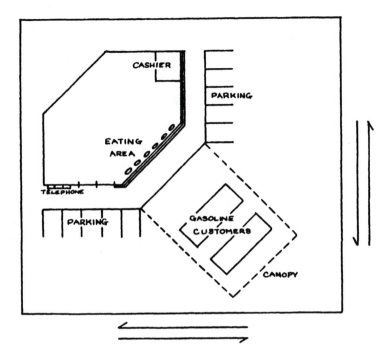

Figure 8−41.

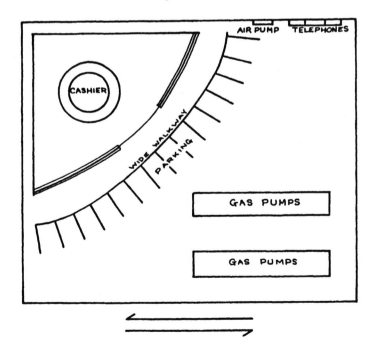

Figure 8−42.

C. Elevated store and cashier locations increase control and customer confidence in safety.
D. Site efficiency, in terms of cost benefit, is high.

Convenience Stores: Kiosk Shaped

Figure 8–43

A. Store oriented to gas sales.
B. 300-degree surveillance for cashier.
C. Late night robbery control through use of bank teller window.
D. Welcoming environment includes high light levels and bright colors.
E. Newer site plans place the car wash to the side instead of the back of the property.
F. Employee compliance with security procedures makes the kiosk store one of the most safe and defensible.

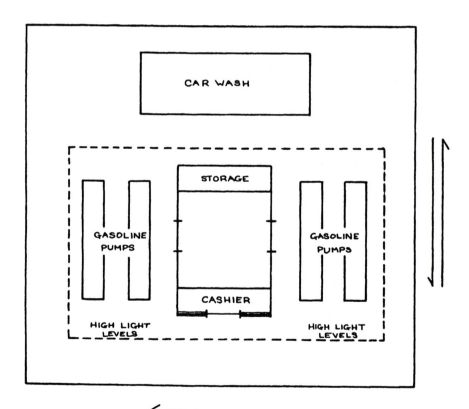

Figure 8–43.

Branch Banks

Poor Design and Use: Figure 8–44

A.   Most branch banks were designed as mini-fortresses reflecting the architect's perception that people would have more confidence that their money was safe.

B.   Corner lots were the most desired to allow for drive-through on the side and back. Engineers desired this to reduce the hazard of vehicles slowing down on the public street to enter a parking area that was visible from the street. Planners desired parking on the side or in back to hide the vehicle. Planners had concluded by the mid to late fifties that cars were ugly and asphalt parking lots were uglier, so they promoted local codes requiring that buildings be placed on the front lot line, so that parking could be hidden behind the structure.

C.   Automatic Teller Machines (ATMs) were originally located adjacent to the secure teller area so that they could be serviced easily, but the traditional design and flow plan caused the secure teller areas to be in

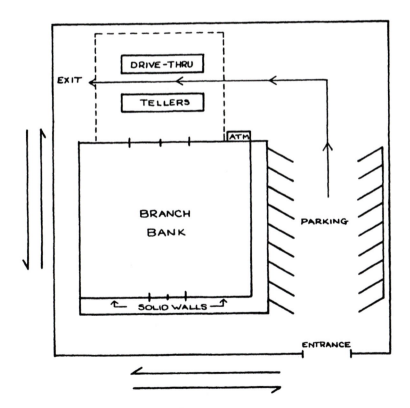

Figure 8–44.

the back of the bank, so ATMs ended up being placed in areas with little or no natural surveillance.

D. Customers have to park on the side or in the back of the bank and then come around on foot to the front or side doors. This is inconvenient and increases their perceived exposure to robbers.

E. Studies have shown that robbers prefer the fortress type branch bank, because they feel that they are less exposed to surveillance from the outside. The fortress design was based on an assumption that went unchallenged for over 30 years.

Good Design and Use: Figure 8–45

A. Bank placed on the rear lot line, allowing customer parking and access from the front.

B. ATM located in area with the greatest natural surveillance and independent from the building. Customers prefer to be able to drive up to the ATM and remain in or close to their vehicle for safety and convenience.

C. Parking should be in front where it is most visible. A curb lane should be used to bring the vehicle deep into the property prior to allowing it

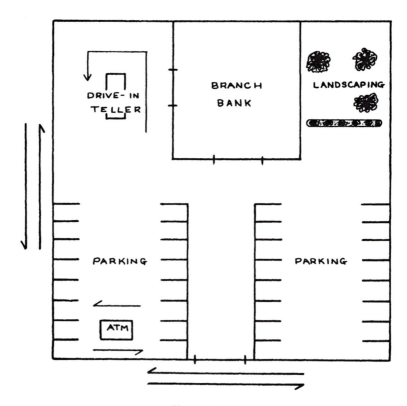

Figure 8–45.

to disburse into the parking area. This will reduce the concern about traffic hazards by increasing the exit speed of the vehicle.

D. The curb laning of vehicle access will serve as a transitional process that forces the user to acknowledge movement from public to semi-public to private space.

E. The building design should emphasize a maximum of glazing to increase the perception of natural surveillance and openness from and to the structure.

F. Abnormal users will feel a greater risk because of the improved natural surveillance and access.

OBJECTIVES FOR RESIDENTIAL ENVIRONMENT

1. *Access control.* Provide secure barriers to prevent unauthorized access to building grounds, buildings, and/or restricted building interior areas.
2. *Surveillance through physical design.* Improve opportunities for surveillance by physical design mechanisms that serve to increase the risk of detection for offenders, enable evasive actions by potential victims, and facilitate intervention by police.
3. *Mechanical surveillance devices.* Provide residences with security devices to detect and signal illegal entry attempts.
4. *Design and construction.* Design, build, and/or repair residences and residential sites to enhance security and improve quality.
5. *Land use.* Establish policies to prevent ill-advised land and building uses that have negative impact.
6. *Resident action.* Encourage residents to implement safeguards on their own to make homes less vulnerable to crime.
7. *Social interaction.* Encourage interaction by residents to foster social cohesion and control.
8. *Private security services.* Determine appropriate paid professional and/ or volunteer citizen services to enhance residential security needs.
9. *Police services.* Improve police service to provide efficient and effective.
10. *Police/community relations.* Improve police/community relations to involve citizens in cooperative efforts with police to prevent and report crime.
11. *Community awareness.* Create neighborhood/community crime prevention awareness to aid in combating crime in residential areas.
12. *Territorial identity.* Differentiate private areas from public spaces to discourage trespass by potential offenders.
13. *Neighborhood image.* Develop positive neighborhood image to encourage residents and investor confidence and increase the economic vitality of the area.

Residential Streets

Figure 8–46

A. Street is quiet with a small amount of through traffic.
B. Residents recognize neighbors' cars and stare at nonresidents who may be passing through or stopping.
C. Gutters are clean and front yards are well maintained, which indicates extended territorial concern. Front porches have furniture and other signs of use.

Figure 8–47

A. A proposed land use change involves the building of a new neighborhood school, which is generally socially desirable.
B. The school generates increased pedestrian and vehicular activity. Nonresident cars will park in front of homes, taking up what had previously been viewed as the proprietary space of residents.

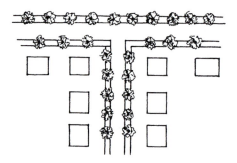

Figure 8–46.

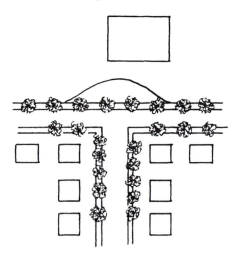

Figure 8–47.

C.   Property value growth and retention will fall. Residents will subconsciously turn their backs to the street and alter their patterns of property use.
D.   The controlling or challenging behaviors of residents (e.g., staring and verbal challenges) will diminish.

Figure 8–48

A.   The neighborhood school is changed to an expanded school that loses its neighborhood identity. Users have very little attachment or concern for the neighborhood.
B.   Traffic increases and more parking activity occurs in the neighborhood. Property values drop and long-term or original residents move out.
C.   New residents accept the changed conditions and exhibit few signs of extended territorial identity and concern.

Figure 8–49

A.   The expanded school is further developed to regional status.
B.   Streets have already been upgraded from residential and subcollector status to the next higher level of traffic flow. Street capacity improvements have resulted in the increase of on-street parking and the removal of the trees. Sidewalks and front yards are pushed closer to the dwelling units.
C.   The neighborhood is already susceptible to zoning change request and the possibility of the development of transient housing, which may be disguised as low income or scattered site publicly supported housing.
D.   Any major land use change will contribute to higher demands for public services, increased housing turnover, and a growing crime rate.

Figure 8–48.

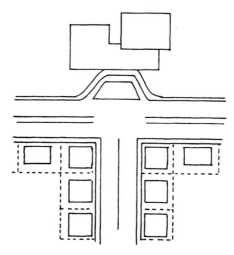

Figure 8–49.

Figure 8–50

A. The encroachment of marginal business and/or transient housing will ultimately be replaced by high density commercial or industrial activities, which will be the only viable land uses once the original site has deteriorated.

B. Vacant or abandoned lots will be used in the interim for overflow parking and unauthorized drug dealing or recreational use. The area

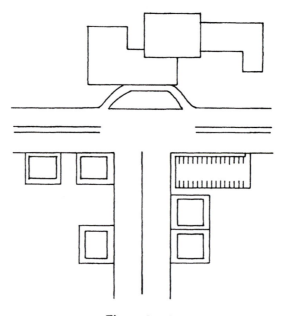

Figure 8–50.

will be perceived as dangerous or undesirable for residential uses. Normal users will avoid the area and abnormal users will feel that they have lower risk of detection or intervention.

C. Some unscrupulous developers will use this process as a means of controlling large parcels of land for long-term development, while capitalizing the long-term plans through the short-term investment in transient housing or marginal commercial activities — both of which help to progressively reduce the property value.

Figure 8–51

A. Access to the new school may be isolated from the contiguous residential streets. School property vehicular access may be planned for an alternative location that may be connected to an existing high-capacity commercially or industrially oriented street.

B. Pedestrian flow through the residential area will still increase, but vehicular and parking activity will be diverted.

Figure 8–52

A. An alternative strategy to the conflict created by the new school would be to create a major set-back to allow for a transition lane and temporary waiting lane for buses and parents who may be awaiting student pickup.

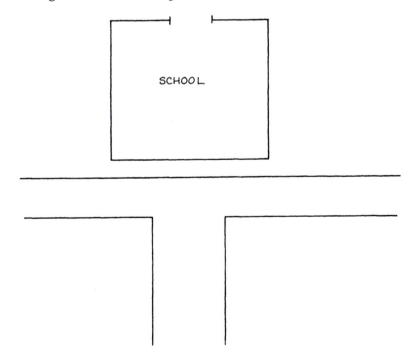

Figure 8–51.

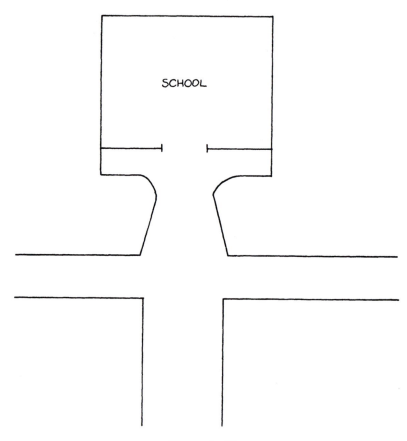

Figure 8–52.

B. Traffic control devices or procedures may be used to direct and divert vehicles from the residential area.

Figure 8–53

A. A partial choker may be used to divert right turn traffic from the affected neighborhood.

Figure 8–54

A. The street affected by the traffic associated with the school may be permanently diverted by closing the street with a cul-de-sac or turnaround T.
B. Emergency vehicle access may be enhanced through the use of drive-over plantings or knockdown gates. Malleable steel pins or links may be used in latching devices or chains to make it easy for emergency vehicles to push open the barriers.

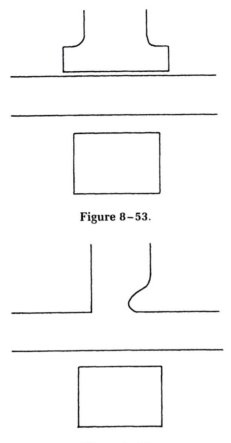

Figure 8–53.

Figure 8–54.

Figure 8–55

A.   The street affected by the traffic associated with the school may be closed in the middle, thus creating a dead end. The middle street closing may use a turnaround ball or a T to facilitate emergency and public service vehicle access.

Figure 8–56

A.   The street affected by the traffic associated with the school may be choked off by the installation of entrance narrowing devices, walls, and columns.

B.   The entrance definition may be physical or symbolic. Columns and entrance definition may he installed without encroaching upon the roadway in situations where the street entrance is too dangerous for a choking effort, or where other factors are involved, such as resident preferences.

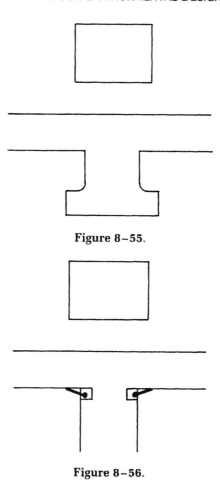

Figure 8-55.

Figure 8-56.

Figure 8-57

A. The street affected by the traffic associated with the school may be choked off with entrance definition devices.
B. The pedestrian walkway may also be upgraded through the installation of paver tiles, or by raising the crosswalk by three inches to serve as a modified speed hump that warns the driver that he is entering a private area.

Residential Development: Curvilinear Streets

Figure 8-58

A. Conventional curvilinear plans minimize unassigned space, which extends territorial concern.
B. Children are more likely to be observed and controlled by residents.

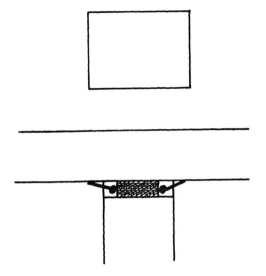

Figure 8–57.

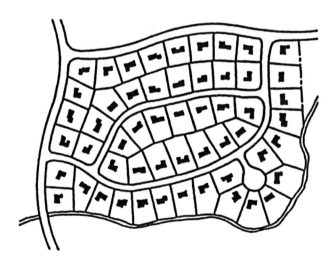

Figure 8–58.

C.   Some bleed-through traffic may occur if drivers become aware that they may avoid the northwest major intersection.

Figure 8–59

A.   Cluster curvilinear streets are presently more appealing because of amenities and green areas, which are marketed heavily by developers. Many local planning regulations require these features in planned unit developments.

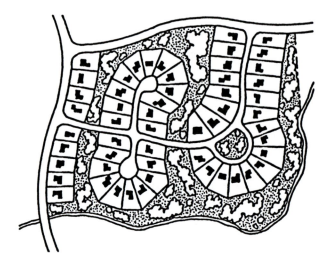

Figure 8–59.

B. The increase in unassigned areas may result in reduced proprietary concern of residents. Unassigned areas may be aesthetically appealing, but residents will feel little attachment and may psychologically turn their backs on activities occurring there.

C. Deed restrictions or covenants are often very strict in terms of what residents may do in the open areas. This further reduces territorial concern.

D. Young people often go unsupervised in the open or green areas. There is some evidence in public housing, as well as in planned developments (cluster concept), that children growing up in undifferentiated environments fail to learn respect for property rights, which negatively affects their values and behavior.

E. CPTED planners may recommend that open areas be assigned to contiguous clusters of homes. Landscaping or other physical changes may be used to establish border definition.

F. Residents may be provided with financial and other inducements to participate in the maintenance of the open or green areas. This participation will increase their proprietary concern for the previously unassigned space.

Figure 8–60

A. A townhouse cluster design is economically viable. Open spaces and amenities are important attractions to buyers.

B. This townhouse development creates an excessive amount of unassigned space that is often protected by strict deed restrictions or covenants.

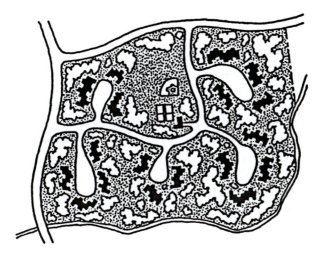

Figure 8–60.

C. Territorial concern is reduced and abnormal users feel safer in accessing the open areas. Young people are less likely to be scrutinized in these areas.

D. The ball field and tennis courts may serve as a magnet to nonresidents. This could produce conflict and reduce the likelihood of controlling behavior by residents. Use by nonresidents will legitimize their presence in the development, which will increase the abnormal users' perception of safety (low risk of detection or intervention). The normal user may feel threatened and therefore exhibit avoidance behavior, which will affect other normal users. Abnormal users will be reinforced by these cues that say that no one owns this space or is willing to challenge the improper use. Normal users may stop using these areas altogether, which has been a problem in public housing and parks.

E. CPTED planners may recommend the assignment of open areas to clusters of buildings. Landscape and other physical changes may be made to enhance border definition.

F. Residents may be induced to participate in maintenance of these areas through financial or other inducements. This will extend proprietary concern for these areas.

G. CPTED planners may recommend the addition of one or two buildings on the north side of the development to provide a natural barrier to potentially conflicting activities. This should appeal to the developer as a profitable move that will produce the added benefits of increased perceptions of safety. CPTED planners may recommend the closure of the internal street in the middle, or at one end, to eliminate through traffic. This may help to eliminate or reduce the probability of drive-by drug sales.

Residential Streets: Options for Private Use

Figure 8–61

A.   Each end of the block is choked off. One end uses a closure of the incoming lane (ingress). The other end closes the outgoing lane (egress).
B.   Play areas are installed to thrust activities more into previously public areas to increase visual and physical attention.
C.   A combination of straight-in and parallel parking is used.

Figure 8–62

A.   Additional crosswalks are added to break the street into four quadrants. This will increase the definition of the pedestrian space in the street.

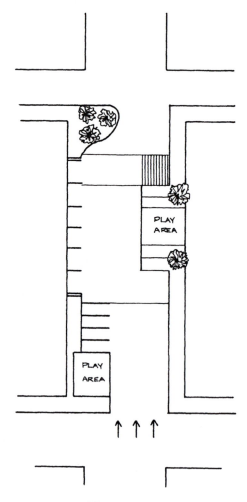

Figure 8–61.

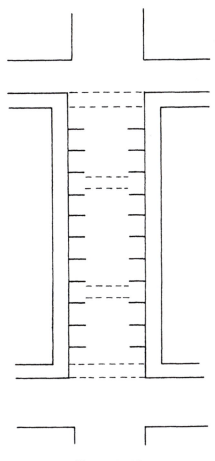

Figure 8–62.

B. Crosswalks should be legally designated under local ordinances to create pedestrian right-of-way.
C. Crosswalks may be raised two to three inches to reinforce the driver's perception of transition.

Figure 8–63

A. A combination of parking styles — parallel and straight-in — may be introduced to create space for more landscaping. This combination of landscaping and parking will narrow the entrance (ingress and egress).
B. Crosswalks should be upgraded to enhance transitional definitions.
C. A middle block or central area should be defined with texture change to be used for occasional block activities. Entrances should be choked off or closed with barricades during planned block parties or functions.

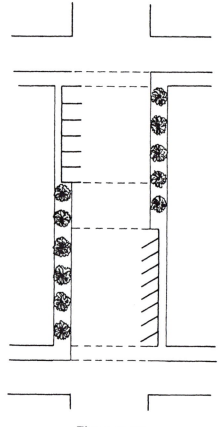

Figure 8–63.

Figure 8–64

A.   One end of the street may be closed by installing a play area with safety barriers.
B.   Parking arrangements may be alternated between angle and parallel to create more parking and to narrow the street.

Figure 8–65

A.   Entrances may be choked to slow down traffic.
B.   A block gathering area may be installed to create a place for parties and other functions. These areas will also further the perception of the block as private.

Figure 8–66

A.   A simple closing will create a cul-de-sac effect that will eliminate through traffic.

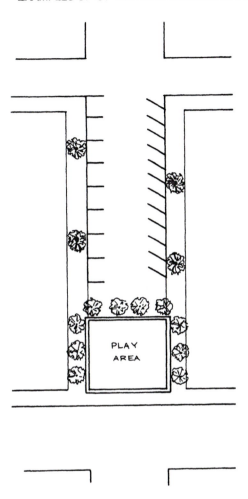

Figure 8–64.

B.   A drive-over (for emergency vehicles) area may be created by reducing the elevation of the center of the planter. Replaceable flowers or bushes may be used to increase the perception of closure in the drive-over area. Another option is to use knockdown bollards.

Figure 8–67

A.   Landscaping improvements may be installed to make the street more appealing for pedestrian activity.
B.   An additional crosswalk may be installed in the middle of the block to enhance pedestrian convenience and to slow down traffic.
C.   Crosswalks should be legally designated under city ordinance. They may also be raised two to three inches to reinforce the driver's perception of transition.

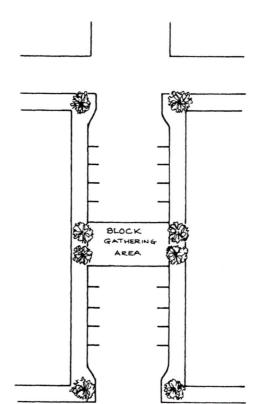

Figure 8–65.

Residential Streets: Recovery of Grid Systems

Figure 8–68

A.　Boundary control is established by creating cul-de-sacs in the middle of most access streets.

B.　Access is limited to two points that connect with internal streets.

Figure 8–69

A.　Internal controls are established by installing a system of diagonal diverters to loop traffic in and out.

B.　Through traffic is denied. The diverter angles should be based upon resident input and an analysis of access needs.

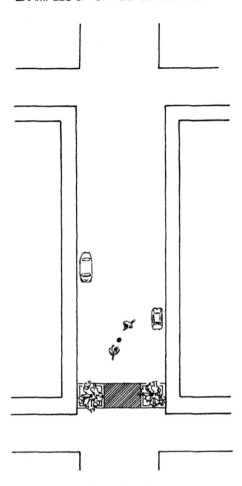

Figure 8–66.

Figure 8–70

A. One-way traffic flows are established to reduce through access.
B. Speed controls should be used to reduce pedestrian and vehicle conflict that may result from higher speeds on the one-way system.
C. Parking plans may be altered to include alternating combinations of angle parking and street landscaping.

Figure 8–71

A. An ad hoc plan of cul-de-sacs, diagonal diverters, and one-way flows to make the streets more private.
B. This approach provides some flexibility for long-term planning.

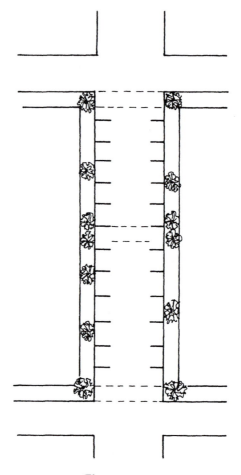

Figure 8-67.

BOUNDARY CONTROL

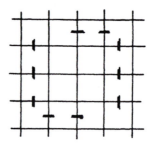

Figure 8-68.

INTERNAL CONTROL

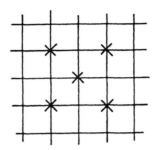

Figure 8–69.

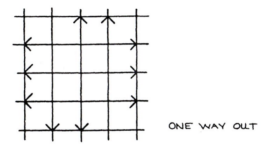

ONE WAY OUT

Figure 8–70.

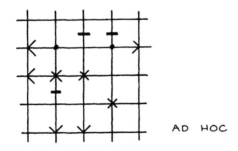

AD HOC

Figure 8–71.

OBJECTIVES FOR SCHOOL ENVIRONMENT

1. *Access control.* Provide secure barriers to prevent unauthorized access to school grounds, schools, or restricted interior areas.
2. *Surveillance through physical design.* Improve opportunities for surveillance by physical design mechanisms that serve to increase the risk of detection for offenders.

3. *Mechanical surveillance devices.* Provide schools with security devices to detect and signal unauthorized entry attempts.
4. *Congestion control.* Reduce or eliminate causes of congestion that contribute to student confrontations.
5. *Psychological deterrents.* Provide psychological deterrents to theft and vandalism.
6. *User monitoring.* Implement staff and student security measures at vulnerable areas.
7. *Emergency procedures.* Provide teachers with means to handle emergency situations.
8. *User awareness.* Initiate programs to promote student awareness of security risks and countermeasures.
9. *User motivation.* Encourage social interaction, social cohesion, and school pride by promoting extracurricular activities, providing amenities, and upgrading the visual quality of the school.
10. *Territorial identity.* Highlight the functional identities of different areas throughout the school to increase territorial identity and reduce confusion.
11. *Community involvement.* Promote public awareness and involvement with school faculty and student achievements and activities.

School Campus Control

Poor Design: Figure 8–72

A. Informal gathering areas are preempted by groups of students who often promote conflict.
B. Isolated areas are used by students who wish to smoke or to engage in unauthorized or illicit behavior.
C. Interlopers or trespassers seek out out-of-sight areas to contact students for drug sales or other improper activities.
D. These areas are very difficult to monitor and control.
E. Most authorities attempt to maintain surveillance of these areas in an attempt to control behavior.

Good Design: Figure 8–73

A. By designating formal gathering areas, all other areas become off limits.
B. Anyone observed in spaces that are not designated as formal gathering areas will be automatically subject to scrutiny.
C. Abnormal users will feel at greater risk and will have few excuses for being in the wrong places.
D. Teachers and administrators assume greater challenging powers by the clear spatial definition.

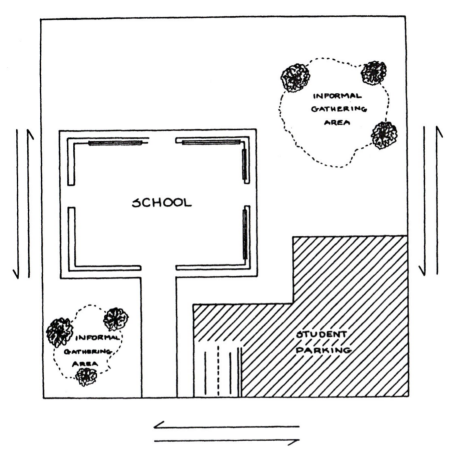

Figure 8–72.

High School Parking Lots

Poor Design: Figure 8–74

A. Multiple access points increase the perception that the parking area is public and provide many escape routes for potential offenders.

B. The location on the periphery of the site reduces any clear transitional definiton of movement from public to private space, thus allowing an abnormal user to feel safe or at low risk of confrontation.

C. The openness of the lot increases the range of excuses for improper use.

Good Design: Figure 8–75

A. Use of barricades to close off unsupervised entrances during low use times controls access and reinforces the perception that the parking area is private.

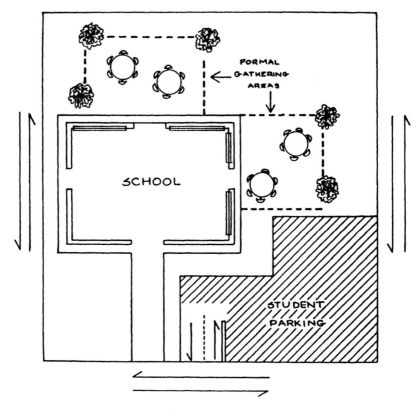

Figure 8–73.

B.   The curb lane in the open entrance forces the user to transition from public to semi-public to private space, with a radical turn into the parking area.

C.   The symbolic isolation creates the perception that escape may be easily blocked.

D.   Violation of the barricade and traffic control devices draws attention to the abnormal user and establishes probable cause sufficient to stop the individual for questioning.

Student Parking and Driver Education Relationships

Poor Design: Figure 8–76

A.   Student parking is an unsafe activity.

B.   Student parking on the periphery of the campus is in an unsafe location.

C.   The isolated location has few opportunities for natural surveillance.

D.   Poor transitional definition creates the perception of safety for abnormal users, and risk for normal users.

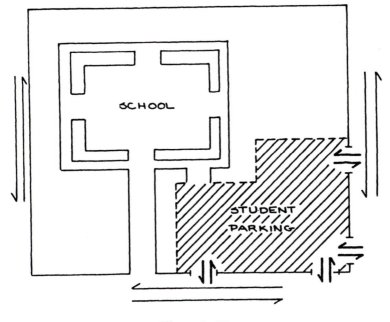

Figure 8–74.

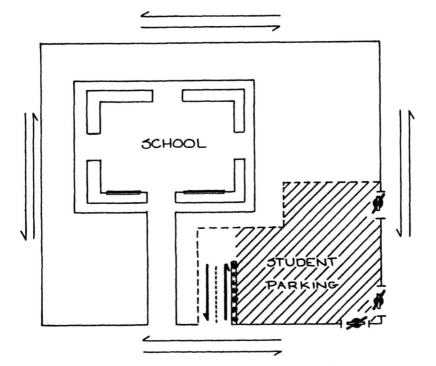

Figure 8–75.

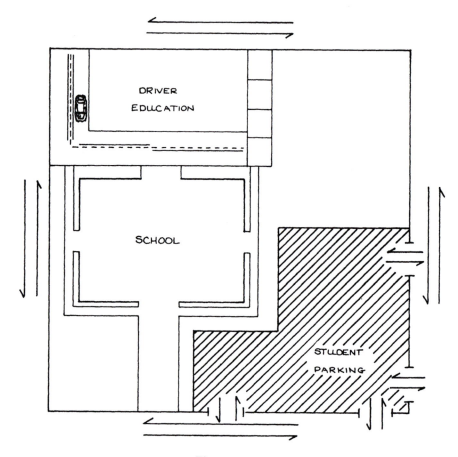

Figure 8-76.

Good Design: Figure 8-77

A. Driver education is a safe activity, monitored by responsible teachers and students.

B. The switch of driver education with student parking in an existing location provides a natural opportunity to put a safe activity in an unsafe location and an unsafe activity in a safe location.

C. The new location for student parking (in this hypothetical example) is in the direct line of sight from office windows.

Courtyards and Corridors

Poor Design and Use: Figure 8-78

A. Many site planners or users of space fail to adequately define the intended purpose and uses of courtyards.

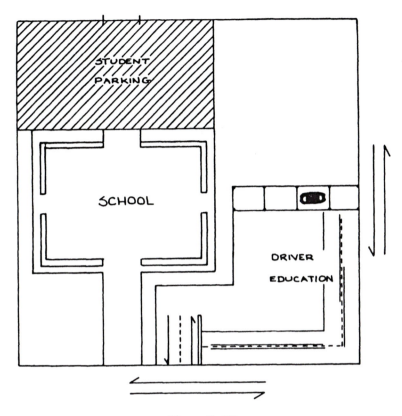

Figure 8–77.

B. Uses could be aesthetics, thermal support of the building, or gathering areas. Each use presents different requirements and space management plans and policies.

C. Corridor and courtyard confusion is exacerbated by the installation of benches and other furnishings along the corridors.

D. Benches are sometimes used as barriers to access to courtyards, with the mistaken idea of protecting the grass from encroachment by students or pedestrians.

E. Corridor/courtyard conflict often leads to congestion, noise, and personal conflict.

F. Groups of students or others will often colonize, or preempt, spaces creating further conflict and fear.

G. Normal users will avoid using these areas. Abnormal users feel safer and at low risk of detection or intervention.

Good Design and Use: Figure 8–79

A. The intended purpose and uses of the courtyards and adjoining corridors are clearly defined in policy and in the physical design.

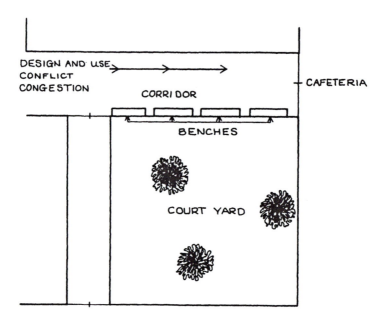

MAIN BUILDING

Figure 8-78.

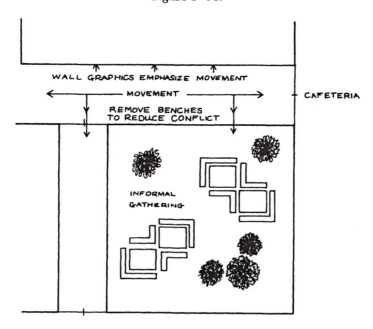

MAIN BUILDING

Figure 8-79.

B. Furnishings for courtyards that are intended for gathering behavior may be designed to break up group size, or to provide only minimal comfort to shorten the staying time.
C. Portable amenities may be used more effectively than permanent ones depending on intended use patterns. Accordingly, physical support is provided only when the specific behavior is desired.
D. Normal users will feel safer in moving through these areas. Abnormal users will be more subject to control and will find it more difficult to preempt these spaces.

School Lunchtime Hallway Use

Poor Design and Use: Figure 8–80

A. The same hallway is used for coming and going.
B. Conflict occurs as groups attempt to go to the cafeteria while others attempt to return to class.

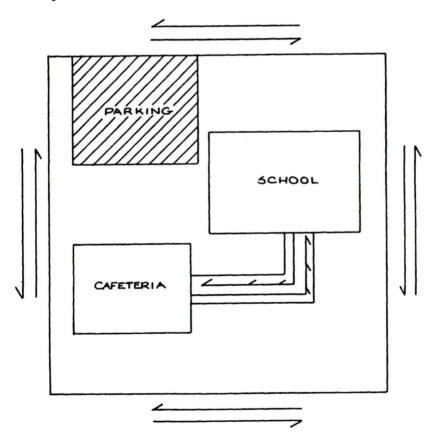

Figure 8–80.

C. The arrival of the first group and the departure of the second are the most controlled because there is no other group moving at the same time. All persons are supposed to be going in the same direction so the hall monitors and administrators are perceived to be more powerful. There is a limited range of excuses for improper behavior.

D. Hall monitors lose control because of the coming and going after the first group eats.

E. It takes longer to get groups, subsequent to the first, through the lunch line, because of the conflict and congestion.

F. Most classroom and locker thefts occur during the lunch period in school systems.

Good Design and Use: Figure 8–81

A. Ingress and egress to the cafeteria may be separated spatially and temporally to define movement relationships.

B. Each group will arrive faster, with fewer stragglers.

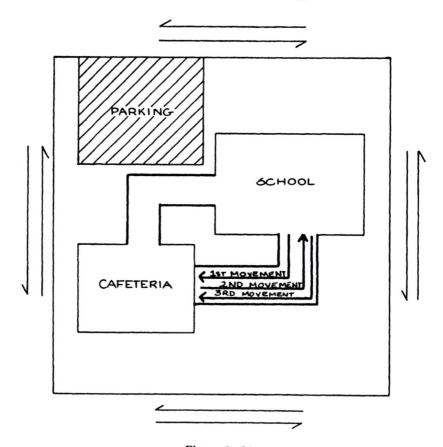

Figure 8–81.

C.   Abnormal users of space will feel at greater risk of detection.
D.   A time, or temporal, separation of movements to and from the classroom area will require the addition of at least five minutes for each shift. This time may be taken from that allotted for eating, since each group will arrive faster and, therefore, be fed faster.

Safe Activities in Unsafe Locations

Poor Design: Figure 8–82

A.   Many noncurricular activities at schools (e.g., military recruiting, college orientation, picture and ring sales, club functions) are assigned to locations in the office, cafeteria, or gymnasium.
B.   Office, cafeteria, and gymnasium areas provide poor design support for these noncurricular activities.
C.   These noncurricular activities often impede the normal operations of the functions of the existing space.

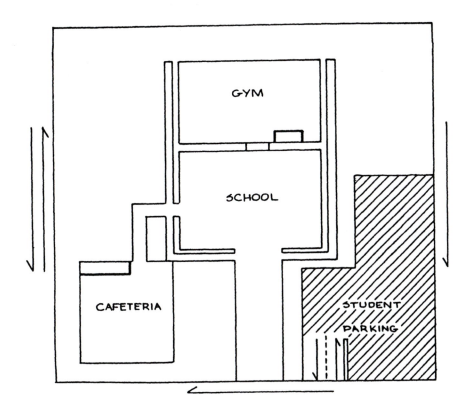

Figure 8–82.

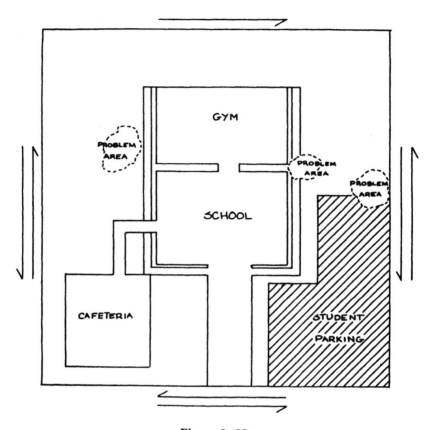

Figure 8–83.

Good Design: Figure 8–83

A. Problem areas on school campuses are well known and easy to map.
B. Problem areas shift with changing groups and trends of supervision.
C. Safe activities may be placed reasonably in many problem areas to attract normal users and displace abnormal or undesirable activity.
D. Normal users will feel safer and abnormal users will feel at greater risk or unsafe.

CONVENTION CENTER AND STADIUM

Convention Center

Poor Design and Use: Figure 8–84

A. Many convention centers are placed purposefully in deteriorated areas to stimulate renewal. They are financed largely by public tax dollars or publicly backed bonds, since normal investors will not take the risk.

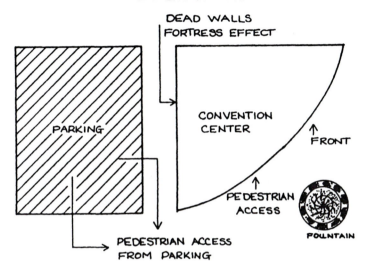

Figure 8–84.

B. Convention centers have suffered from fortress designs, which must reflect the designer's negative perception of the location, as well as the unique logistics requirements of convention activities.

C. Parking and pedestrian access are impeded by the fortress designs and by the deteriorated condition of surrounding areas.

D. Local codes often require parking to be placed behind structures and obscured by landscaping.

E. Local codes generally will require the creation of plazas and open sitting areas. Developers are influenced to install fountains to enhance the aesthetics of an open area, but experience has shown that fountains and amenities in open areas attract vagrants, especially if they have already become established as the indigenous population.

F. Convention centers and their related parking structures usually are not designed to contain a variety of pedestrian-oriented businesses at the ground level, which would attract people all day and on weekends.

Good Design and Use: Figures 8–85 and 8–86

A. Change local codes to allow parking in front of convention centers, where it is safer.

B. Delay installation of permanent amenities and fountains until the intended user population has clearly taken control of the site.

C. Thrust the convention center and parking structures into the airspace above, and place businesses and nightclubs at the ground level to increase year-round and evening activity. This will improve business and increase the number of normal users, who will feel and act safer.

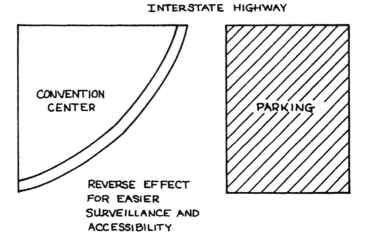

Figure 8–85.

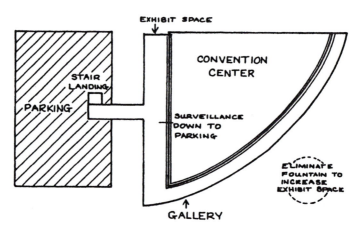

Figure 8–86.

D.   Consider altering the exterior and use patterns of existing sites by adding galleries to offset fortress effects and increase both real and perceived surveillance opportunities. Galleries may be used to increase outdoor activities for exhibits and vendors, thus putting safe activities in what had been perceived to be unsafe locations.

Stadium Entrance and Ticket Control

Poor Design and Use: Figure 8–87

A.   Traditional designs provide no transition from undifferentiated parking and informal gathering areas to the entrance and ticket control functions.

STADIUM

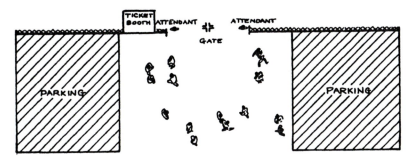

Figure 8-87.

B. Groups of students and others tend to congregate in front of entrance locations, which produces fear and concern for adults and young people who wish to enter the stadium.
C. Ticket booth personnel and gate attendants cannot see over the groups of bystanders.
D. Normal users feel the lack of control and avoid these areas or pass through them quickly, thus reinforcing the control by abnormal users.

Good Design and Use: Figure 8-88

A. A funnel design forces informal gathering behavior farther out into the parking area.

STADIUM

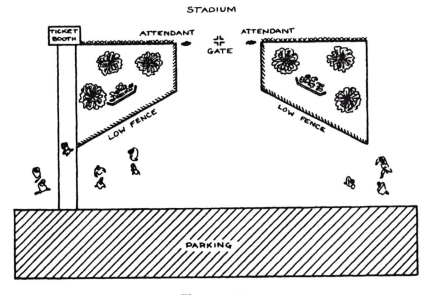

Figure 8-88.

B.   Gathering behavior is more difficult deeper into the parking area because of the perceived pedestrian/vehicular conflict.

C.   Gate attendants have greater line of sight control of the parking lot and pedestrian areas.

D.   The range of excuses for different behaviors narrows with the width of the funnel as one approaches the gate. Attendants have more power to exert their influence over persons seeking entry as they are channeled into the funnel.

E.   Normal users feel safer as they approach the entrance because of the narrow definiton of behavior deep into the funnel—movement only.

9

CPTED Implementation

PROGRAM PLANNING

Planning is a process of self-examination, confronting difficult choices, and establishing priorities. Planning addresses the following questions:

- Where are we now?
- Where do we want to be?
- How do we get there?
- How do we measure progress?

The principal reason why community activities and programs have failed in the past is that they were never implemented. This may seem overly simplistic, but there are volumes of research literature that describe the failure of attempts to implement new social and community-based concepts in terms of the lack of cooperation and planning. Most of these activities consumed many local resources and time but failed to deliver any services or achieve any objectives.

New activities or programs start with great expectations and excitement. This leads to a second phase, which is a period of concern. Things do not seem to be happening the way in which they were planned. Eventually, it is clear that the plans have broken down and there is much embarrassment. A hunt for the guilty is immediately carried out to forestall criticism from the community or from those who would have been served by the new activity. Even after the guilty are identified as the key players and decisionmakers responsible for the plan's failure, there is a tendency to punish the innocent. This is done by declaring that the program or concept is not feasible or that the recipients of the services abused the privilege. Accordingly, the services will have to be denied to everyone.

Among the reasons why new programs or services are not implemented are the following:

- *Inadequate problem assessment.* Everyone thinks that they know what the problem is, so there is the tendency to skip this step.

- *Undiagnosed organizational needs and capabilities.* There is the assumption that the organizations and individuals involved have the skills and resources to take on new activities.
- *Solutions that do not fit the problems.* This is the tendency to have untried, trendy, or favorite solutions looking for problems to address.

One of the best ways to overcome these problems is to conduct a community self-assessment that incorporates the information that is collected as part of the analysis process. The self-assessment process must involve the community, public policymakers, and the key staff from public and private agencies that will be required to coordinate services and activities. The main objectives of the community self-assessment are to:

- identify the strengths and weaknesses of the present community responses to crime and safety problems
- compile a community resource inventory
- identify organizational capabilities that must be developed or enhanced

There are a number of important reasons for going through the self-assessment process prior to making any plans or commitments to programs or activities. Following are descriptions of these reasons:

- *Authority.* The self-assessment establishes the credibility and objectivity of the interagency committee's findings and recommendations for action. It substitutes facts for beliefs in dealing with issues and problems that are usually politically and socially sensitive. How can this process be criticized when it is members of the community or organization who are publicly identifying strengths, weaknesses, and needs for responding to crime and safety problems?
- *Liability.* In a general sense, the self-assessment process establishes due diligence by proving that all things reasonable were done to make the right decisions. How can the process be faulted if things do not go well during implementation, when a systematic and organized approach was followed to determine what needs to be done and how to do it?
- *Budget.* It is extremely difficult to increase budgets or to add new items to existing budgets for programs and activities that are not yet proven or guaranteed to be successful. Financial resources are easily developed when there is an overwhelming demand or public support for a new program or activity. The self-assessment helps to legitimize the need for the commitment of resources by demonstrating that an exhaustive effort was made to identify the needs of the community.
- *Scope of activities.* The self-assessment helps to increase confidence and credibility in the plan of action, which in turn helps to remove restraints to the range of activities that are undertaken. Caution is usually associated with fear of failure and results in weak or ineffectual

commitments to getting the job done. Programs fail because they are never implemented sufficiently to prove their worth.

- *Discovery.* The systematic and unbiased approach to "turning over all of the stones" usually provides startling revelations about assets and capabilities that already exist in the community. It is common for the interagency steering committee to discover that there are more local resources than there is need, that the real problem is lack of coordination. Additionally, it is common to discover that there is more community support than assumed by elected officials or by self-proclaimed community leaders.

The self-assessment process may be compared to the medical model of identifying problems and solutions. This is a process of diagnosis, prognosis, and prescriptive action:

- *Diagnosis (Dx).* The process of taking a series of measurements and observations about community or organization needs, agency activities, and results. The observations are made in terms of the elements and key components of the CPTED concept.
- *Prognosis (Px).* The development of an overall understanding of the health, the strengths, and the needs of the community or organization in terms of crime and safety-related problems and current responses.
- *Prescriptive (Rx).* The specific actions that are required to meet the goals and objectives established during the prognostic stage of the self-assessment and planning process.

The medical model provides insights into the phenomenon of why programs fail. It happens too often in social and community programs that problems are defined in the language of solutions. Popular solutions do not always fit the problem. Popular programs treat the symptoms instead of eliminating the problems that produce the symptoms. Another metaphorical analogy from the medical field that may be applied to social programs is that "the operation was a success, but the patient died!" The self-assessment process is one sure means of ensuring that the plan of action is reasonable and appropriate.

The medical model translates into three basic steps required to be completed in planning:

1. *Normative.* Is the process devoted to providing answers to the question "What should we be doing and why?" The information that is developed during the *diagnostic* step is used to help answer these questions. It is important to set aside discussions about solutions to avoid missing some obvious discovery opportunities.
2. *Strategic.* Is the process associated with developing answers to the question "What can we do and how?" These questions help to examine

alternatives and to ensure that final decisions are based upon good *prognostic* information.

3.   *Operational.* Is the process directed toward answering the question "What will we do and when?" Building upon the answers to the questions in the previous two steps, the *prescriptive* step outlines specific action to be taken.

The most important tasks to be completed in the planning process can be listed as follows:

- Collect data and survey existing conditions (Dx)
- Analyze data and identify all opportunities and limitations (Dx)
- Formulate goals and objectives (Px)
- Generate alternative concepts (Px)
- Develop each concept into a workable solution (Px)
- Evaluate alternative solutions (Px)
- Translate solutions into policies, plans, guidelines, and programs (Rx)

IMPLEMENTATION

CPTED Task Force

The interagency or organizational steering committee that was set up to conduct the self-assessment and develop the plan of action will have to provide leadership and oversight for the implementation process. The committee or council will need to be composed of chief executives of the key agencies, community representatives, and staff from the agencies involved. The same mix is required for an organizational level committee. It is recommended that the interagency be divided into at least two groups: policy level and staff.

The participants at the policy level should meet regularly to approve plans and activities that are developed by the members of the staff group. The policy group must have the authority to appoint persons to work groups to complete tasks that are required for implementing the program. Work groups should be used to carry out discrete tasks as well as to provide ongoing planning, coordination, and evaluation.

The most important activities and tasks of the steering committee are:

- conduct and periodically update the self-assessment of crime problems and needs in the community or organization
- identify goals and objectives for improvement
- publish the community or organization self-assessment report
- designate working groups and responsibilities for the implementation of the planned improvements

- provide oversight to implementation activities and develop remedial action as necessary

Program Management

It is clear that there will be many activities and tasks involved in the implementation of a CPTED program. The interagency or intra-organizational nature of the program will make coordination even more difficult. Accordingly, an individual program manager or program management committee should be appointed to provide the ongoing coordination, scheduling, and monitoring of activities. Several persons who possess good management skills and who are placed in high-level staff positions in the key agencies may serve in a program management work group that is authorized by the policy-level steering committee.

The program management function includes the following requirements:

- system design and planning
- coordination
- training
- assistance
- monitoring
- management
- handling highly complex or unique tasks that may not be delegated

Meetings

Meetings should be conducted on a regular basis so that participants can plan their schedules around meeting times. An agenda should be prepared for each meeting containing distinct tasks and expectations for results or outcomes of the meeting. One strategy for maintaining attendance and interest in the meetings is to establish a rotating position of chairperson who is responsible for planning and running the meeting. This rotating position could be filled by the various interagency members in turn, which will help ensure that everyone participates and understands the importance of coordination.

Planning for Change

First and foremost in planning for change is the need to *control expectations.* This is necessary to ensure that support will be there for the program when it is needed. It is important to avoid the creation of unrealistic goals or timetables for action. It is equally important for the interagency steering committee to establish and stick to a reasonable schedule of activities.

Another important admonition in planning for change is the need to avoid the tendency to seek out *canned goods* or *instant recipes*. It is easy to skip the dull drudgery of developing a program from scratch by going elsewhere and lifting out someone else's program. This can spell disaster because outside programs may not be adaptable. Moreover, the adoption of a "canned program" will leave the participants with very little understanding of the intricacies and nuances of the program operation. This knowledge is critical when it comes time to fix problems.

There is a tendency for program planners to feel the need to either rush the planning process or to go too slowly. Some people may feel the need to rush through planning in order to get the program or services in place. This may result in much embarrassment and failure when it is discovered that the wrong solutions or methods are being used. Conversely, a planning committee that equates length of time with good planning may never get the job done and lose community support in the meantime. Therefore, it is recommended that both pitfalls be avoided by adopting a *development strategy* that balances the importance of careful planning with early experimentation and testing of new concepts or methods. Instead of rushing to get to final form or never getting there, it can be made clear that the program is still in the developmental process that includes learning about and revising the services and procedures as they are implemented. This will improve the cooperation and collaboration needed from the persons who will carry out or receive the new services.

Finally, one of the primary impediments to planning for change is the issue of *evaluation*. Evaluation can be a trap if it is done poorly or if it is connected to some unrealistic anticipated outcomes. Evaluation that is conducted by outsiders may appear to be more objective, but it does little to assist the program planners in remedial improvements. Program planners lose a lot of time educating the outside evaluators about the project activities and services. Evaluation that is conducted internally provides direct feedback to program planners and administrators. Accordingly, evaluation should be considered as a tool for program planning and monitoring. Outcomes will still be measured and objectivity may be assessed through audits of project data by any interested outside parties.

Mission Statements, Goals, and Objectives

Mission statements are used to define the scope of responsibility and interest of a program or service. The mission statement stakes the claim or territory of the program. It also provides a formal reminder for all concerned individuals of the purpose of the program. *Goals* are more specific statements used to identify program components or intended areas of accomplishment. *Objectives* are the steps or milestones that must be reached in attaining an individual goal. The use of these terms furnishes a hierarchy for planners and managers to use in determining the priorities and interrelationships of program activity.

The importance of having well-defined objectives cannot be overstated. To the extent that objectives are not established or are poorly defined, the project will suffer from incomplete planning, uncertain execution, and difficulty in evaluating progress. Following are several requirements for setting objectives:

- *Measurable.* Objectives should be phrased in concrete, measurable terms, so that their achievement at project completion can be demonstrated.
- *Related to time.* Progress toward the achievement of objectives is difficult to assess unless there is an understanding of when the full objective will be reached.
- *Related to cost.* Objectives must clearly relate to project costs and expenditures so that activities may be assessed or evaluated in terms of return on investment.

Goals and objectives should be re-assessed periodically to ensure that they still reflect the wishes and needs of the community. Changes in the political climate and the funding process, or those brought on by internal project assessment, may require some changes in the focus of the program. However, some caution should be used in making changes that are inconsistent with the original mission statement.

Time and Task Planning

There are many excellent tools for time management and task planning available in manuals or computer programs. Spreadsheets may be used to plan activities as well as expenditures. A variety of charts may be used to develop an understanding of program activities. Some of these techniques incorporate dependency networks and critical path analysis to assist in task planning and the setting of priorities.

Agreements

Some communities have rushed into interagency agreements and discovered that everything needed to be changed once the program was planned. Others have found that agency heads were very hesitant to sign an agreement because they were not clear about the commitments they were making. The best approach is to commit to a process that incorporates two agreements. First, is the *agreement to agree* that commits the participants and agencies solely to the community self-assessment process. There is the expectation that this will lead ultimately to a plan of action and a final interagency agreement to implement the plan of action. The second or *formal interagency agreement* may be signed long after the program has commenced and the partners are sure what their commitments entail.

EVALUATION AND MONITORING

Evaluation is defined as a process of making judgments about the worth of something. In the present context, it involves a systematic examination of project activities and the impact these activities have on the objectives of the project. Evaluation efforts are directed at the documentation of changes or improvements and at a determination of the extent to which those effects may be attributed to project implementation.

Evaluation can be of assistance to administrators and project staff by providing feedback on the efficacy of the project (or specific project activities), thus guiding decisions related to project management. Evaluation also can serve as a vehicle for technology transfer, documenting techniques successfully employed within a project.

The involvement of the staff in the evaluation process is critical, because project staff are the ones who are most knowledgeable about project operations. The project manager will, in most cases, be responsible for planning and managing the evaluation efforts.

Summary of Evaluation Steps

- Define goals and objectives of the project.
- Define evaluation criteria appropriate to the goals.
- Identify and define target population.
- Identify important project variables (i.e., how does the project work and what makes it work?).
- Choose the appropriate evaluation design(s).
- Identify data sources and data points appropriate to evaluation criteria, target population, and design.
- Consult with staff concerning data and collection procedures.
- Collect data.
- Analyze data.
- Formulate conclusions.
- Present recommendations for change.

Types of Evaluation

There are several types of evaluation that are relevant to the CPTED program. Formative, program monitoring, process, impact, or intensive evaluation can all be used effectively in the program. These approaches can be summarized as follows:

- *Formative evaluation.* This is used to develop and pretest concepts during the planing process. Meta-evaluations are conducted to help construct strategies that may be part of an overall program.

- *Program monitoring evaluation.* Here the focus is on measuring change. It is the least expensive of evaluations, but it can provide decision-makers with important information regarding the progress of each project.
- *Process evaluation.* This is concerned with the operations of the various project components that account for the success of a project. A relatively simple evaluation process would provide a well-documented description of the project activities, specification of the project recipients, identification of the time period involved, definition of the project locale, and discussion of intended and unintended effects.
- *Impact (or intensive) evaluation.* This allows the evaluator to draw conclusions about the causal relationship between project activities and various impact measures. An impact evaluation requires a research design that allows the evaluator to make comparisons between the effects of the presence and absence of program activities.

Evaluation Design

Evaluation designs vary in the degree to which they allow project effects to be isolated and separated from factors outside the operation and control of the project. Four evaluation designs are outlined below. This is only one topology of designs and is not meant to be inclusive.

- *Pretest/posttest design before and after comparison.* This design consists primarily of a comparison of data collected on evaluation criteria prior to project initiation with those collected at project conclusion. This design is the simplest and least expensive. It does not, however, allow causal linkages to be drawn between observed changes and project implementation (i.e., it does not rule out the possibility that outside factors effected the change).
- *Pretest/posttest with a comparison group.* Through the use of a comparison group, this design allows greater confidence that observed changes are in fact due to the program and not to outside factors. Obviously, the similarity of the comparison and target group is critical to the evaluation results.
- *Controlled experimentation with random assignment of available population to target and comparison group.* This is the most sophisticated and expensive of the designs. It compares preselected, similar groups, some within the target groups served population and some within the comparison group. The critical aspect of the design is the random assignment of participants to the groups prior to program implementation.
- *Time series.* This design compares data collected after project initiation with estimates of what the data would be if trends from past years were to continue.

Evaluation Objectives

A final issue in the evaluation of programs relates to how objectives are set for the program, which in turn become the focal point for the evaluation. Externally produced objectives will always evoke a conservative response on the part of program planners. Outside evaluators will negotiate with program planners to produce a set of objectives that are often easily measurable but that may not be as valuable as those that are harder to measure. Internally produced evaluations on the other hand may be accused of being biased, but this depends upon the motivations for the evaluation.

The program planner who defines objectives for the purpose of guiding the activities of the project will set higher standards than when the objectives are used to make external judgments of achievement. Accordingly, the development of objectives must be conducted in the context of program planners' wanting to determine if they accomplished their desired results. Evaluations must be developed according to accepted standards, but the effort must be an integral component of program development and implementation, something that is a proprietary concern of the program specialists.

Evaluation is an essential component of program development, implementation, and management. It is an ongoing management tool that is central to the process of communications. The creators and staff of programs must be integrally involved in the evaluation process. Moreover, the method must suit the program and its process.

10

Twenty Questions Often
Asked About CPTED

1. What is CPTED and how does it differ from traditional approaches to crime and loss control?

CPTED is a natural approach to crime and loss control that differs from traditional approaches by placing most of its emphasis on human activities and how they become exposed to crime and loss. Traditional approaches to crime and loss control center on the offender, the offense, and the offender's background. The objective has been to control crime by identifying and apprehending the offender. Moreover, most contemporary approaches to crime prevention focus on the offender by trying to deny access to a victim through physical barriers.

For the past 150 years, criminology has failed to deal effectively with crime because of its limited emphasis on the criminal event, the criminal, and the criminal's behavior. Criminologists have attempted to explain crime through legal, social, psychological, biological, and political theories, all of which deal with the offender as the focal point. It is now commonly accepted that there are many causes of crime, but few successful approaches to treatment of offenders. However, it is also commonly accepted that most criminals decide to commit crimes based upon opportunity that is inherent in how human space is design or being used.

By placing a primary emphasis on the human activity and its objectives, CPTED generates a greater interest among residents, business, government, and community leaders. Crime prevention, security, and law enforcement professionals find that their efforts are more readily accepted when they use CPTED to help improve the quality of life and attainment of the objectives of human activities, while reducing their exposure to crime and loss victimization.

2. How does the CPTED concept differ from the contemporary approaches to procedural and physical security?

The simplest response to this question is that CPTED differs from procedural and physical security by its primary emphasis on natural strategies. Natural strategies are aimed at integrating and incorporating behavior

211

management into the design of human activity and physical resources. Procedural and physical security are well defined and sophisticated processes, but they rely on the expenditure of resources that are intended solely to protect persons and property, in the place of helping to attain their objectives.

3. Do CPTED concepts conflict with building code requirements for safety and accessibility for physically challenged persons?

The answer is no! This is, perhaps, the most misunderstood aspect about CPTED among the lay public as well as public safety professionals. It is often used to avoid dealing with security and safety issues. A fundamental understanding of the concepts and requirements of CPTED will reveal that there is no conflict between CPTED solutions to problems and concern for safety and accessibility.

One common misinterpretation of life safety codes is that it is illegal to secure exit doors in schools, malls, and office buildings. A legal solution is the use of magnetic locks that delay egress for up to 30 seconds, depending on the occupancy. Once an attempt is made to exit, an alarm is activated locally or sent to a central monitoring station. The door will not open until the preprogrammed delay unless there is a general fire alarm, a power failure, or the magnetic lock mechanism detects smoke. Another common misinterpretation, in this case of accessibility requirements, is that ramps have to be enclosed with opaque walls. This isolates the legitimate user of an accessibility ramp and it actually contributes to more discomfort for the user because of the tendency for the walls to accumulate waste materials and debris along the lower edges where the wheel chairs have to pass or crutches and canes have to establish a secure hold. Finally, many people think it is illegal to install maze entrances in public or school toilets because the trash bins can become sources of fire and smoke. These facilities in fact may have open, maze-type entrances if they have sprinkler systems, fire retardant walls, or have magnetic holders that allow outer doors to close when there is a smoke source present.

4. Is there a relationship between the design and use of space and the opportunity for criminal activities?

Yes! Criminals or improper users of space look for the chance to commit unwanted acts based upon opportunity that is inherent in how space is designed and used. Human history is replete with examples of how the environment was used to effect certain behaviors or to prevent undesired acts. The early Mayans built zig-zag walls around their habitats to discourage intruders. The walls required the intruders to expose their backs as they attempted to scale the walls. The stations of the Washington, D.C., subway system have curved walls next to the pedestrian platforms that are impossible to reach, thus preventing graffiti. Studies of criminal assaults and rape show that offenders prefer heavily landscaped pathways to provide concealment and the element of surprise.

5. How does the design and use of the physical environment affect the behavior of normal and abnormal users of space?

In opposite ways! The environmental cues that make a normal user feel safe will have the opposite effect on the abnormal users. These cues will make the abnormal user feel at greater risk of detection or apprehension. The users of space react to how others are behaving, or to the absence of others. They also react to perceptions of barriers, to entrapment, and to evidence of ownership. The only environmental cue that has the same effect upon both normal and abnormal users of space is *distance*. The farther one is from a potential threat, the easier it is to manage. This is why CPTED planners will generally try to give the normal or desired user of space more distance in which to make choices. Conversely, the CPTED planner tries to take distance away from abnormal or undesired users of space to reduce their choices and to make them feel more conspicuous.

6. What is the difference between organized, mechanical, and natural approaches to crime and loss control?

Organized approaches to security are labor intensive; they require the use of people to protect other people and property. These approaches may be characterized by the use of guards or hall monitors in schools and shopping centers. The personnel costs for these security methods are additional to the normal resource costs for human activities. They are there to protect, not to carry out the human function. Mechanical approaches are hardware or capital intensive. These security approaches rely on barriers, alarms, and camera systems to protect people and property. In opposition to these two approaches, the natural approach merely introduces behavior management into what was going to be done anyway. The smart planner tries to make the maximum use of natural strategies first rather than automatically relying on the additional costs of organized and mechanical approaches. It is clear that organized and mechanical approaches to security and safety work better in an environment that has made the most of incorporating natural strategies into the design and use of the spaces.

7. In what ways will natural approaches to crime and loss control contribute to the attainment of profit, productivity, and quality of life?

The answer is that, by focusing efforts on using natural strategies to increase the attainment of the objectives of the human activity, profit, productivity, and quality of life will increase. Human activities that are successful in meeting their objectives almost always result in a reduced exposure to crime and loss. Why? Because successfully managed space and human resources increases the quality of supervision and control, thus decreasing opportunity for abnormal behavior or undesired activities.

8. Are there historical precedents for the use of CPTED concepts and strategies?

Yes! Archeological evidence demonstrates that Germanic tribes used hierarchies of space to defend habitats nearly 200,000 years ago. The ruins of Pompeii and similar ruins in the American Southwest more than a

1,000 years later reveal that hierarchies of space were well defined. Clear transitions from private to semi-private to public space were very important for security by defining who belonged in what space and when. The archeological and historical planning reveal that tribes or communal groups recognized that there was an appropriate number of people who could live together in harmony. Too few could not survive the rigors of nature. Too many resulted in a breakdown of social control. Native Americans realized that too great of a concentration of people in one place rapidly diminished natural resources, so they went through a constant process of winnowing down large assemblies to workable sizes.

9. Will concerns about aesthetics or appearance be sacrificed by the use of CPTED concepts and strategies?

Of course not! One major misconception is that all CPTED planners do is cut bushes and close streets. On the contrary, CPTED planners introduce new dimensions in the planning of aesthetics by incorporating behavior management into design and space use plans. Strategic horticulture has turned out to be a major CPTED tool that is used to define space and to promote desired behaviors. The effective use of color and light can enhance behavior management in positive ways.

10. Is it expensive for a building owner or manager to use CPTED concepts and strategies?

No. Experience has demonstrated that CPTED concepts can save money and resources when incorporated into conceptual plans for facilities. Many design efficiencies are inherent in the use of the CPTED process to help determine what is appropriate for spaces. Natural strategies reduce the extra costs of organized and mechanical security. Retrofit strategies have helped to reduce management and security costs. Where the use of a CPTED strategy results in an increase in cost, usually during the initial investment, there is always a significant return on investment due to increased profitability and reduced liability.

11. Is CPTED limited in value only to the planning of new facilities?

No! It has proven its usefulness in all types of facilities. Since CPTED relies on good common sense, it is clear that it may be useful in nearly every human endeavor.

12. May CPTED concepts be used in planning major events, or are these strategies limited to the built environment?

CPTED strategies have been used, sometimes without formal attribution, for the management of events throughout human history. CPTED has been used in major events since the 1972 Republican and Democratic political conventions in the United States. CPTD was used during the 1979 Pan American Games and in the 1982 World's Fair in Knoxville, Tennessee. The 2000 Olympic Games scheduled for Sydney, Australia, have very carefully and cleverly incorporated CPTED into nearly every phase of planning for transportation and for housing and athletic venues. The successes have been measured in increased profits, reduced incidents, and an improvement to the accessibility and enjoyment of the events. It is a documented fact that the careful incorporation of CPTED and planning of law enforcement services for the World's Fair in Knoxville resulted in the savings of approximately $750,000 of a law enforcement services budget of $835,000. Similar dramatic savings were experienced wherever CPTED was used appropriately. How can this be? It is simple: CPTED is founded on good planning and a commitment to doing what is appropriate. Experience has demonstrated that breakdowns in security at major events have been a direct result of poor event planning and management.

13. *How does CPTED relate to local government functions of planning, housing, traffic control, and downtown revitalization?*

Totally! CPTED is a benign approach to improving good planning. Accordingly, CPTED is compatible with every type of planning model, including functional planning, livable cities, urban villages, neotraditionalism, new urbanism, and transportation-oriented development.

14. *Are CPTED concepts of value in the design and management of interior spaces?*

Yes! It is another common misconception that CPTED is only an outdoors or site planning concept, perhaps because its contemporary stimulus has come from urban planners. However, the interior design of workspaces and schools has had many successes in improving quality of life, productivity, and safety. Convenience stores have been leaders in the interior use of CPTED. Malls and shopping centers have dramatically altered interior uses. Sales have been enhanced and losses reduced. Many designers and decorators have discovered that Feng Shui, the Chinese art of promoting the sense of harmony by careful arrangement of the spatial environment, is closely aligned with CPTED concepts. Interior design research has demonstrated that the more employees who share a common work space and the less differentiated it is, the lower will be their morale, the lower the productive output, and the greater the tolerance of dishonesty.

15. *Do CPTED concepts have any value in dealing with concerns about youth development and delinquency prevention?*

Very much so! CPTED concepts in public housing, more commonly known as "defensible space," have demonstrated that children who grow up in large, undifferentiated spaces are less likely to develop a respect for property values and rights, they exhibit more disruptive behavior in school, and they experience more maladaptive behavior as adults. CPTED in school design and management has had a dramatic impact on increased achievement and reduced behavioral problems. CPTED has worked in parks, recreation facilities, and in retail environments where children spend a considerable amount of time, often unsupervised by their parents.

16. *Who should use CPTED concepts?*

Everyone! Everybody has to be concerned about the effective and productive use of space. And everyone should be concerned about safety and security. Interestingly, CPTED is very important in the design and management of juvenile detention, group home, and correctional facilities. It would be hard to identify a profession or a human activity that does not have a responsibility and interest in safety and security.

17. What are the important steps required in conducting a CPTED review of proposed site plans or of existing facilities?

The Three D approach to the assessment of the built environment or proposed events has proven to be the most straightforward and simplest to use. This process starts with designation of purpose. It is not enough to name the human function. The behavioral objectives of the function or activity must be clearly articulated. Once the behavioral objectives are clear the designated purpose must be defined in terms of rules, laws, signs, and cultural practices to reinforce the desired behaviors. Designation and definition lead to the design phase where decisions have to made along two dimensions: physiological and psychological functions. The physiological dimension supports and facilitates carrying out the human function. The psychological dimension focuses on controlling behavior. The Three D process is divided into a series of diagnostic questions that may be used to assess proposed plans, as well as existing facilities.

18. What types of data are required to conduct CPTED assessments?

Five types of data are required: crime/incident; demographics; land use; observations; and user or resident input. Each of these types of data has its unique value, but all are required to provide a clear picture of the extent to which the basic concepts of CPTED are operating as desired. Observations conducted in a systematic manner by a team composed of a mixture of professions are of immeasurable value. With a minimum of training and orientation, an interdisciplinary team of persons can conduct an adequate CPTED assessment.

19. Can CPTED concepts and strategies be used to help eliminate or control problem businesses and high-crime housing locations?

Yes! CPTED concepts rely upon the effective use of ordinances and codes to maintain territorial control and order. Zoning, business regulation, architectural guidelines, traffic laws, housing codes, and life safety requirements are all tools that may be used to control problem situations. A history of code violations can open the door for an interdisciplinary team to exercise powers of local government in a process that is referred to as "intrusive code enforcement." There are literally thousands of examples of the successful use of local codes and ordinances by CPTED teams to clean up problem neighborhoods and businesses.

20. Do CPTED concepts conflict with the increasingly popular planning processes identified as new urbanism, neotraditional planning, livable cities, and transportation-oriented development?

The answer is an emphatic no! The key is to understand that CPTED is linked to a commitment to good planning, to using a process for determining what is appropriate for an individual site or human activity. The CPTED process relies upon the requirement to carefully orchestrate planing activities and to integrate the best of all planning models. The misconceptions about CPTED have their roots in conflicts over the use of strategies and in the failure to recognize that CPTED is a *planning process*. Strategies will change as new technologies and methods are developed. The process has and will always be the same. Community planners and builders 5,000 years ago were using the same commonsense process that is inherent in contemporary CPTED programs. This process is based upon an understanding of human nature and how people respond to the environment.

11

CPTED in the 21st Century: The Past Is Prologue

CPTED has its origins in the early history of the development of communities. The conscious planning of human habitats to include identity and protection goes back as far as our knowledge of human existence. Early Sumerian codes (4000 B.C.) identified the importance of respect for property rights. The Code of Hammurabi (2000 B.C.) introduced the responsibilities of builders to their clients and specified punishments for failure to comply. Archeological evidence suggests that humans were actively identifying ways to control their environment as much as 400,000 years ago.

The future of CPTED may be revealed through the past. Eighth-century Chinese practitioners of Feng Shui sought to increase the sense of harmony by controlling the spatial environment, from the smallest rooms up to the planning of cities. Plains dwellers in North America from the 8th to the 11th centuries developed hierarchies of family and community identity and protection through the design of living space. The cliff dwellers (U.S. Mesa Verde National Park) built impregnable living areas in the faces of cliffs that were accessible only by ladders and entrances that could be sealed.

Modern warfare has demonstrated how design can counter an enemy's technological and numerical superiority. Both the cities of Hue, Viet Nam, and Kuwait City, Kuwait, are of traditional French design with twisting, narrow streets that allowed for a small number of defenders to block the movements of large numbers of opposing troops. Residential development after World War II replaced grid-pattern streets with the curvilinear street, which has improved safety, security, neighborhood identity, and property value.

Contemporary research generally supports the notion that space that is widely shared by people, and poorly identified, will result in low morale, reduced productivity, and greater tolerance of misbehavior. Respect for property values and rights is difficult to instill in youth, when ownership and transition from public to private space is confused.

CPTED in the 21st century will not forget the lessons from the past. But the transition to a new century will be one that points toward an explosion of technological and space management advances in the use of the environment to promote behavior that is desired and conducive to human existence.

THE TRANSITION TO THE FUTURE OF CPTED

CPTED is a self-evident concept that has been used successfully for many years. Research and assessment over the past 30 years have confirmed the utility of what many people think is just good, common sense. The greatest impediment to the widespread use of CPTED is ignorance. Most people have never heard of CPTED. Some of the few who have heard of CPTED have attempted to exploit it, without developing an understanding of the concept. Others have attempted to pass it off as another fad that will go away with time.

The following are the factors necessary for CPTED to make the transition to wide acceptability and use:

- *Education and training.* CPTED must be included in professional and academic education and training. Legislators, planning board members, and professional societies need to become oriented toward CPTED immediately so that their future decisions reflect a commitment to its concepts.
- *Codes.* Current codes governing all aspects of the physical environment need to be improved to incorporate CPTED concepts.
- *Design review.* CPTED concepts need to be included in an expanded concept of design review, which emphasizes interagency and interdisciplinary approaches to making better decisions about the design and use of the environment.
- *Code enforcement.* The uneven and inconsistent enforcement of existing codes is a major cause of the deterioration of our communities. Interdisciplinary approaches to code enforcement must be used as a tool in prevention of decay and revitalization of those communities.
- *Litigation.* The courts are rapidly becoming a tool for forcing people to make better decisions about human space. It is human nature to overlook all of the good reasons for doing things right in the first place (e.g., quality of life, profit, aesthetics, reduced victimization, and loss) and wait for the civil law to require that changes be made, often at great cost.
- *Documentation.* CPTED successes must be documented in multimedia presentations that ensure a wide dissemination of the concepts and a permanent record of how to use those concepts to avoid repeating past mistakes.

CPTED IN THE NEW MILLENNIUM

Once CPTED has become a well-known concept, it will contribute to an explosion of technological and space management advances in the use of the environment. The concepts of CPTED in the new millennium will promote behavior that is desired and conducive to human existence.

The following are a few of the many topics areas related to CPTED that will be part of the ongoing development of human experience in the early 21st century.

Information and Communications Technology

- information system superhighways
- merger of radio/telephone/television technology
- 70 million persons in the United States projected to be carrying personal communications systems (PCS) by 2010
- finger spellers for the visually challenged
- microcircuit implants to enable sight for the totally blind
- audio-loops for hearing impaired
- holographic technology — 3D imaging
- microspace implants of microchips for information storage and retrieval; voice-activated entry and security systems

Housing

- shuffle-housing for changing needs of second and third generations of extended families
- co-housing for the maintenance of identity and control for family and near-family groups
- detachable housing for changing urban scenes
- collapsible housing for unattended protection and storage
- adjustable room size for smaller, more defensible space
- movable yards with window or dumbwaiter access
- floating communities

Transportation

- hover cars
- service/frontage and residential through-pass roads
- adjustable streets
- instant cul-de-sacs
- automatic speed/collision controls
- robotics

- digital camera-controlled auto pilot for hands-free navigation
- infrared and radar for collision avoidance
- integrated gas- and battery-operated vehicles for up to 200-miles-to-the-gallon efficiency
- standard use of GPS and concierge service for obtaining directions and monitoring the safety of the vehicle and occupants
- particle beam conversion of humans and transport
- virtual reality trips for shopping, medical care, and recreation

Institutional

- biospheres
- closed school campuses
- behavioral space management/design
- remote services/monitoring/treatment
- robotics/bionics

Commercial/Retail/Industrial

- disposable businesses
- disposable centers
- remote shopping
- instant products
- information/communications

Social Recognition/Control

- behavior incentives
- visual accessibility
- property values/rights
- legendary health rediscoveries (e.g., kudzu)

Materials/Construction

- force fields
- electronic implants in construction
- durable materials
- adjustable walls and windows
- behavior-directed products/devices
- behavior/threat-directed fenestration controls

Changes in the 21st century like those just listed will have dramatic effects on the reduction of exposure of people to victimization. Of course, with the introduction of each new technology, there is the possibility of new, unpredicted exposures to victimization. Accordingly, it will be a continuing challenge to CPTED planners and specialists to be involved in the development and application of these new technologies. One way or another, the technologies will develop. The CPTED perspective can help to improve the overall value of new technologies and social change.

Appendix A:
Broward County School
CPTED Matrix

Table A-1   Broward County School CPTED Matrix

Crime Environment	Crime Environment Problem	CPTED Strategies	CPTED Design Directives
School grounds: Assault Bicycle theft Breaking and entering Vandalism	Design of and procedures for bus loading areas prohibit teacher surveillance, increase supervision ratio, impede pedestrian traffic flow, and cause congestion. Confrontations, thefts and vandalism occur.	Redesign bus loading zone and revise procedures to increase surveillance area for natural surveillance, control pedestrian flow, and decrease ratio of students to supervisors.	Create one zone in a surveillance area for loading and unloading students, limited in size to a maximum of 4–5 buses. Require bus drivers to allow students to enter or leave their bus only when in a specified loading zone. Create a bus queuing zone for waiting buses that is convenient to the unloading zone. Require teachers on monitoring assignment at the bus loading zone to direct the movement of buses and to disperse each group of students from the bus loading area before allowing another group to load or unload.

Location of informal gathering areas (natural and designated) promotes the preemption of space, interferes with traffic flow, and prohibits natural surveillance. Assaults occur.	Relocate informal gathering areas near supervision or natural surveillance.	Move benches and physical amenities that support informal gatherings from undefined areas to courtyards.
		Relocate the student smoking zone to the interior courtyards.
	Redesign informal gathering areas to promote orderly flow and breakup the preemption of space by groups.	Remove conventional picnic tables and benches.
		Install new tables and benches that physically divide space and the size of groups.
		Position amenities to create multiple access and passageways.
Design, use, and location of facilities has created	Provide functional activities in unused or misused	Place ticket booths in problem areas.

(continued overleaf)

Table A-1 (continued)

Crime Environment	Crime Environment Problem	CPTED Strategies	CPTED Design Directives
	isolated and blind spot areas that are difficult to survey (due to design and/or nonuse because of fear or avoidance). Assaults, thefts, and vandalism occur.	problem areas to promote natural surveillance, increase safe traffic flow, and attract different types of users.	Create mini-plazas in courtyards. Organize a student/faculty committee to assist in the design and coordination of miniplaza activities.
	Design and border definition of campus creates unclear transitional zone definition. Breaking and entering, theft, and vandalism occur.	Provide clear border definition of transitional zones for access control and surveillance.	Install low hedging, flower beds, or ornamental fencing along borders. Organize a student/faculty committee to assist in the design and coordination of border definition activities.
	Location and positioning of school physical plant prohibit natural surveillance (off hours) by local residents and passersby. Breaking and	Provide functional community activities on school campus (off hours) to increase surveillance through effective use of facilities.	Create a police "school precinct" office. Install audio burglar alarm system.

entering, theft, and vandalism occur. (One half of vandalisms are incident with breaking and entering.)	Overcome distance and isolation by improving communications to create rapid response to problems (and its perception) and more effective surveillance.	Provide portable radios to deans, school resource persons, and custodians.
Design, use, and location of bicycle compounds or parking areas on school grounds prohibit natural surveillance and limit proper use because of students with variable hours. Thefts of bicycles occur.	Redesign bicycle parking areas to provide levels of security consistent with variable access needs of students.	Create a fenced bicycle parking area (secure area).
		Create an open bicycle parking area located in a place with good natural surveillance (nonsecure area).
		Assign bicycle students to either secure or nonsecure parking area on the basis of schedule.
		Install ground-level locking devices in each bicycle parking area.
		Set a policy requiring students to utilize a bicycle locking cable or chain.

(continued overleaf)

Table A-1 (continued)

Crime Environment	Crime Environment Problem	CPTED Strategies	CPTED Design Directives
Parking lots: Assault Theft Breaking and entering Vandalism	Location and design of student parking near bus-loading areas without restricting borders promotes unmanaged pedestrian use of parking areas, promotes preemption of space by groups, and prohibits natural surveillance. Assaults, breaking and entering, thefts, and vandalism occur (affected by bus-loading procedures).	Relocate and/or redesign bus-loading and parking lot access procedures to reduce necessity for pedestrian use of lot, reduce congestion in transitional zones, and support strict definition of parking lot use.	Switch locations between student parking and driver education range. Designate accessways to the student parking lot that avoid the bus-loading zone.
	Design and location of parking lots provide unclear definition of transitional zones and unmanaged access by vehicles and pedestrians, students, and nonstudents. Breaking and entering, thefts, vandalism, and trespassing occur.	Provide natural border definition and limit access to vehicular traffic in student parking to clearly define transitional zones, to reroute ingress and egress during specified periods, and to provide natural surveillance.	Install hedges around parking lots. Install aesthetically pleasing gates on vehicular access points. Set policies to limit student pedestrian use of the parking lots.

Location of informal gathering areas designated as smoking zones in open corridors adjacent to parking lots and visible from public thoroughfares prohibits natural surveillance, attracts outsiders, and is an impediment to school policies restricting student use of parking lots during school hours. Breaking and entering, thefts, and vandalism occur.	Relocate informal gathering areas to places with natural surveillance, that are isolated from the view of public thoroughfares and designed to support informal gathering activities.	Secure gates at external vehicular access points during school hours; leave internal access points open.
		Organize a student/faculty committee to assist in the design and coordination of the border definition and parking lot access control activities.
		Create mini-plazas.
		Relocate the student smoking zone to the mini-plazas.
		Organize a student/faculty committee to assist in the design and coordination of the mini-plaza activities.
Isolation of student parking lots (some locations) prohibits any natural	Relocate student parking (or part of) to areas with natural surveillance	Switch locations between student parking and the driver education range.

(continued overleaf)

Table A-1 (continued)

Crime Environment	Crime Environment Problem	CPTED Strategies	CPTED Design Directives
	surveillance. Variable student hours limit use of fencing and gates. Breaking and entering, thefts, and vandalism occur.	and/or relocate safe activities in juxtaposition with student parking to increase natural surveillance.	
		Redesign parking lots to provide levels of security consistent with variable access needs of the students.	Create a fenced parking area (secure) that is locked during school day.
			Create an open parking area (nonsecure) in a place with good natural surveillance.
			Assign parking to either the secure or nonsecure area on the basis of student schedule.
			Reroute vehicular access to nonsecure parking area through internal parts of school ground before entering the parking lot.

Locker room: Theft Breaking and entering	Design and use of lockers (by multiple assignment) disperses students throughout area, reduces surveillance, and increases territory for teacher supervision. Breaking and entering and thefts occur.	Redesignate use of space to increase territorial concern, to increase the defined purpose of space, and to reduce area requiring surveillance.	Set policy limiting student pedestrian use of parking lots. Assign lockers by section separately for each class.
	Similar design of lockers creates confusion and decreases natural surveillance by creating unclear definition of transitional zones. Breaking and entering and theft occur.	Provide clear definition of transitional zones and use of space for easy recognition of bona fide users.	Color code locker sections uniquely for each class.
	Isolation of locker area while class is in gymnasium or on playing field eliminates natural surveillance. Breaking and entering and thefts occur.	Provide functional activities in problem areas to increase natural surveillance.	Relocate a teacher planning area to the physical education offices. Assign teachers to the planning area during all classes.

(continued overleaf)

Table A-1 (continued)

Crime Environment	Crime Environment Problem	CPTED Strategies	CPTED Design Directives
Corridors: Assault	Design and use of corridors provide blinds spots and isolated areas that prohibit natural surveillance. Assaults, threats, and extortions occur.	Provide functional activities (or redesignate use) in blind spots or isolated areas to increase natural surveillance (or the perception thereof).	Relocate teacher planning areas.
			Redesign blind spot areas to provide storage spaces for clubs and/or the school administration.
		Remove obstacles to natural surveillance (increase perception of openness).	Install windows in walls along problem corridors.
			Install windows in walls of exterior stairwells.
	Class scheduling promotes congestion in certain areas at shift changing that decreases supervision capabilities and produces inconvenience. Assaults and confrontations occur.	Revise class scheduling and management procedures to avoid congestion, to decrease supervision ratio, and to define time transitions.	Provide a 3–5 minute shift change hiatus between lunch periods.
	Location of benches and/or other amenities in corridors creates misused space and congestion. Corridor locations are lacking in natural	Relocate informal gathering areas to areas with natural surveillance that are designed to support that activity.	Remove benches and other physical amenities from crowded corridors.

surveillance because of design. Assaults and confrontations occur.

Location and use of corridors for functions other than pedestrian passage such as smoking zones promotes preemption of space by groups and unsurveillable misused space. This misused space supports behavior that attracts outsiders to the external corridors designated as smoking areas. Assaults, confrontations, and other illegal activities occur.

Design and definition of corridor areas do not support a clear definition of the dominant function of that space (i.e., passage). Unclear transitional zones produce behaviors conducive to assault and confrontation.

Relocate activities and functions from misused space to areas designed to support these activities and to provide natural surveillance.

Provide clear definition of the dominant function (and intended use of space) and clearly define transitional zones to increase territorial concerns and natural surveillance.

Move the student smoking zones from corridors to mini-plazas.

Revise school policy to restrict student use of the outside corridor previously designated for smoking.

Provide cafeteria food at the gymnasium snack bar.

Provide multiple access to the snack bar and install queuing lanes.

Place graphic designs in stairwells and corridors defining the intended function of these spaces.

Color code various sections of the school and use graphics and art designs uniquely for each functional component of the school.

(continued overleaf)

Table A-1 *(continued)*

Crime Environment	*Crime Environment Problem*	*CPTED Strategies*	*CPTED Design Directives*
			Organize student/faculty committees by functional component to select and coordinate the graphic design and color coding activities.
Restrooms: Assault Extortion	Location of restrooms near external entrances and exits isolates them from normal school-hour traffic flow and prohibits surveillance. Assaults occur.	Limit access to isolated areas during specific times for access control and to reduce the need for surveillance.	Install collapsible gates at restroom entrances for locking during problem periods.
	Privacy and isolation required for internal design provides blind spots that reduce surveillability on the part of students and supervisory personnel (i.e., exterior door and anteroom wall). Assaults occur.	Remove obstacles to natural surveillance to decrease fear, increase use, and increase risk of detection.	Remove entrance doors to restrooms. Eliminate unnecessary portions of anteroom walls.

Classrooms: Assault	Design requirements for classrooms produce isolation of individual classes, resulting in high student to teacher ratios and little external natural surveillance (real or perceived) when class is in session. Assaults occur. Theft occurs when class is empty.	Remove obstacles to natural surveillance to increase risk of detection and to reduce perception of isolation.	Install windows in classroom walls and doors.
		Overcome distance and isolation by improving communications to create rapid response to problems, the perception of rapid response, and more effective surveillance.	Provide portable radios to deans, school resource persons, and custodial personnel.
			Install audio alarm systems in problem classrooms for after hours.
	Location and design definition of multiple purpose classrooms produces unclear transitional zones, decreases territorial concern, and decreases natural surveillance. Thefts occur.	Extend the identity of surrounding spaces to multiple purpose space to increase territorial concern and natural surveillance.	Color code and graphically identify multiple purpose classrooms with adjacent spaces.
		Provide functional activity in problem areas to increase territorial concern and natural surveillance.	Relocate a teacher planning area to each multi-purpose classroom.

(continued overleaf)

Table A-1 *(continued)*

Crime Environment	*Crime Environment Problem*	*CPTED Strategies*	*CPTED Design Directives*
	Class shift procedure during lunch hour produce unclear time transition and definition of groups; decreases control and increases student-to-teacher ratio. Many classroom thefts are committed by classcutters.	Revise class scheduling and movement procedures to define time for class shifts, making surveillance and supervision of classcutters easier.	Provide a 3–5 minute shift change hiatus between lunch periods.

Appendix B:
CPTED Training Outline

GOALS AND OBJECTIVES

Goals

The goals of this module on Crime Prevention Through Environmental Design (CPTED) are to alter and expand the participants' perception of immediate physical environment. By altering the perception of the physical environment, the participant will be more capable of understanding the direct relationship of the environment to human behavior and to crime. An increase in this basic understanding should result in the increased likelihood of the individual to confidently question or challenge decisions that affect her immediate environment — particularly those that may have a direct bearing on the safety of the individual, her family, and neighborhood.

An understanding of the direct relationship of the environment — its design and management — to human behavior is a prerequisite to increasing the success of citizens' efforts in crime prevention. It is the key to effective community organization, because it gives citizens power to protect and control their physical environment and quality of life. CPTED is not the total or exclusive answer for a community seeking to eliminate or reduce environmental obstacles to social, cultural, or managerial control.

Learning Objectives

CPTED does not require an extensive technical background or understanding. But, to be effective as a community strategy, basic CPTED concepts must be understood by as many people as possible, even if that understanding is in layperson's terms. Otherwise, true public policy setting will remain in the hands of technocrats and politicians.

The following learning objectives should be considered as the absolute minimum for successful completion of this module:

1. The participant should be able to recall the meaning of the acronym CPTED: Crime Prevention Through Environmental Design.
2. The participant should recognize the underlying premise of CPTED and recall the two underlined words in the definition as key CPTED descriptors. The CPTED premise is "that the proper design and effective use of the built environment can lead to a reduction in the incidence and fear of crime — and to an increase in the quality of life."
3. The participant should be able to recognize and define (in a brief one-sentence definition or example) the three basic CPTED strategies of natural access control, natural surveillance, and territorial reinforcement.
4. The participant should be able to distinguish (by definition or example) between the organized, mechanical, and natural crime prevention strategy classifications.
5. The participant should be able to recall the reference to the CPTED approach to space assessment and list the components:

   Reference   3-D Concept
   Components   Designation
                   Definition
                   Design

6. The participant should be able to demonstrate his new awareness and understanding of CPTED concepts by providing a descriptive example of a good and a bad CPTED setting in at least one of the following types of locations:

   - a residential neighborhood that is near a major street intersection
   - neighborhood park
   - neighborhood schools
   - public parking lots
   - public housing area
   - industrial/commercial center

7. The participant should be able to describe the functions and location of the following types of information:

   - crime analysis data
   - demographic data
   - land use
   - observations
   - resident or user interviews

8.   The participant should be able to draw a simple map of her residential
     or business neighborhood showing:

     - street layout
     - land use
     - pedestrian and vehicular usage
     - crime (or fear) problem areas
     - current boundaries of geographic, ethnic, or neighborhood identities

These learning objectives represent the minimum that is required to develop efficiency and skill in the use of CPTED concepts. Meeting them would be a clear indication of the ability to perceive the relationship of the environment to human behavior — particularly criminal behavior. It should not be expected that any sort of brief overview presentation (e.g., one lasting 30 minutes) is sufficient for individuals to fully understand the concepts of CPTED. A longer period of a combined seminar and workshop — preferably with a field trip or exercise — is best. However, some change in individuals' appreciation of the human/environment interaction can be expected even after a relatively short, nonparticipatory session.

Appendix C:
School CPTED Survey

SCHOOL SECURITY SURVEY FORM[1]

I. School Data
    A. School
    B. School number
    C. By
    D. Date
    E. School level
        1. High school _____
        2. Junior high _____
        3. Elementary _____
        4. Vocational _____
        5. Other _____
    F. Student population _____
    G. Premise type
        1. Single story _____
        2. Multiple story _____
        3. Enclosed design _____
        4. Tropical (open) _____
        5. Fortress _____
        6. Other _____
    H. Hours _____
    I. Busing % _____
II. Neighborhood Area
    A. Neighborhood type
        1. Commercial _____
        2. Industrial _____

---

[1] Adapted from School Security Survey Form, TDC Associates. Reston, VA, 1982.

       3. Residential _____
       4. Other _____
- B. Housing _____
       1. Single _____
       2. Multiple _____
       3. High rise _____
       4. Low rise _____
       5. Public _____
       6. Other _____
- C. Businesses
       1. Fast food _____
       2. Convenience _____
       3. Shopping center _____
       4. Services _____
       5. Other _____
- D. Streets
       1. Major arterial(s) _____
       2. Business _____
       3. Residential _____
       4. Mixed _____
       5. 2-Lane _____
       6. 4-Lane _____
       7. Signals _____
       8. Other _____
- E. Institutions
       1. Church(s) _____
       2. Schools
          Public _____
          Private _____
       3. Social club _____
       4. Hospital _____
       5. Recreational _____
       6. Other _____
- F. Police reporting area _____
- G. Comments _____
       _____

III. Interview Comments (Principal or Designer)
- A. Problems
       1. _____
       2. _____
       3. _____
       4. _____
- B. Needs
       1. _____
       2. _____

        3.   ————————————

        4.   ————————————

IV. Survey Items

  A. Neighborhood

     1. Contact   S ——— U ——— NA ———
     2. Businesses   S ——— U ——— NA ———
     3. Traffic flows   S ——— U ——— NA ———
     4. Social   S ——— U ——— NA ———
     5. Other ———   S ——— U ——— NA ———
     6. Comments ——————————————

  B. School grounds border definition

     1. Fences   S ——— U ——— NA ———
     2. Foliage/trees   S ——— U ——— NA ———
     3. Gathering areas   S ——— U ——— NA ———
        Informal   S ——— U ——— NA ———
        Formal   S ——— U ——— NA ———
     4. Bus (loading zones) S ——— U ——— NA ———
     5. Police access   S ——— U ——— NA ———
     6. Furniture/amenities S ——— U ——— NA ———
     7. Other ———   S ——— U ——— NA ———
     8. Comments ——————————————

  C. Parking lot(s)   *Teachers*

     1. Street(s)
        Access   S ——— U ——— NA ———
        Surveillance   S ——— U ——— NA ———
     2. Building(s)
        Access   S ——— U ——— NA ———
        Surveillance   S ——— U ——— NA ———
     3. Conflict with
        Bus zone   S ——— U ——— NA ———
        Gathering areas   S ——— U ——— NA ———
        Rec./DE   S ——— U ——— NA ———
        Other ———   S ——— U ——— NA ———
     4. Comments ——————————————

                           Students

     1. Street(s)
        Access   S ——— U ——— NA ———
        Surveillance   S ——— U ——— NA ———
     2. Building(s)
        Access   S ——— U ——— NA ———
        Surveillance   S ——— U ——— NA ———
     3. Conflict with
        Bus zone   S ——— U ——— NA ———
        Gathering areas   S ——— U ——— NA ———

	Rec./DE	S ___ U ___ NA ___
	Other ___	S ___ U ___ NA ___

4. Comments _____

D. Building(s) *Access*

1. Roof   S ___ U ___ NA ___
2. Windows   S ___ U ___ NA ___
3. Entrances   S ___ U ___ NA ___
4. Comments _____

Surveillance

1. Roof   S ___ U ___ NA ___
2. Windows   S ___ U ___ NA ___
3. Entrances   S ___ U ___ NA ___

E. Key control

1. Great grand master   S ___ U ___ NA ___
2. Grand master   S ___ U ___ NA ___
3. Master   S ___ U ___ NA ___
4. Individual   S ___ U ___ NA ___
5. Zone control   S ___ U ___ NA ___
6. Assignment list   S ___ U ___ NA ___
7. Restrictions   S ___ U ___ NA ___
8. Other ___   S ___ U ___ NA ___
9. Comments _____

F. Security Systems

1. Electronic   S ___ U ___ NA ___
2. Trailer   S ___ U ___ NA ___
3. Fences   S ___ U ___ NA ___
4. Locking systems   S ___ U ___ NA ___
5. Other ___   S ___ U ___ NA ___
6. Comments _____

G. Classrooms

1. Windows   S ___ U ___ NA ___
2. Interior doors   S ___ U ___ NA ___
3. Exterior doors   S ___ U ___ NA ___
4. Windows in doors   S ___ U ___ NA ___
5. Proprietary space   S ___ U ___ NA ___
6. Multiple purpose   S ___ U ___ NA ___
7. Other ___   S ___ U ___ NA ___
8. Comments _____

H. High-value areas (doors, windows, locks, location procedures)

1. Computers   S ___ U ___ NA ___
2. Business machines   S ___ U ___ NA ___
3. Audio/visual   S ___ U ___ NA ___
4. Shop/vocational   S ___ U ___ NA ___

    5.   Other _____   S _____ U _____ NA _____
    6.   Comments _____

I. Corridors
    1.   Lockers   S _____ U _____ NA _____
    2.   Lighting   S _____ U _____ NA _____
    3.   Surveillance
        General   S _____ U _____ NA _____
        Classrooms   S _____ U _____ NA _____
        Offices   S _____ U _____ NA _____
    4.   Shop/vocational   S _____ U _____ NA _____
    5.   Other _____   S _____ U _____ NA _____
    6.   Comments _____

J. Stairwells
    1.   Interior   S _____ U _____ NA _____
    2.   Exterior   S _____ U _____ NA _____
    3.   Fire   S _____ U _____ NA _____
    4.   Comments _____

K. Restrooms
    1.   Location(s)   S _____ U _____ NA _____
    2.   Entrance design   S _____ U _____ NA _____
    3.   Interior access   S _____ U _____ NA _____
    4.   Other _____   S _____ U _____ NA _____
    5.   Comments _____

L. Locker room(s)
    1.   Location(s)   S _____ U _____ NA _____
    2.   Surveillance
        Interior   S _____ U _____ NA _____
        Exterior   S _____ U _____ NA _____
    3.   Doors   S _____ U _____ NA _____
    4.   Windows   S _____ U _____ NA _____
    5.   Equipment storage S _____ U _____ NA _____
    6.   Lockers
        Layout   S _____ U _____ NA _____
        Assignment   S _____ U _____ NA _____
    7.   Other _____   S _____ U _____ NA _____
    8.   Comments _____

M. Cafeteria
    1.   Equipment   S _____ U _____ NA _____
    2.   Storage   S _____ U _____ NA _____
    3.   Queuing   S _____ U _____ NA _____
    4.   Table arrangements S _____ U _____ NA _____
    5.   Surveillance   S _____ U _____ NA _____
    6.   Patio/gathering area access S _____ U _____ NA _____

      7. Other _____   S _____ U _____ NA _____

      8. Comments _____

N. Other areas

      1. Portables   S _____ U _____ NA _____

      2. Athletic/recreational   S _____ U _____ NA _____

      3. Storage   S _____ U _____ NA _____

      4. _____   S _____ U _____ NA _____

      5. _____   S _____ U _____ NA _____

      6. _____   S _____ U _____ NA _____

      7. Comments _____

O. Administrative

      1. Inventory control   S _____ U _____ NA _____

      2. Facility management   S _____ U _____ NA _____

          Scheduling   S _____ U _____ NA _____

          Hours   S _____ U _____ NA _____

          Functional layout   S _____ U _____ NA _____

          Productivity   S _____ U _____ NA _____

          Surveillance   S _____ U _____ NA _____

      3. Maintenance   S _____ U _____ NA _____

      4. Programs   S _____ U _____ NA _____

          Incentive   S _____ U _____ NA _____

          Student patrol   S _____ U _____ NA _____

          Other _____   S _____ U _____ NA _____

      5. Staff   S _____ U _____ NA _____

          Hall duty   S _____ U _____ NA _____

          Planning areas   S _____ U _____ NA _____

          Other _____   S _____ U _____ NA _____

      6. Comments _____

V. Priority Recommendations

  A. Physical space

      1. Remove _____

         _____

      2. Repair _____

         _____

      3. Replace _____

         _____

      4. Install _____

         _____

      5. Reallocate _____

         _____

      6. Other _____

         _____

  B. Management (policy, procedure, personnel allocation, neighborhood programs, or other)

VI. Security Plan
   A. Neighborhood _____

   B. Perimeter _____

   C. Grounds _____

   D. Parking (vehicle and bicycle) _____

   E. Building access _____

   F. Building exterior _____

   G. Building interior (classrooms, corridors, restrooms, offices) _____

   H. High-value areas _____

   I. Protection of persons _____

   J. Special events _____

   K. Other _____

VII. School Incident Map

A. Target incidents	*Last year*	*Year-to-date*
1. Breaking and entering	_____	_____
2. Vandalism	_____	_____
3. Theft	_____	_____
4. Arson/fire	_____	_____
5. Staff assault	_____	_____
6. Assault/battery	_____	_____
7. Sex offense	_____	_____
8. Drugs/alcohol	_____	_____
9. Bomb	_____	_____
10. Weapons	_____	_____
11. Other	_____	_____

Appendix D: CPTED Design Directives for Dormitory and Student Lounges

Table D-1 Interior Spaces

Environment	Environment Goal	CPTED Strategies	CPTED Design Directives
Rooms	Increase surveillance of room entrances.	Promote natural concern for room entrances with neighbors.	Avoid isolating an individual entrance at the end of a hall or head of stairs.
Hallways	Enhance territorial concern for hallways.	Provide a clearly identifiable zone that is shared by a small number of rooms.	Reduce the number of rooms sharing a common hallway.
			Provide transitional definition moving from stair landings, lounges and restrooms, to resident's rooms.
			Assign wall space to immediate residents for decoration and territorial identity.

(continued overleaf)

Table D–1   (*continued*)

Environment	Environment Goal	CPTED Strategies	CPTED Design Directives
	Increase natural surveillance of hallways.	Promote natural surveil to increase the perception of risk by abnormal users.	Place window walls at ends of hallways to increase natural illumination and visibility.
			Place windows in doors of stair landings.
			Position lounge areas to provide direct line of sight to hallways; use windows in walls.
			Illuminate walls in hallways to increase perception of width and safety.
Stair systems	Increase natural surveillance of stairs.	Increase the perception of surveillance of interior stairs to make abnormal users feel more subject to scrutiny and challenge.	Design wrought iron or see-through wood railings for stairs and landings to increase visibility.
			Provide landings with visibility to lobby areas.
			Place windows in landings of all stairs (outside).
Restrooms	Enhance natural surveillance and access control.	Increase convenience of access.	Place restrooms in central areas.
			Reduce the number of residents sharing a common restroom.

		Increase the perception of natural surveillance and access control.	Install maze entrances to restrooms; avoid double door entry systems.
			Refrain from placing restrooms near stairs or exterior doors.
Lounges/ study areas	Enhance the territorial nature and identity of dormitory lounge areas.	Assign lounge areas to definite groupings of rooms.	Reduce the number of persons sharing a common lounge.
			Involve residents in the decoration and adornment of their lounge areas.
	Increase the natural surveillance of lounges and contiguous hallways.	Place lounges in strategic locations with visibility of hallways and stairs.	Install windows in inner and outer walls of lounges.
		Increase the use of lounges through enhancements to decor, amenities, and environmental systems.	Design lighting systems and select window coverings to limit the desirability of closing blinds.
			Install floor, wall, and ceiling systems to reduce the effects of noise.
Laundry	Enhance the effect of laundry usage on natural surveillance and access control.	Increase convenience of laundry locations.	Place laundries in central locations near major activity areas. Refrain from isolating laundries in remote areas.
		Increase perception of surveillance.	Maximize the use of glazing in outer walls.

(continued overleaf)

Table D-1   (*continued*)

Environment	Environment Goal	CPTED Strategies	CPTED Design Directives
			Provide intense illumination.
			Increase number of machines to reduce the need for late night or odd hour usage.
Resident assistant room location	Increase the perception of natural surveillance and access control on the part of the abnormal or undesired users of space.	Place safe activities in potential problem locations.	Place apartments in strategic locations; place windows in walls overlooking entrances and lobbies.
		Improve accessibility of managers/ resident assistants to students.	Place resident assistants' rooms at the entry points of each floor.
			Provide a visible sitting and waiting area in front of manager's apartments.
Lobbies/ Vestibules	Increase the transitional definition of movement from public to semi-public to private space.	Make potential abnormal users feel less comfortable and more subject to scrutiny by acknowledging transition through space.	Create minor obstacles or passage points to prevent easy movement from very public areas to lobbies.
			Change the texture, width, and border definition of sidewalks as they move from parallel

		passage to building approaches.
Improve natural access control.	Increase proprietary concern by residents over general use and access areas	Assign lobby walls and vestibule areas to dorm residents for reasonable decoration/ adornment
Increase natural surveillance.	Increase the perception of visibility from and to buildings.	Maximize the use of glazing and wall-mounted lighting.
Telephones/ Telephone Rooms	Reduce the propensity for public telephone locations increase vulnerability of normal users, and to legitimize loitering behavior of abnormal users.	Place unsafe activities in safe locations to extend the natural surveillance of the safe location over the unsafe activity (telephones).	Locate public telephones in well-used hallways and controlled areas away from restrooms.
		Provide natural barriers to conflicting activities.	Refrain from placing public telephones in or near entrances to buildings.
Apartment units	Enhance natural surveillance of individual room doors and restrooms.	Provide direct view from living room and kitchen areas.	Design bedroom and restroom entrances to cluster around living rooms and kitchens.
	Increase natural access control of main entrances to individual apartments.	Orient entrances toward high activity areas.	Provide windows at each apartment that are directed toward entry door(s).
	Increase territorial identity of common exterior entrances, foyers landings, and shared hallways.	Reduce number of residents sharing a common exterior entry	Separate landing and exterior stair systems to emphasize access to a small number of apartments

Table D–2   Exterior Spaces

Environment	Environment Goal	CPTED Strategies	CPTED Design Directives
Entrances	Enhance territorial identity of entrances.	Provide transitional definition of approaches to main entrances to identify movement from public to private space.	Set back sidewalks that are parallel to buildings to provide distance as transitional definition.
			Ensure a reasonable length for approach sidewalks.
	Increase surveillance of entrances.	Provide observation from room windows and approaches.	Increase the length of line of sight from approaches to entrances.
			Place windows overlooking entrances.
			Use glazing material in entry doors and adjacent panels.
	Increase natural access control of entrances.	Control building access through space management strategies and juxtapositioning with safe activities.	Reduce ingress/egress to one entry during vulnerable times.
			Architecturally celebrate and define the preferred and primary entry point
			Place a job function or other safe activity near primary entry points
Windows	Increase perception of natural surveillance from windows.	Increase opportunities for occasional surveillance through the	Place windows in walls overlooking isolated areas.

		planning of window locations.
		Place windows in all external stair systems.
	Increase the perception of natural surveillance through the management of window blinds and lighting.	Use adjustable venetian or mini-blinds on all windows, including bedrooms.
		Direct outdoor lighting away from windows, especially bedroom, to influence residents to leave windows loosely curtained, or blinds partially open, to increase the perception of surveillance from apartments.
Balconies/ Galleries	Enhance natural surveillance of pathways, isolated areas and parking lots.	Increase the perception of surveillance from balconies, patios, and galleries.	Install balconies and open galleries as often as possible.
		Increase the visibility of patio/balcony entry points to rooms/apartments from ground levels and adjacent buildings.	Using railings that allow visibility, in the place of walls or continuous wood fencing.
			Orient patios, balconies and galleries to allow for direct line of sight to outdoor pathways and areas.

(*continued overleaf*)

Table D-2 (*continued*)

Environment	Environment Goal	CPTED Strategies	CPTED Design Directives
Outdoor stair systems	Increase perception of natural surveillance.	Increase visibility of stairs and landings by open design.	Use wrought iron or wood railing to improve visibility.
	Increase natural access control.	Orient stair/landing directions to route persons past surveillance opportunities.	Place stairs in direct view of windows or activities.
Loading/ Passenger drop-off zones	Enhance territorial concern and natural surveillance through the strategic placement of loading/drop-off zones.	Increase visibility of loading zones from building entrances.	Identify a special loading zone for each building.
			Provide for direct line of sight from building entrances to loading zone.
Lighting	Increase natural surveillance through effective use of lighting.	Increase the perception of natural surveillance to make normal users feel safe and abnormal users feel at greater risk.	Provide for standard levels of light for all paths, sidewalks, bicycle parking, and isolated areas.
	Ensure that lighting enhances human activities and does not become an impediment.	Set lighting levels to meet the objectives of each human activity, in terms of effective illlumination and perceptions of safety.	Reduce lighting glare on bedroom and living room windows to ensure that residents do not obscure their windows at night from the view of walkways, open entrances, and parking.

Table D–3   Immediate Vicinity

Environment	Environment Goal	CPTED Strategies	CPTED Design Directives
Building groupings	Increase territorial identity of housing areas.	Orient buildings into distinctive clusters.	Face buildings toward court yards with entrances in line in line of sight of all buildings; keep number of buildings sharing a common courtyard to a minimum.
		Provide natural border definition of controlled space.	Plan landscaping and topographical features to reinforce borders of building clusters.
	Overcome isolation of building groups through improved natural surveillance.	Provide for natural surveillance of perimeter areas of building groups/clusters.	Orient balconies and windows to provide effective over views of unassigned space.
Courtyards	Enhance territorial identity of building groups through the use of individualized courtyards.	Design courtyards to serve as the focal point for access to buildings.	Route all pedestrian approaches through court yards.
		Increase natural surveillance and access control through courtyard planning.	Identify and celebrate entrance points to courtyards to provide a sense of arrival that signifies movement from public to semi-public space.
Sidewalks	Increase the safety of sidewalks through natural surveillance.	Increase the reality and perception of natural surveillance through sidewalk route planning and landscape maintenance.	Route sidewalks close to roadways and/or high activity areas.

(*continued overleaf*)

Table D-3   (*continued*)

Environment	Environment Goal	CPTED Strategies	CPTED Design Directives
			Reduce landscape impediments to sidewalk visibility.
			Provide transitional thinning of underbrush and foliage, especially in curves and bends.
	Enhance territorial concern through the routing of sidewalks.	Use the public sidewalk to define the perimeters of controlled space.	Refrain from placing parallel sidewalks near bedroom windows or entrances to residential units.
Landscaping	Enhance territorial identity through landscape planning.	Define pedestrian approaches with landscape.	Install landscaping to define borders of private spaces and to signify transitional movement from public to private space.
	Increase natural surveillance through landscape planning and maintenance.	Reduce barriers to visibility through routine trimming and maintenance of trees and bushes.	Establish maximum height standards for bushes and shrubs; establish minimum height standards for tree foliage (lower level).
			Implement landscape management procedures that require periodic thinning and replacement at the end of the useful life of the plant, shrub, or tree.

			Integrate illumination planning with landscape maintenance activities to enhance and maximize the free flow of light.
Bicycle shelters, racks, and posts	Enhance natural surveillance opportunities for bicycle storage areas.	Provide convenient access to bicycle parking.	Install bicycle racks and posts near all building entrances.
		Increase natural surveillance of bicycle parking by effective placement and design.	Relocate existing bicycle shelters, racks, and posts to locations that are directly in view of ongoing activities.
Lighting pedestrian ways and approaches to buildings	Enhance natural surveillance and safety through illumination of pedestrian ways.	Provide lighting of all pathways and building approaches at the human scale.	Increase lighting at the ground level without over illuminating upper-floor windows.
		Plan lighting to direct pedestrians along areas with high volume activities.	Create corridors of light along roadways and other pedestrian paths connecting colleges, the student center, and library facilities.
	Increase territorial identity through illumination of controlled spaces.	Plan for specific areas to become "islands of light."	Illuminate the lower levels of buildings and adjacent grounds, extending the light to perimeter areas.
Coffee Shops	Increase natural surveillance of college grounds	Place coffee shops in central locations to serve as a magnet	Maximize the use of windows and glazing material to

(*continued overleaf*)

Table D–3 (*continued*)

Environment	Environment Goal	CPTED Strategies	CPTED Design Directives
	through the effective location, design, and management of coffee shops.	for evening activities.	increase visibility from and into coffee shops.
			Illuminate the immediate are of the coffee shop to provide an "island of light" for the students.
Trash bins/ Disposal areas	Increase natural surveillance of trash disposal areas.	Improve the accessibility of trash disposal areas.	Place trash bins in prominent locations within view of windows and high activity areas.
		Increase the visibility of trash bins.	Design trash bin enclosures to psychologically screen instead of physically obscure.
			Refrain from isolating trash bins by location and design.
Outdoor amenities	Enhance natural surveillance of outdoor picnic and sitting areas.	Ensure visibility of outdoor sitting areas by locating them near activities.	Install amenities in college courtyards.
		Increase the accessibility and convenience of picnic areas to ensure high levels use.	Install amenities in direct view of windows.
			Refrain from designing or installing any features that block natural surveillance.

Table D-4 General Area

Environment	Environment Goal	CPTED Strategies	CPTED Design Directives
Parking	Increase natural surveillance of remote parking lots.	Place safe activities in areas that have little opportunities for natural surveillance.	Relocate guard booths from perimeter entry points to the intersections of the entrances of remote lots.
		Remove obstacles to natural surveillance.	Redesign landscape plans to reduce the negative effect of foliage and topographical features on direct visibility from adjacent streets and structures.
	Increase natural access control of parking areas located near buildings.	Provide border control and clear transitional definition in movement from public streets and semi-public access roads to private parking areas.	Design and manage parking lots so that some ingress/egress points may be closed during vulnerable periods to reduce the possibility of cruising by abnormal users.
	Increase the perception of risk of detection and scrutiny of abnormal users of parking areas.	Plan for new parking areas to be located in areas of high visibility.	Place parking in front of buildings and windows, and landscape appropriately to provide minimal screening for aesthetics.
Traffic Levels/ Direction	Increase natural access control through traffic management.	Reduce vehicular access to controlled points at night.	Route all traffic past guard booths.

(*continued overleaf*)

Table D–4   (*continued*)

Environment	Environment Goal	CPTED Strategies	CPTED Design Directives
Sidewalks and Pedestrian Paths	Increase natural surveillance along sidewalks and pedestrian paths.	Remove obstacles to natural surveillance.	Provide transitional landscape control along all wooded and obscured pedestrian paths to increase fields of view.
	Increase accessibility and convenience to sidewalks along road ways.	Develop a pedestrian pathway master plan.	Install intense lighting at the human scale along all critical pathways.
			Install sidewalks along all roadways.

Appendix E:
Convenience Stores and
Gas Stops CPTED
Assessment Form

Date: _____
Name of Reviewer _____

Natural Surveillance — NSU
Natural Access Control — NAC
Territorial Concern — TER

I. Demographics
   A. Name of Site _____
   B. Location _____
   C. Jurisdiction _____
   D. Customers

Type/#	Repeat	Nonrepeat
Resident	_____	_____
	_____	_____
	_____	_____
Nonresident	_____	_____
	_____	_____
	_____	_____
Drive	_____	_____
	_____	_____
	_____	_____
Walk	_____	_____
	_____	_____
	_____	_____

Type/#   Repeat   Nonrepeat
Commuter _____   _____

Visitor   _____   _____

F. Police services _____
G. Fire services _____
H. Number of employees _____
I. Hours of operation _____
J. CPTED/Security
    Advantages _____
    _____

    Disadvantages _____
    _____

    Precautions _____
    _____

    Recommendations _____
    _____

II. Neighborhood/Area
    A. Residential % _____
    B. Commercial/Retail _____
    C. Industrial _____
    D. Streets by type _____
        _____

        Private _____   Residential _____
        Service _____   Subcollector _____
        Collector _____   Major coll. _____
        Expressway _____   Interstate _____

    E. Proximity to expressways _____

    F. Access to transportation (by type) _____

    G. Lighting _____

    H. Demographics _____

    I. Vehicle approaches _____

J. Pedestrian approaches _____

K. Other _____

L. CPTED/Security _____
    Advantages _____
    _____

    Disadvantages _____
    _____

    Precautions _____
    _____

    Recommendations _____
    _____

III. Site Plan
    A. Acreage _____
    B. Topographical features _____
    _____

    C. Green areas
        Public _____
        Semi-public _____
        Private _____
    D. Recreation _____
    _____

    E. Landscape _____
    F. Access to contiguous properties _____
    _____

    G. Fences/Walls/Natural barriers _____
    _____

    H. Border definition _____
    _____

    I. Lighting (type, mounts, location) _____
    _____

    J. Type of store _____
    K. Parking _____
    L. Pumps (visual access) _____
    M. CPTED/Security
        Advantages _____
    _____

Disadvantages _____
_____
_____

Precautions _____
_____
_____

Recommendations _____
_____
_____

IV. Buildings/Exterior
   A. # by type _____
   B. Station (by type) _____
   C. Scale (# of buildings, size, volume) _____
       _____
       _____

   D. Use patterns/Users _____
       _____
       _____

   E. Sitting/Gathering areas _____
       _____
       _____

   F. Vehicle approaches _____
       _____

   G. Vehicle drop-off _____
       _____

   H. Pedestrian approaches _____
       _____

   I. Telephones _____
       _____

   J. Lighting — public areas _____
       _____

   K. Lighting — service areas _____
       _____

   L. Doors/Entrances/Exits _____
       _____
       _____

M. Windows/Openings _____

_____

_____

N. Service areas _____

_____

_____

O. Public transit stops _____

_____

P. Connections/Other buildings _____

_____

Q. Life safety codes/Issues _____

_____

R. Trash enclosures _____

S. Carwash (visual access, glazing) _____

_____

_____

T. Other _____

_____

_____

U. CPTED/Security
   Advantages _____

_____

_____

   Disadvantages _____

_____

_____

   Precautions _____

_____

_____

   Recommendations _____

_____

_____

V. Parking
   A. Type (s) _____

_____

_____

   B. Characteristics
      Ingress/Egress _____

_____

_____

Surface _____

_____

Enclosures/Structures _____

_____

units (by type) _____

Access to public _____

Visual access _____

C. Porch design/Size _____
D. CPTED/Security
    Advantages _____

_____

Disadvantages _____

_____

Precautions _____

_____

Recommendations _____

_____

VI. Interior
  A. Layout/Type _____

  B. Scale _____

  C. Waiting/Seating _____

  D. ATM machines _____

  E. Other businesses _____

  F. Movement areas/Corridors _____

  G. Observation areas/Opportunities
     Offices _____
     Windows _____
     Balconies/terraces _____
     Stairs _____
     Other _____

H. Decorations (fountains, planters, sculptures) _____
    _____
    _____
    _____
    _____

I. Gondolas/Shelves/Racks _____
    _____
    _____

J. Cashier location/Work area (risers, barriers) _____
    _____

K. Food service — seating _____
    _____

L. Food service — movement areas _____
    _____

M. Restrooms _____
    Locations _____

    Entry design _____

    Layout/Fixtures _____

    Materials _____

N. Telephones _____

O. Lighting _____
    _____

P. Service/Maintenance _____
    _____

Q. Administrative offices (location, access, fenestration, proximity,
    and visual access)
    _____
    _____
    _____

R. CPTED/Security
    Advantages _____
    _____
    _____

Disadvantages _____

_____

_____

Precautions _____

_____

_____

Recommendations _____

_____

_____

VII. Materials
   A. Interior _____

_____

   B. Exterior _____

_____

   C. Paint _____

_____

   D. Lighting
       Type _____
       Mount _____
       Comments _____

_____

_____

   E. Other _____

_____

_____

   F. CPTED/Security
       Advantages _____

_____

_____

       Disadvantages _____

_____

_____

       Precautions _____

_____

_____

       Recommendations _____

_____

_____

VIII. Security
   A. Systems (alarms, safes, timers, mirrors, EAS) _____

_____

   B. Guards (proprietary, contract, etc.) _____

_____

_____

C. Leasee/Concession _____

D. Police _____

E. Key control _____

F. Access control _____

G. Cash control _____

H. Training _____
I. CPTED/Security
    Advantages _____

    Disadvantages _____

    Precautions _____

    Recommendations _____

IX. Crime Patterns/Security Incidents (attach reports/maps to Section XII.)
A. Crime report _____

B. Crime map (spot map of incidents) _____

C. Fear map (spot map of fear locations) _____

D. Land-use map (local area) _____

E. Pedestrian activity map _____

F. Vehicle parking/Movement map _____

G. Other _____

H. CPTED/Security _____
    Advantages _____

Disadvantages _____

_____

Precautions _____

_____

Recommendations _____

_____

X. Priority Recommendations
Physical Space
A. Replace _____

_____

_____

_____

B. Repair _____

_____

_____

_____

C. Remove _____

_____

_____

_____

D. Install _____

_____

_____

_____

E. Re-allocate _____

_____

_____

_____

F. Other _____

_____

_____

_____

Management
A. Policies _____

_____

_____

_____

B. Procedures _____
_____
_____
_____

C. Personnel _____
_____
_____
_____

D. Neighborhood programs _____
_____
_____
_____

E. Other _____
_____
_____
_____

XI. Security Plan
A. Neighborhood _____
_____
_____
_____

B. Perimeter _____
_____
_____
_____

C. Grounds _____
_____
_____
_____

D. Parking _____
_____
_____
_____

E. Building access _____
_____
_____
_____

F. Building exterior _____
_____
_____
_____

G. Building interior _____
_____
_____
_____

H. High-value areas _____
_____
_____
_____

I. Protection of persons _____
_____
_____
_____

J. Special events _____
_____
_____
_____

K. Others _____
_____
_____
_____

XII. CPTED Matrices and Drawings (attach to form and provide any comments in this section)

_____
_____
_____
_____
_____
_____
_____
_____
_____
_____

Appendix F:
Rail, Transit, and Terminal CPTED Assessment Form

Date: _____

Name of Reviewer _____

Natural Surveillance — NSU
Natural Access Control — NAC
Territorial Concern — TER

I. Demographics
    A.   Name of Site _____
    B.   Location _____
    C.   Jurisdiction _____
    D.   Age % under _____ _____ _____ _____ over 65 _____
    E.   Customers/Riders/Visitors

Type/#	Repeat	Nonrepeat
Resident		
Nonresident		
Drive		
Walk		
Commuter		
Visitor		
Other		

    F.   Police services _____
    G.   Fire services _____
    H.   CPTED/Security
          Advantages _____
          _____

Disadvantages _____

Precautions _____

Recommendations _____

II. Neighborhood/Area
   A. Residential % _____
   B. Commercial/Retail _____
   C. Industrial _____
   D. Streets by type _____

   Private _____   Residential _____
   Service _____   Subcollector _____
   Collector _____   Major coll. _____
   Expressway _____   Interstate _____

   E. Proximity to expressways _____

   F. Access to transportation (by type) _____

   G. Lighting _____

   H. Demographics _____

   I. Vehicle approaches _____

   J. Pedestrian approaches _____

   K. CPTED/Security
       Advantages _____

       Disadvantages _____

       Precautions _____

   Recommendations _____

   _____

   _____

III. Grounds
   A. Acreage _____
   B. Topographical features _____

   _____

   C. Green areas
        Public _____
        Semi-public _____
        Private _____
   D. Recreation _____

   _____

   E. Landscape _____
   F. Access to contiguous properties _____

   _____

   G. Fences/Walls/Natural barriers _____

   _____

   H. Border definition _____

   _____

   I. Lighting (type, mounts, location) _____

   _____

   _____

   J. CPTED/Security
        Advantages _____

        _____

        _____

        Disadvantages _____

        _____

        _____

        Precautions _____

        _____

        _____

        Recommendations _____

        _____

        _____

IV. Buildings/Exterior
   A. Terminal (by type) _____
   B. Station (by type) _____
   C. Scale (# of buildings, size, volume) _____

   _____

   D. Use patterns/Users _____

   _____

E. Sitting/Gathering areas _____

F. Sitting/Gathering areas _____

G. Vehicle approaches _____

H. Vehicle drop-off _____

I. Pedestrian approaches _____

J. Telephones _____

K. Lighting-public areas _____

L. Lighting-service areas _____

M. Doors/Entrances/Exits _____

N. Windows/Openings _____

O. Service areas _____

P. Rail/Transit approaches _____

Q. Connections/Skywalks _____

R.   Life safety codes/issues _____

_____

S.   Other _____

_____

T.   CPTED/Security
Advantages _____

_____

Disadvantages _____

_____

Precautions _____

_____

Recommendations _____

_____

V. Parking
A.   Type(s) _____

_____

B.   Characteristics
Ingress/Egress _____

_____

Surface _____

Enclosures/Structures _____

_____

units (by type) _____

Proximity to terminal/station _____
Access to public _____

Visual access _____

C.   CPTED/Security
Advantages _____

_____

Disadvantages _____

_____

Precautions _____

Recommendations _____

VI. Interior
  A. Layout/Type _____

  B. Scale _____

  C. Waiting/Seating _____

  D. Ticket sales _____

  E. Information booths _____

  F. Movement areas/Corridors _____

  G. Observation areas/opportunities
     Offices _____
     Windows _____
     Balconies/terraces _____
     Stairs _____
     Other _____
  H. Landscape (fountains, planters, sculptures) _____

  I. Concessions/Retail _____

  J. Commercial/Mixed uses _____

  K. Food service — Seating _____

  L. Food service — Movement areas _____

M. Restrooms/Showers _____
   Locations _____

   _____

   Entry design _____

   _____

   Layout/Fixtures _____

   _____

   Materials _____

   _____

N. Lockers _____

   _____

O. Vertical access
   Stairs/Stair systems _____

   _____

   Escalators _____

   _____

   Elevators _____

   _____

P. Queing areas _____

Q. Turnstiles/Fare controls _____

   _____

   _____

   _____

R. Connections/Skywalks _____

   _____

S. Lighting _____

   _____

   _____

T. Service/Maintenance _____

   _____

   _____

U. Baggage/Package handling _____

   _____

   _____

V. Administrative offices (location, access, fenestration, proximity, and visual access)

   _____

   _____

   _____

W. Currency handling areas/Issues _____

   _____

   _____

X. Security offices/Stations _____

   _____

_____

VII. Materials
   A. Interior _____

   B. Exterior _____

   C. Paint _____

   D. Lighting
       Type _____
       Mount _____
       Comments _____

   E. Other _____

   F. CPTED/Security
       Advantages _____

       Disadvantages _____

       Precautions _____

       Recommendations _____

VIII. Security
   A. Systems _____

   B. Guards (proprietary, contract, etc.) _____

   C. Leasee/Concession _____

   D. Police _____

   E. Key control _____

   F. Access control _____

G. Other _____

_____

H. CPTED/Security
    Advantages _____

_____

    Disadvantages _____

_____

    Precautions _____

_____

    Recommendations _____

_____

IX. Crime Patterns/Security Incidents (attach reports/maps to Section XII)
    A. Crime report _____

_____

    B. Crime map (spot map of incidents) _____

_____

    C. Fear map (spot map of fear locations) _____

_____

    D. Land-use map (local area) _____

_____

    E. Pedestrian activity map _____

_____

    F. Vehicle parking/movement map _____

_____

    G. Other _____

_____

    H. CPTED/Security
        Advantages _____

_____

        Disadvantages _____

_____

        Precautions _____

_____

        Recommendations _____

_____

_____

X. Priority Recommendations
   Physical Space
   A. Replace _____
   _____
   _____
   _____
   _____

   B. Repair _____
   _____
   _____
   _____
   _____

   C. Remove _____
   _____
   _____
   _____
   _____

   D. Install _____
   _____
   _____
   _____
   _____

   E. Re-allocate _____
   _____
   _____
   _____
   _____

   F. Other _____
   _____
   _____
   _____
   _____

   Management
   A. Policies _____
   _____
   _____
   _____

   B. Procedures _____
   _____
   _____
   _____

   C. Personnel _____
   _____
   _____
   _____

D. Neighborhood programs _____
_____
_____
_____

E. Other _____
_____
_____
_____

XI. Security Plan
A. Neighborhood _____
_____
_____

B. Perimeter _____
_____
_____

C. Grounds _____
_____
_____

D. Parking _____
_____
_____

E. Building access _____
_____
_____

F. Building exterior _____
_____
_____

G. Building interior _____
_____
_____

H. High value areas _____
_____
_____

I. Protection of persons _____
_____
_____

J.   Special events _____
    _____
    _____
    _____

I.   Others _____
    _____
    _____
    _____

XII. CPTED Matrices and Drawings (attach to form and provide any comments in this section)

_____
_____
_____
_____
_____
_____
_____
_____
_____
_____
_____
_____

Appendix G:
Malls and Shopping Centers CPTED Assessment Form

Natural Surveillance — NSU
Natural Access Control — NAC
Territorial Concern — TER

I. Demographics
  A. Name of site _____
  B. Location _____
  C. Jurisdiction _____
  D. Type: Mall_____ Strip_____ Neighborhood_____ Intermediate_____
     Regional_____ Renewal (downtown)_____ Urban village_____
  E. Customers/Visitors

Type/#	Repeat	Nonrepeat
Resident	____	____
Nonresident	____	____
Drive	____	____
Walk	____	____
Commuter	____	____
Visitor	____	____

  F. Police _____
  G. Fire _____
  H. EMS _____
  I. Number of employees _____
  J. Hours of operation _____
  K. CPTED/Security
     Advantages _____
     _____

Disadvantages _____

_____

Precautions _____

_____

Recommendations _____

_____

II. Area/Neighborhood
   A.   Residential% _____
   B.   Commercial/Retail _____
   C.   Industrial _____
   D.   Streets by type _____

   _____

   Private _____   Residential _____
   Service _____   Subcollector _____
   Collector _____   Major collector _____
   Expressway_____   Interstate _____

   E.   Proximity to expressways _____

   _____

   F.   Access to transportation (by type) _____

   _____

   G.   Lighting _____

   _____

   H.   Demographics _____

   _____

   I.   Vehicle approaches _____

   _____

   J.   Pedestrian approaches _____

   _____

   K.   Other _____

   _____

   L.   CPTED/Security
        Advantages _____

   _____

        Disadvantages _____

   _____

        Precautions _____

   _____

Recommendations _____

_____

_____

III. Site Plan
   A.   Acreage _____

   B.   Topographical features _____

       _____

   C.   Site plan _____

       _____

   D.   Footprint _____

       _____

   E.   Green areas
       Public _____
       Semi-public _____
       Private _____
   F.   Recreation _____
   G.   Landscape _____
   H.   Access to contiguous properties _____
   I.   Outlot uses _____
   J.   Reservoir roads _____
   K.   Ring roads _____
   L.   Fences/Walls/Natural barriers _____
   M.   Border definition _____
   N.   Lighting (type, mounts, location) _____
   O.   Parking _____
   P.   Other _____
   Q.   CPTED/Security
       Advantages _____

       _____

       Disadvantages _____

       _____

       Precautions _____

       _____

       Recommendations _____

       _____

IV. Buildings/Exterior Features
   A.   # by type _____

   B.   Scale (# of buildings, size, volume) _____

   C.   Use patterns/Users _____

D. Sitting/Gathering areas _____

E. Vehicle approaches _____
_____

F. Vehicle drop-offs _____
_____

G. Pedestrian approaches _____
_____

H. Telephones _____
_____

I. Lighting — public areas _____
_____

J. Lighting — service areas _____
_____

K. Doors/Entrances/Exits _____
_____

L. Windows/Openings _____

M. Service areas _____

N. Public transit stops _____

O. Connections/Other buildings _____

P. Life safety codes/Issues _____
_____

Q. Trash enclosures _____

R. Other _____

S. CPTED/Security

Advantages _____
_____

Disadvantages _____
_____

Precautions _____
_____

Recommendations _____
_____
_____

V. Parking

A. Type (s) _____
_____

B. Characteristics

Ingress/egress _____

Surface _____

Enclosures _____

# of units (by type) _____

Access to public _____

       Right of reasonable public access _____

       _____

       Visual access _____

       Islands _____

       Walkways _____

  C. Other _____

       _____

  D. CPTED/Security

       Advantages _____

       _____

       _____

       Disadvantages _____

       _____

       _____

       Precautions _____

       _____

       _____

       Recommendations _____

       _____

       _____

VI. Interior

  A. Layout/Type _____

  B. Scale _____

  C. Waiting/Seating _____

       _____

  D. ATM machines _____

  E. Arcades _____

  F. Food courts _____

       Seating _____

       Pathways/Movement areas _____

       Service areas _____

       Restrooms _____

       Telephones _____

  G. Theaters _____

  H. Clubs/Entertainment _____

   I. Movement areas/Corridors (main, approach) _____

   J. observation areas/opportunities _____

       Offices _____

       Windows _____

       Balconies/Terraces _____

       Stairs _____

       Escalators _____

       Elevators _____

       Other _____

  K. Decorations (fountains, planters, sculptures) _____

    L. Vendor carts _____

    M. Special events _____

    N. Restrooms _____

          Locations _____

          Entry design _____

          Layout/Fixtures _____

          Materials _____

    O. Telephones (location, proximity to seating, planters) _____

_____

    P. Lighting _____

_____

    Q. Service/Maintenance access _____

    R. Administrative offices (location, access, fenestration, proximity, and visual access) _____

_____

_____

    S. Other _____

    T. CPTED/Security

          Advantages _____

_____

_____

          Disadvantages _____

_____

_____

          Precautions _____

_____

_____

          Recommendations _____

_____

_____

VII. Materials

    A. Interior _____

    B. Exterior _____

    C. Paint _____

    D. Lighting _____

          Type _____

          Mount _____

          Comments _____

    E. Other _____

    F. CPTED/Security

          Advantages _____

_____

_____

          Disadvantages _____

_____

Precautions _____

_____

Recommendations _____

_____

VIII. Security
   A. Systems (alarms, safes, timers, mirrors, EAS, etc.) _____

   B. Guards (proprietary, contract, etc.) _____

   C. Leasee/Concession _____

   D. Police _____

   E. Key control _____

   F. Access control _____

   G. Cash control _____

   H. Training _____

   I. Other _____

   J. CPTED/Security
      Advantages _____

_____

      Disadvantages _____

_____

      Precautions _____

_____

      Recommendations _____

_____

IX. Crime Patterns/Security Incidents (attach reports/maps to Section XII)
   A. Crime report _____

   B. Crime map (spot map of incidents) _____

   C. Fear map (spot map of fear locations) _____

_____

D.   Land-use map (local area) _____

E.   Pedestrian activity map _____

F.   Vehicle parking/ Movement map _____

G.   Other _____ __

H.   CPTED/Security
     Advantages _____

     Disadvantages _____

     Precautions _____

     Recommendations _____

X. Priority Recommendations
   Physical Space
   A.   Replace _____

   B.   Repair _____

   C.   Remove _____

   D.   Install _____

   E.   Re-allocate _____

F. Other _____

Management
A. Policies _____

B. Procedures _____

C. Personnel _____

D. Neighborhood programs _____

E. Other _____

XI. Security Plan
A. Neighborhood _____

B. Perimeter _____

C. Grounds _____

D. Parking _____

_____

_____

E. Building access _____

_____

_____

F. Building exterior _____

_____

_____

G. Building interior _____

_____

_____

H. High value areas _____

_____

_____

I. Protection of persons _____

_____

_____

J. Special events _____

_____

_____

K. Others _____

_____

_____

XII. CPTED Matrices and Drawings (attach to form and provide any comments in this section)

_____

_____

_____

_____

_____

Appendix H: Apartments and Public Housing CPTED Assessment Form

Date: _____
Name of Reviewer _____

Natural Surveillance — NSU
Natural Access Control — NAC
Territorial Concern — TER

I. Demographics
   A. Name of site _____
   B. Location _____
   C. Jurisdiction _____
   D. # of units _____
   E. Residents _____
   F. Age % under 18 ___ 18–25 ___ 26–45 ___ 45–65 ___ over 65 ___
   G. Race/Sex/Ethnic origins

	Female	*Male*
Anglo	_____	_____
	_____	_____
	_____	_____
Hispanic	_____	_____
	_____	_____
	_____	_____
Afro-Am.	_____	_____
	_____	_____
	_____	_____

	Female	*Male*
Asian	_____	_____
_____	_____	_____
_____	_____	_____
Native Am.	_____	_____
Other ____	_____	_____

H. Police services _____

I. Fire services _____

J. CPTED/Security

    Advantages _____

    _____

    Disadvantages _____

    _____

    Precautions _____

    _____

    Recommendations _____

    _____

II. Neighborhood

A. Residential % _____

B. Commercial/Retail _____

C. Industrial _____

D. Streets by type _____

    _____

Private _____	Residential _____
Service _____	Subcollector _____
Collector _____	Major coll. _____
Expressway _____	Interstate _____

E. Proximity to expressways _____

F. Access to transportation (by type) _____

G. Lighting _____

H. Demographics _____

I. CPTED/Security

    Advantages _____

    _____

Disadvantages _____

_____

Precautions _____

_____

III. Buildings
   A. Flats high/Garden _____
   B. Townhouses _____
   C. Maisonettes _____
   D. Single family _____
   E. Duplex or higher _____
   F. Stairs _____
   G. Elevators _____
   I. A.D.A. (e.g., ramps) _____
   J. CPTED/Security
      Advantages _____

_____

Disadvantages _____

_____

Precautions _____

_____

Recommendations _____

_____

IV. Grounds
   A. Acreage _____
   B. Topographical features _____

_____

   C. Yards
      Public _____
      Semi-public _____
      Private _____
   D. Recreation _____
   E. Gardens _____
   F. Landscape _____
   G. Access to contiguous properties _____

_____

   H. Fences/Walls/Natural barriers _____

_____

   I. Border definition _____

_____

    J. Lighting (type, mounts, location) _____

_____

_____

    H. CPTED/Security
        Advantages _____

_____

_____

        Disadvantages _____

_____

_____

        Precautions _____

_____

_____

        Recommendations _____

_____

_____

V. Interior Streets
    A. Pattern _____
    B. Ingress/Egress (to outside) _____

_____

    C. Parking _____
        Ingress/Egress _____
        Street _____
        Court _____
        Cluster _____
        Pads _____
        Enclosures/Roof _____
        Conflict _____

_____

        # per unit _____
        Proximity to units _____
        Access to public _____
    D. CPTED/Security
        Advantages _____

_____

        Disadvantages _____

_____

        Precautions _____

_____

        Recommendations _____

_____

VI. Units
  A. Floor plan _____
  B. Private space — balcony/patio/stoop _____

  C. Pedestrian approaches _____

  D. Sidewalks and proximity _____

  E. Fenestration
       Doors and frames _____
       Windows _____
       Screens _____
       Materials _____
       Comments _____
  F. Locks
       Doors _____
       Windows _____
       Storage areas _____
       Other _____
  G. Materials
       Interior _____

       Exterior _____

       Paint _____

  H. Lighting
       Type _____
       Mount _____
       Comments _____
   I. Visual accessibility _____

   J. CPTED/Security
       Advantages _____

       Disadvantages _____

       Precautions _____

Recommendations _____

_____

_____

_____

VII. Security
    A.   Systems _____

    _____

    B.   Guards _____

    _____

    C.   Block/Neighborhood associations _____

    _____

    D.   Police/Sheriff _____

    _____

    E.   Key control _____

    _____

    F.   CPTED/Security
         Advantages _____

    _____

    _____

         Disadvantages _____

    _____

    _____

         Precautions _____

    _____

    _____

         Recommendations _____

    _____

    _____

VIII. Common Buildings
    A.   Office _____
    B.   Meeting _____
    C.   Recreation _____
    D.   Laundry _____
    E.   Maintenance _____
    F.   CPTED/Security
         Advantages _____

    _____

    _____

         Disadvantages _____

    _____

    _____

         Precautions _____

    _____

    _____

Recommendations _____
_____
_____
_____

IX. Crime Patterns/Security Incidents (attach reports/maps to Section XII)
A. Crime report _____
_____

B. Crime map (spot map of incidents) _____
_____

C. Fear map (spot map of fear locations) _____
_____

D. Land-use map (local area) _____
_____

E. Pedestrian activity map _____
_____

F. Vehicle parking/movement map _____
_____

G. Other _____
_____

H. CPTED/Security
Advantages _____
_____
_____

Disadvantages _____
_____
_____

Precautions _____
_____
_____

Recommendations _____
_____
_____

X. Priority Recommendations
Physical Space
A. Replace _____
_____
_____
_____
_____

B. Repair _____
_____
_____
_____
_____

C. Remove _____
    _____
    _____
    _____
    _____

D. Install _____
    _____
    _____
    _____
    _____

E. Re-allocate _____
    _____
    _____
    _____
    _____

F. Other _____
    _____
    _____
    _____
    _____

Management
A. Policies _____
    _____
    _____

B. Procedures _____
    _____
    _____

C. Personnel _____
    _____
    _____

D. Neighborhood programs _____
    _____
    _____

E. Other _____
    _____
    _____

XI. Security Plan
    A. Neighborhood _____
        _____

_____
_____
_____

B. Perimeter _____
_____
_____

C. Grounds _____
_____
_____

D. Parking _____
_____
_____

E. Building access _____
_____
_____

F. Building exterior _____
_____
_____

G. Building interior _____
_____
_____
_____

H. High value areas _____
_____
_____

I. Protection of persons _____
_____
_____

J. Special events _____
_____
_____

I. Others _____
_____
_____
_____

XII. CPTED Matrices and Drawings (attach to form and provide any comments in this section)

_____

_____

_____

_____

_____

_____

_____

_____

_____

_____

_____

_____

Glossary

area analysis An early step in the design process in which the existing and proposed internal and external relationships are mapped and articulated. This expands upon the earlier stage of site analysis.

astragal The vertical bar or member that joins the closure of double doors. It may be secured to one door or to the floor and overhead support structure (frame). The astragal is important to door security.

average daily trips (ADT) A measure of the vehicle flow on streets, especially residential types. High ADTs are an indication of a range of potential problems.

average time per visit (ATPV) A measure used to assess the marketing effectiveness of a mall or shopping center. The length of time per customer visit provides an indication of the potential level of impulse buying.

azimuth The compass reference on site plans or maps used to define boundary lines.

barricade A portable device used to temporarily close a street or walkway. CPTED planners are using barricades to divert traffic and to permanently close streets.

bench mark Point of reference from which measurements are made.

berm The use of mounds of earth to provide border definition of properties or to contribute to the aesthetic requirements of a landscape plan.

blueprints The common reference to a copy or facsimile of a set of original drawings or working plans of a building or site. The common method of reproduction produces a blue color on the original.

bubble charts A sometime reference to the area analysis conducted by the architect. Circles and ellipses (bubbles) are drawn in various sizes to represent activities planned for a site or structure. These bubbles are then moved around to simulate the best spatial relationships.

charette A multidisciplinary workshop for making planning and design decisions, generally conducted on a project site. The term comes from the French word for a little wagon that was used to deliver sections of plans as they were drafted by architects who lived all over Paris.

codes These are the standards and requirements enacted by local and state legislative bodies to govern land use and building.

crime prevention fence Any fence that may be seen through. Other fences obscure natural surveillance. Pedestrians do not feel safe walking next to a continuous fence.

cul-de-sac The circular turnaround at the end of a street. The adjacent lots are subdivided to provide a maximum number of frontages on the circle.

curb cuts The openings along curb lines for driveways and vehicular entrance/exit to parking lots.

curtain walls Buildings that use windows or walls that are not part of the load-bearing system. These buildings appear often as window-walls or glass-walls.

elevation This term is used in a variety of ways. It is a reference to height. It is also a reference to the page or pages in a set of blueprints in which the view is looking at a structural element.

exposure An important consideration in site planning. The designer has to consider the effects of orientation to the sun and to the elements. Landscape plans are affected by exposure. Evergreens are often used to shield buildings from northern exposures, whereas deciduous trees are used on the south side.

facade The front of a building or structure.

fenestration The manner in which a building is designed to take advantage of natural illumination.

fire lane The access areas adjacent to buildings that are reserved for fire apparatus. These areas are mandated by local laws.

glazing The transparent material used for windows and doors. It may be glass or some form of plastic.

gondola A free-floating shelf or rack in a convenience store. It is not up against a wall or window.

hip roof A tented style of roof that has sloping ends that offset sloping sides.

HVAC The blueprint and engineering reference to heating, ventilating, and air conditioning systems of a building.

impulse buying A customer is induced to make an unintended or unplanned purchase. These buyers react strongly to environmental conditions.

international style This style of architecture dominated the design of office buildings for a number of decades until the late 1970s. The style was characterized by smooth, sleek, vertical lines of buildings, later criticized as unimaginative.

life safety codes Locally adopted codes that are used on national standards. These codes relate to fire and emergency access/escape plans. These codes are criticized occasionally for conflicting with good security procedures.

light The section of a window system through which light passes, normally the pane.

lintel The horizontal structural support above a door or arch. These features are sometimes enhanced aesthetically to define the private entrance. Entrance system design is an important aspect of CPTED territorial concepts.

mansard roof A top structure that uses two angles from the peak to the side. The most common form makes the second pitch become part of the side walls (as in Burger King and other fast food restaurant buildings).

matrix presentation The use of a cross-tabular approach to presenting ideas and recommendations. This approach reduces report preparation time and makes reports easier to understand. It also reduces the length of reports.

mullion The central post in a casement window. This term is sometimes used to refer to a central anchor post for double doors (usually called an astragal). The mullion is an important component of window security.

north indicator The reference to the direction of due north on site plans and drawings.

original drawings These are the official drawings or plans for a site or a structure. Blueprints are copies of original drawings.

pilotis construction An early 20th-century style that emphasized the lifting of the building into the airspace, with structural support emanating from a central pile (hence pilotis).

pitched roof A traditional or tented style that is most effective for small structures or dwelling units.

plan This term is used in a variety of ways. It may be a reference to a design or blueprint for action. It may document local decisions and future actions. It is commonly defined as the page or pages of a set of drawings in which the view is looking downward at the dimensions of a site or floor of a structure.

planting strip The grassy area found between the sidewalk and curb along city streets.

plot/plat Both words refer to the site or lot drawing that legally defines the location and boundaries of the property.

post-modern deconstruction style This style breaks with all conventions. Buildings are made to appear unfinished. Structural components are left visible. Cross-sections of wall and roofs are often revealed.

post-modern style This style was established in reaction to many decades of the modern, or international, style. This style breaks the tradition of smooth, sleek buildings. Mixtures of various styles are used without regard for convention. Structural components are emphasized in the use of exterior columns and the appearance of strong walls and foundations.

preapplication process The informal discussions and information gathering activities conducted by builders and developers prior to the filing of formal applications for building permits, zoning changes, or code variances. This is a critical time for both the developer and local government. Mistakes and high costs may be avoided at this point through effective communications. The CPTED planner can be most effective at this stage, since the various parties are still conceptualizing their plans. Past the conceptual stage, plans and designs are difficult to change.

public housing The term refers to housing projects that have been built wholly or in part with federal funds. Other funding has been supplied through local governments. Public housing projects were developed mostly just before and after World War II. Federal policy regarding housing is presently controversial.

PUD Planned Unit Development is a reference to a major land use plan that is submitted for approval by local officials. These plans are generally designated for major residential uses that include a comprehensive design for all services and requirements (e.g., traffic, sewage, and utilities).

purposeful buying The shopper arrives at a business area with a predetermined purchase in mind. These buyers react differently to environmental conditions than do others.

scale A unit of measurement. It also is used as a reference to the orientation, or siting, of a building. Another use of this term is in reference to the triangular-shaped measurement instrument used to integrate architectural and engineering references on a site plan or set of blueprints.

scattered site housing A newer concept of publicly supported housing that emphasizes the dispersal of housing units to properties with a range of 4–16 units. The number of units will vary, but the policy is to spread the units throughout the community.

section This term has a number of meanings. A section is a surveyor's term for a 640-acre plot. A section refers to the page or pages in a set of blueprints in which the view is looking through a part or structural element (as in cross-section).

Section 8 housing A later public housing approach that used federal funds to subsidize rents for lower income families who were living in privately owned apartment complexes. The major distinction is the ownership of the property.

site analysis One of the preliminary stages in the planning for a structure or other construction. Basic information is collected about soil, water, drainage, topographic features, and exposure.

spatial data management The organization of data and information into a one-page or screen format. Related items are grouped and graphic techniques are used to demonstrate interrelationships. A matrix is a simple form of this concept. The "cluttered desk" is often an example of a finely organized "visual" inventory of information. Spatial-data management is best symbolized in the expression "Out of sight, out of mind."

street hierarchy The system used to identify streets that range from private roads to interstate highways. The general hierarchy includes: private, residential, sub-collector, collector, arterial, service road, limited access, and interstate highway.

striping The painted lines used to designate driving lanes and parking spots.

topo A slang reference to a topographical map that presents the contours and geographical descriptions of any site.

traffic separator The heavy cement islands that are used as safety barriers between oncoming or converging traffic, mostly at construction sites or where median width is too narrow. These devices are now used to divert vehicles from direct access to building entrances to prevent car bombing attacks.

twenty-five percent greenspace requirements A contemporary water control policy directed toward the management of groundwater and groundwater run-off. This general planning requirement affects decisions about parking lots and other design features of properties.

variance The granting of any exception to local codes and building requirements.

working plans An often misleading reference to the final set of drawings and specifications for a building or site. These are the formal documents that a builder uses to guide the construction of a structure. Many persons think that the reference to working plans means that they are in draft form or are preliminary.

zero-lot line A reference to the placement of a building on the lot line, usually on the rear or side.

Bibliography

A Police Guide to Surveying Citizens and Their Environment, Bureau of Justice Assistance monograph. Washington, DC: U.S. Department of Justice, Office of Justice Programs, October, 1993.

Angel, S. *Discouraging Crime Through City Planning*. Berkeley: University of California, 1969.

Appleyard, D. *Liveable Streets*, Berkeley, California: University of California Press, 1981.

Baumer, T. and Hunter, A. "Street Traffic, Social Integration and Fear of Crime." Working paper of the *Reactions to Crime Project*. Evanston, Illinois: Northwestern University Center for Urban Affairs, January 1978.

Becker, F.D. *Design for Living*. Ithaca, New York: Center for Urban Development Research, May 1974.

_____. "The Effect of Physical and Social Factors on Residents' Sense of Security in Multi-Family Housing Developments." *Journal of Architectural Research*, February 1975, *4*(1), 18–24.

Bevis, C. and Nutter, J.B. *Changing Street Layouts to Reduce Residential Burglary*. St. Paul, Minnesota: Governor's Commission of Crime Prevention and Control, 1977.

Bickman, L. "Dormitory Density and Helping Behavior." *Environment and Behavior*, December 1973, *5*(4), 465–490.

Block, R. "Community, Environment, and Violent Crime." *Crime Prevention Through Environmental Design Panel*. Atlanta: American Society of Criminology, 1977.

Brantingham, P.L. and Brantingham, P.J. "Residential Burglary and Urban Form." *Urban Studies*, October 1975, 273–285.

_____. "A Theoretical Model of Crime Site Selection." *Proceedings of the American Society of Criminology*, Atlanta, Georgia, November 18, 1977.

_____. "Notes on the Geometry of Crime." *International Symposium on Selected Criminological Topics*, University of Stockholm, August 1978.

_____. "A Theoretical Model of Crime Site Selection" in M.D. Krohn and R.L. Akers (eds.), *Crime, Law and Sanctions: Theoretical Perspectives*. Beverly Hills: Sage Publications, 1978.

_____. "Crime, Occupation and Economic Specializatin: A Consideration of Inter-metropolitan Patterns" in K.D. Harries and D.E. Georges (eds.), *Crime: A Spatial Perspective*. New York: Columbia University Press, 1980.

_____. "Housing Patterns and Burglary in a Medium-Sized American City" in J.E. Scott (ed.), *Criminal Justice and Planning*. New York: Praeger, 1980.

315

Brantingham, P.L., Brantingham, P.J., and Molumby, T. "Perceptions of Crime in a Dreadful Enclosure." *Ohio Journal of Science*, November 1977, *77*(6), 256–261.

Brantingham, P.J. and P.L. ed., *Environmental Criminology*, Beverly Hills, CA: Sage, 1981.

Brill, W.H. "Security in Public Housing: A Synergistic Approach" in *Deterrence of Crime in and around Residences: Papers presented at the Fourth National Symposium on Law Enforcement Science and Technology*. University of Maryland, May 1–3, 1972.

Brill and Associates. *Victimization, Fear of Crime, and Altered Behavior: A Profile of Four Housing Projects in Boston*. Washington, DC: W.H. Brill, 1975.

_____. *Comprehensive Security Planning: A Program for Capper Dwellings, Washington, D.C.* Washington, DC: Department of Housing and Urban Development, Office of Policy Development and Research, 1977.

_____. *Comprehensive Security Planning: A Program for Murphy Homes, Baltimore, Maryland*. Washington, DC: Department of Housing and Urban Development, Office of Policy Development and Research, 1977.

_____. *Victimization, Fear of Crime, and Altered Behavior: A Profile of the Crime Problem in Murphy Homes, Baltimore, Maryland*. Washington, DC: Department of Housing and Urban Development, Office of Policy Development and Research, 1977.

_____. *Victimization, Fear of Crime, and Altered Behavior: A Profile of the Crime Problem in Capper Dwellings, Washington, D.C.* Washington, DC: Department of Housing and Urban Development, Office of Policy Development and Research, 1977.

_____. *Comprehensive Security Planning: A Program for William Nickerson Gardens, Los Angeles, California*. Washington, DC: Department of Housing and Urban Development, Office of Policy Development and Research, 1977.

_____. *Phipps Plaza South Safety and Security Analysis and Recommendations*. Annapolis, Maryland: W.H. Brill, 1977.

_____. *Architectural Analysis and Design Recommendations to Convert Tasker for the Senior Citizen*. Philadelphia: Philadelphia Housing Authority, 1977.

Brower, S. *Street Front and Backyard: Two Ways of Looking at Neighborhood Open Spaces*. Baltimore, Maryland: Baltimore City Department of Planning, 1977.

Brown, B.B. and Altman, I. "Territorial and Residential Crime: A Conceptual Framework." *Crime Prevention Through Environmental Design Theory Compendium*. Arlington, Virginia: Westinghouse National Issues Center, 1978.

_____. "Territoriality, Defensible Space and Residential Burglary: An Environmental Analysis." *Journal of Environmental Psychology*, 1983, *3*, 203–220.

Brown, R.H., Burton, V., and Prater, W. *An Analysis of Incidence of Crime with Selected Socio-Economic Variables in Durham, North Carolina*. Durham: North Carolina Central University, June 1976.

Capone, D.L. and Nichols, W., Jr. "Urban Structure and Criminal Mobility." *Criminal Behavior and the Physical Environment, American Behavioral Scientist*, 1976, 20.

Cardarelli, A.P. *Crime in Boston: An Analysis of Serious Crime Patterns Within 81 Neighborhoods*. Boston: A Report of the Mayor's Office of Justice Administration, 1971.

Carter, G.M. *Designing Safe Environments IV: Sample Size Requirements*. Unpublished manuscript, Santa Monica, California: Rand Corporation, June 1978.

Carter, R.L. "The Criminal's Image of the City." Doctoral dissertation, University of Oklahoma, 1974.

Carter, R.L. and Hill, K.Q. *Criminals' and Non-Criminals' Perceptions of Urban Crime*. Houston: University of Texas as Clear Lake, 1976.

_____. "The Criminal's Image of the City and Urban Crime Patterns." *Social Science Quarterly*, 1976, 57.

_____. "Area Images and Behavior: An Alternative Perspective for Understanding Crime" in D.E. Georges and K.D. Harries (eds.), *Crime: A Spatial Perspective*. New York: Columbia University Press, 1981.

Chaiken, J.M. "What's Known About Deterrent Effects of Police Activities." *The Rand Paper Series*. Santa Monica, California: The Rand Corporation, November 1976.

Chenoweth, R.E. "The Effects of Territorial Markings on Residents of Two Multi-family Housing Developments: A Partial Test of Newman's Theory of Defensible Space." Doctoral dissertation, University of Illinois, 1977. *Dissertation Abstracts International*, 1978, *38*, 5088 (University Microfilms No. GAX78-03955).

Clarke, R.V.G. *Crime Prevention Through Town Planning and Architecture: International Comparison (Including Social Structure, Synopsis and Outlook in United Kingdom; Defensible Space and Vandalism: The Lessons From Some Recent British Studies.)* London: Home Office Research Unit.

Clarke, R.V. ed., *Situational Crime Prevention: Successful Case Studies*, New York, NY: Harrow and Heston, 1982.

Clay, P.L. *A Safe Place to Live: Security in Multi-Family Housing*. Roxbury, Massachusetts: The Lower Roxbury Community Corporation, March 1972.

Cohen, L.E. and Felson, M. *"Social Change and Crime Rate Trends: A Routine Activities Approach,"* American Sociological Review, 1979, vol. 44, pp. 588–608.

Conklin, J.E. "Crime Prevention Through Environmental Design" in *Crime Prevention Through Environmental Design Theory Compendium*. Arlington, Virginia: Westinghouse National Issues Center, 1978.

Cooper, J. *Environmental Factors Relating to Violence: A Second Report of Mayor Lastman's Committee on Violence*. Borough of North York, Toronto, 1974.

Crime Prevention Through Environmental Design, Crime Prevention Through Environmental Design in Convenience Stores (video), Tallahassee, FL: Office of the Attorney General, 1988.

Crow, W.J. and Brill, J.C. *Robbery Deterrence: An Applied Behavioral Science Demonstration*. La Jolla, California: Western Behavioral Sciences Institute, September 1975.

Crowe, T.D. *Crime Prevention Through Environmental Design: A Training Manual*. Washington, DC: U.S. Department of Justice, 1982.

_____. "Clean, Well-lighted Places: A Natural Approach to Retail Security." *International Security Review*, London, England, 1988.

_____. "An Ounce of Prevention: A New Role for Law Enforcement." *FBI Bulletin*. Washington, DC: Federal Bureau of Investigation, October 1988.

Crowe, T.D., Pesce, E., and Reimer, A. *Crime Prevention Through Environmental Design: School Demonstration Plan*. Westinghouse Electric Corporation, 1976.

Crowe, T.D. *Crime Prevention Through Environmental Design*, Stoneham, MA: Butterworth-Heinemann, 1991.

Crowe, T. "Designing Safer Schools," School Safety, Fall 1990, pp. 9–13.

Dean, L.M., Pugh, W.M., and Gunderson, E.K. "The Behavioral Effect of Crowding." *Environment and Behavior*, September 1978, 419–431.

Dietrick, B. "The Environment and Burglary Victimization in a Metropolitan Suburb." Paper presented to the annual meeting of the American Society of Criminology, Atlanta, Georgia, November 16–20, 1977.

Dingemans, D.J. "Defensible Space Design in the California Townhouse." *California Geographer*, 1978.

———. "Evaluating Housing Environments for Crime Prevention." *Crime Prevention Review*. Los Angeles: Office of the Attorney General, State of California, July 1978, 5(4), 7–14.

Dingemans, D.J., Garfield, S., and Olson, T. *Defensible Space in Suburban Townhouse Design: A Case Study of Six California Developments*. Davis, California: Institute of Government Affairs, University of California, May 1977.

Duffala, D.C. "Convenience Stores, Armed Robbery and Physical Environmental Features." *Criminal Behavior and the Physical Environment; American Behavioral Scientist*, 1976, 20(2), 227–247.

Duhl, L.J. "The Possibilities of Minimizing Crime-Inducing Factors by the Design and Construction of City Areas." Paper presented at *The National Symposium on Science and Criminal Justice*, Washington, DC, June 22–23, 1966.

Dunn, C.S. "The Analysis of Environmental Attribute/Crime Incident Characteristic Interrelationships." Doctoral dissertation, State University of New York. *Dissertation Abstracts International*, 1977 (University Microfilms).

Fabbin, J. "Crime Prevention Through Physical Planning." *Crime Prevention Review*, April 1974, 1(3), 1–7.

Fairley, W. and Liechenstein, M. *Improving Public Safety in Urban Apartment Dwellings*. New York: Rand Institute, 1971.

Feeney, F. and Nair, A. *The Geography of Robbery*. Davis, California: University of California, 1974.

Felson, M. "Routine Activities and Crime Prevention in the Developing Metropolis," *Criminology*, 1987, Vol. 25 pp. 911–931.

Fennelly, L. ed., Handbook of Loss Crime Prevention, 3rd. ed., Boston, MA: Butterworth-Heinemann, 1996.

Fitch, J.M. *American Building: The Environmental Forces That Shape It*. Boston: Houghton Mifflin, 1972.

Fleissner dan and Fred Heinzelmann, *Crime Prevention Through Environmental Design and Community Policing*, Washington, D.C.: U.S. Department of Justice, National Institute of Justice, August 1996.

Fowler, F. and Mangione, T.W. *Implications of Map and Fear Data for Crime Control Design*. Boston: Center for Survey Research, The University of Massachusetts/ Boston; the Joint Center for Urban Studies of MIT; and Harvard University, 1974.

———. *Reducing Residential Crime and Fear: The Hartford Neighborhood Prevention Program*. Boston: Center for Survey Research, The University of Massachusetts/ Boston; the Joint Center for Urban Studies of MIT; Harvard University; and Hartford Institute of Criminal and Social Justice, August 1979.

Franck, K.A. "Community by Design: A Study of Moderate-Income, Federally Assisted Housing Developments." Doctoral dissertation, The City University of New York, 1978.

Fremont/Richmond Police Departments. *Crime Prevention/Reduction of Services and Environmental Design*. Fremont, California: The Police Foundation, 1972.

Gardiner, R.A. "Crime and the Neighborhood Environment." *HUD Challenge*, February 1976, *8*, 9–13.

_____. *Environmental Security Report for South New Town*. Cambridge, Massachusetts: Richard Gardiner and Associates, 1976.

_____. *Environmental Security Planning: Redesign for Safe Neighborhoods*. Cambridge, Massachusetts: Richard Gardiner and Associates, 1977.

Gold, R. "Urban Violence and Contemporary Defensive Cities." *American Institute of Planners Journal*, 1970, *36*, 146–159.

Goldberg, F. and Michelson, W. "Defensible Space as a Factor in Combatting Fear Among the Elderly: Evidence from Sherbourne Lanes." *Crime Prevention Through Environmental Design Theory Compendium*. Arlington, Virginia: Westinghouse National Issues Center, 1978.

Goldstein, H. *Problem — Oriented Policing*, New York, NY: McGraw-Hill, 1989.

Gordon, R.A. "Issues in the Ecological Study of Delinquency" in M.E. Wolfgang et al. (eds.), *The Sociology of Crime and Delinquency*. New York: John Wiley & Sons, 1970.

Gray, C.M. and Joelson, M.R. "The Impact of Crime on Housing Values and Property Tax Revenues." Paper presented to the annual meeting of the American Society of Criminology, Atlanta, Georgia, November 1978. Minneapolis: Minnesota Crime Prevention Center, 1978.

Greebie, B. "An Ethological Approach to Community Design" in W. Preiser (ed.), *Environmental Design Research, 1*. Stroudsburgh: Dowden, Hutchinson & Ross, 1973.

Greenberg, S.W. and Roehe, W.M. "Neighborhood Design and Crime," *American Psychological Association*, Winter, 1984.

Gordon, C.L. and Brill, W. *The Expanding Role of Crime Prevention Through Environmental Design in Premises Liability*, Washington, D.C.: U.S. Department of Justice, National Institute of Justice, April 1996.

Hand, L. "Cincinnati Housing Authority Builds Safety into Project." *HUD Challenge*, March 1977.

Harries, K.D. "Spatial Aspects of Violence and Metropolitan Population." *Professional Geographer*, February 1973, *25*(1), 1–6.

_____. "Cities and Crime: A Geographic Model." *Criminology*, November 1976, *14*(3), 369–386.

Hawaii University. *Offenses and Environments: Analysis of Crime in the City and County of Honolulu*. Honolulu: Hawaii University, 1974.

Heald, K.A. *Designing Safe Environments: III Testing Procedures*. Unpublished manuscript. Santa Monica, California: Rand Corporation, July 1978.

Jacobs, J. *The Death and Life of Great American Cities*. New York: Vintage Books, 1961.

Jeffrey, C.R. "Criminal Behavior and the Physical Environment." *American Behavioral Scientist*, 1972, *20*, 149–174.

_____. *Crime Prevention Through Environmental Design* (2nd edition). Beverly Hills: Sage Publications, 1977.

Kaplan, S. "Defensible Space: A Review." *Architectual Forum*, May 1973, 138(5).

Katz. "Patterns of Arrest and the Dangers of Public Visibility." *Criminal Law Bulletin*, 1973, *4*, 311–324.

Kelling, G.L. and Coles, C.M. *Fixing Broken Windows*, New York, NY: The Free Press, 1996.

Kirmeyer, S.L. "Urban Density and Pathology: A Review of Research." *Environment and Behavior*, June 1978, *10*(2), 247–269.

Knowles, E.S. "Boundaries Around Social Space." *Environment and Behavior*, December 1972, 437–445.

Lander, B. "An Ecological Analysis of Baltimore" in M.E. Wolfgang et al. (eds.), *The Sociology of Crime and Delinquency.* New York: John Wiley & Sons, 1970.

Latane, Z. and Darley, J.M. *The Unresponsive Bystander: Why He Doesn't Help.* New York: Appleton Century Crofts, 1970.

Laymon, R.S. *Architectural Design and Crime Prevention.* Washington, DC: National Institute of Law Enforcement and Criminal Justice, U.S. Department of Justice, 1974.

Lee, Y. and Egan, F. "The Geography of Urban Crime: The Spacial Pattern of Serious Crime in the City of Denver." *Proceedings of the Association of American Geographers*, 1972, *4*, 59–64.

Lentz, P., Sternhall, R., and Lyle, C. *The Limits of Lighting: The New Orleans Experiment in Crime Reduction.* The Mayor's Criminal Justice Coordinating Council, April 1977.

Letkemann, P. *Crime at Work.* Englewood Cliffs: Prentice Hall, 1973.

Lewis, H. *An Analysis of Public Safety as Related to the Incidents of Crime in Parks and Public Areas.* U.S. Department of Transportation (NTIS No. PB220770).

Ley, D. and Cybriwsky, R. "The Spacial Ecology of Stripped Cars." *Environment and Behavior*, March 1974, *6*(1), 53–67.

Liechenstein, M. *Designing for Security.* New York: The Rand Corporation, 1971.

———. *Reducing Crime in Apartment Dwellings: A Methodology for Comparing Security Alternatives.* New York: Rand Institute, 1972.

Lorenz, M.H. *Draft Workbook for Defensible Industrial Space: Case Study of Crosstown Industrial Park, Parcel 1.* Roxbury, Massachusetts: Community Development Corporation of Boston, May 1977.

Luedtke and Associates. *Crime and the Physical City.* Detroit: Luedtke and Associates, 1970.

Malt, H.L. "Neighborhood Streets — Accessory or Deterrent to Crime." *American County*, May 1971, *36*(5).

Malt, H.L., Associates. *An Analysis of Public Safety as Related to the Incidence of Crimes in Parks and Recreation Areas in Central Cities.* Prepared for the Department of Housing and Urban Development. Washington, DC: H.L. Malt Associates, 1972.

———. *Tactical Analysis of Street Crimes.* Prepared for the City of Jacksonville, Florida, Office of the Sheriff. Washington, DC: H.L. Malt Associates, 1973. Mann, L. and Hageirk, G. "The New Environmentalism: Behaviorism and Design." *Journal of the American Institute of Planners*, September 1971.

Marcus, C.C. and Sarkissian, W. *Housing as if People Mattered*, Berkley, CA: University of California Press, 1986.

Mauer, E.C. "Housing Project Safety Restored." *Journal of Housing*, June 1971, *28*, 282.

Mawby, R.I. "Defensible Space: A Theoretical and Empirical Appraisal." *Urban Studies*, 1977, *14*, 169–179.

Mayhew, P., Clarke, R.V., Sturman, A, and Hough, J.M. *Crime as Opportunity.* London: Her Majesty's Stationery Office, 1976 (Home Office Research Study No. 34).

Molumby, T. "Patterns of Crime in a University Housing Project." *American Behavioral Scientist*, 1976, *20*, 247–259.

_____. "Evaluation of the Effect of Physical Design Changes on Criminal Behavior." Doctoral dissertation, St. Ambrose University, 1981.

Morris, T. *The Criminal Area: A Study in Social Ecology.* London: Routledge & Kegan Paul, 1958.

Mullins, P. and Robb, J.H. "Residents' Assessment of a New Zealand Public-Housing Scheme." *Environment and Behavior*, December 1977, *9*(4), 573–624.

Musheno, M.C., Levine, J.P., and Palumbo, D.J. *Is "Defensible Space" a Defensible Theory?: An Evaluation of Closed-Circuit Television as a Crime Prevention Strategy.* Presented at the National Conference on Criminal Justice sponsored by the Law Enforcement Assistance Administration, Washington, DC, February 1977.

_____. "Television Surveillance and Crime Prevention: Evaluating an Attempt to Create Defensible Space in Public Housing." *Social Science Quarterly*, 1978.

National Crime Prevention Institute, *Understanding Crime Prevention,* Stoneham, MA: Butterworth Publishers, 1986.

Newman, O. *Defensible Spaces: Crime Prevention Through Urban Design.* New York: Macmillan, 1972.

_____. *Architectural Design for Crime Prevention.* New York: New York University, March 1973. (U.S. Government Printing Office.)

_____. *Improving Residential Security, a Design Guideline.* Washington, DC: Department of Housing and Urban Development, December 1973.

_____. *Design Guidelines for Creating Defensible Space.* Washington, DC: Law Enforcement Assistance Administration, April 1976.

Nieburg, H.L. "Crime Prevention by Urban Design." *Society.* November/December 1974, 41–47.

Normandeau, A. "Trends and Patterns in Crimes of Robbery." Doctoral dissertation, University of Pennsylvania, 1968.

Pablant, P. and Baxter, J.C. "Environmental Correlates of School Vandalism." *American Institutes of Planning,* July 1975, 270–279.

Palen, J.J. *Density, Crowding and Pathology: Research and Reappraisal.* Milwaukee: Urban Research Center and Department of Sociology, University of Wisconsin-Milwaukee, 1978.

Patterson, A.H. "Crowding, Crime and the Designed Environment: A Social Control Perspective." Paper presented at the American Psychological Association Meeting, 1975.

_____. *Territorial Behavior and Fear of Crime in the Elderly.* University Park: The Pennsylvania State University, 1977.

_____. "Crime and Fear Among the Elderly: The Role of the Physical and Social Environment." *Crime Prevention Through Environmental Design Theory Compendium.* Arlington, Virginia: Westinghouse National Issues Center, 1978.

Pesce, E.J., Kohn, I.R., and Kaplan, H.M. *Crime Prevention Through Environmental Design: Final Report, Phases II and III, July 1976–1978.* Arlington, Virginia: Westinghouse Electric Corporation, July 1978.

Phillips, G.H., Kreps, G.M., and Moody, C.W. *Environmental Factors in Rural Crime.* Wooster, Ohio: Ohio Agricultural Research and Development Center, November 1976 (Research circular 224).

Plaster, S. and Carter, S. *Planning for Prevention, Sarasota, Florida's Approach to Crime Prevention Through Environmental Design,* Florida Criminal Justice

Executive Institute, Florida Department of Law Enforcement, Tallahassee, Florida, 1993.

Pope, C.E. *Crime-Specific Analysis: The Characteristics of Burglary Incidents.* Washington, DC: U.S. Department of Justice, 1977.

_____. *Crime-Specific Analysis: An Empirical Examination of Burglary Offender Characteristics.* Washington, DC: U.S. Department of Justice, 1977.

Poyner, B. *Design Against Crime: Beyond Defensible Space*, London, Butterworths, 1983.

President's Commission of Law Enforcement and Administration of Justice. *Task Force Report: Crime and Its Impact — An Assessment.* Washington, DC: U.S. Government Printing Office, 1967.

Pyle, G.F. *The Spatial Dynamics of Crime.* Chicago: Department of Geography, University of Chicago, Research Paper #159, 1974.

_____. "Spatial and Temporal Aspects of Crime in Cleveland, Ohio." *American Behavioral Scientist*, November/December 1976, *20*, 175–198.

Rainwater, L. "The Lessons of Pruitt-Igoe." *Public Interest*, Summer 1967, *8*, 116–126.

Reiss, A.J. "Environmental Determinants of Victimization by Crime and Its Control: Offenders and Victims." *Crime Prevention Through Environmental Design Theory Compendium.* Arlington, Virginia: Westinghouse National Issues Center, 1978.

Rengert, G.F. "The Journey of Crime: An Empirical Analysis of Spatially Constrained Female Mobility." Paper presented at the 1975 annual meeting of the Association of American Geographers at Milwaukee. Philadelphia: Temple University, 1975.

Reppetto, T.A. "The Control of Street Robbery: Some Strategic Considerations" in Law Enforcement Assistance Administration (ed.), *Research on Street Crime Control.* Washington, DC: T.A. Reppetto, June 1973.

_____. *Residential Crime.* Cambridge, Massachusetts: Ballinger, 1974.

_____. "Crime Prevention and the Displacement Phenomenon." *Crime and Delinquency*, April 1976, 22(2).

_____. *Report on Offender Interviews in Hartford.* New York: John Jay College of Criminal Justice, 1977.

Rizzo, M. "The Cost of Crime to Victims: An Empirical Analysis." *Journal of Legal Studies*, January 1979.

Rosenthal, S.J. et al. *Developing a Comprehensive Security Program for Public Housing.* Philadelphia: The Housing Management Institute Center for Social Policy and Community Development, Temple University, 1974.

Sagalyn et al. *Residential Security.* Washington, DC: National Institute of Law Enforcement and Criminal Justice, 1973.

Scarr, H.A. *Patterns of Burglary.* National Institute of Law Enforcement and Criminal Justice. Washington, DC: Government Printing Office, 1972.

Schmitt, R. "Density, Delinquency and Crime in Honolulu." *Sociology and Social Research*, *41*, 274–276.

Schneider, A.L. "Evaluation of the Portland Neighborhood-Based Anti-Burglary Program" in Pascal (ed.), *Racial Discrimination in Economic Life.* Lexington: Lexington Books, 1972.

Seattle Law and Justice Planning Office. *Burglary Reduction Program: Final Report.* Prepared for the U.S. Department of Justice, Law Enforcement Assistance Administration. Seattle: Seattle Law and Justice Planning Office, February 24, 1975.

Shaw, C.R. and McKay, H.D. *Juvenile Delinquency and Urban Areas.* Chicago: Chicago University Press, 1969.

Smith, M.S. *Crime Prevention Through Environmental Design in Parking Facilities*, Washington, D.C.: U.S. Department of Justice, National Institute of Justice, April 1996.

Smith, T.S. "Inverse Distance Variations for the Flow of Crime in Urban Areas." *Social Forces*, June 1976, *54*(4), 802–815.

Sommer, R. "Developing Proprietary Attitudes Toward the Public Environment." *Crime Prevention Through Environmental Design Theory Compendium*. Arlington, Virginia: Westinghouse National Issues Center, 1978.

Southern California Association of Governments. *Handbook of Crime Prevention Bulletins: Crime Prevention Through Physical Planning*. Los Angeles: Southern California Association of Governments, 1971.

Spivak, M. "Listen, Hide, Build, Sing and Dig: The Political Collapse of a Playground." *Landscape Architecture*, July 1969.

Sternlieb, G., Burchell, R.W., and Casey, S. *Municipal Crime Rates and Land Use Patterns*. New Brunswick, New Jersey: Prepared for Westinghouse Electric Corporation, Public Applied Systems, January 1978.

Struder, R.G. "Behavior Technology and the Modification of Criminal Behavior Through Environmental Design and Management." *Crime Prevention Through Environmental Design Theory Compendium*. Arlington, Virginia: Westinghouse National Issues Center, 1978.

Swartz, R.D. "Mitigating Through Traffic in Residential Areas: Issues and Perspectives." *Transportation Quarterly*, October 1985.

Tata, R., Vanhorn, S., and Lee, D. "Defensible Space in a Housing Project: A Case Study from a South Florida Ghetto." *Professional Geographer*, August 1978, *27*, 297–303.

Taylor, R.B. and Harrell, A.V. *Physical Environment and Crime, A Final Summary Report Presented to the National Institute of Justice*, Washington, DC: U.S. Department of Justice, National Institute of Justice, May 1996.

Taylor, R.B., Gottfredson, S., et al. *Toward a Resident-Based Model of Community Crime Prevention: Urban Territoriality, Social Network and Design*. Baltimore, Maryland: The Center for Metropolitan Planning and Research, Johns Hopkins University, December 1979.

Tien, J.M., O'Donnell, V.R., Barnett, A.K., and Mirchandane, P.B. *Street Lighting Projects: National Evaluation Program, Phase I, Final Report*. Cambridge, Massachusetts: Public Systems Evaluation, Inc., July 1977.

Turner, S. "Delinquency and Distance" in M.E. Wolfgang and T. Sellin (eds.), *Delinquency: Selected Studies*. New York: John Wiley & Sons, 1969.

_____. "The Ecology of Delinquency" in M.E. Wolfgang and T. Sellin (eds.), *Delinquency: Selected Studies*. New York: John Wiley & Sons, 1969.

U.S. Congress Senate Select Committee on Small Business. Crime *Against Small Business*. Washington, DC: Government Publishing Office, 1969.

U.S. Department of Commerce. *The Role of Behavioral Science in Physical Security: Proceedings of the First Annual Symposium — April 29–30, 1976*. Washington, DC: National Bureau of Standards, November 1977.

Verbrugge, L.B. and Taylor, R.B. *Consequences of Population Density: Testing New Hypotheses*. Baltimore, Maryland: The Center for Metropolitan Planning and Research, Johns Hopkins University, 1976.

Voss, H. *Ecology, Crime and Delinquency*. New York: Meredith Corporation, 1971.

Weinstein, N.D. "The Statistical Prediction of Environmental Preferences: Problems of Validity and Application." *Environment and Behavior*, December 1976, *8*(4), 611–627.

Wekerle, G.R. and Whitzman, C. *Safe Cities: Guidelines for Planning, Design and Management*, New York, NY: Van Nostrand Reinhold, 1995.

Westinghouse National Issues Center. *Crime Prevention Through Environmental Design: Final Report on Schools Demonstration, Broward County, Florida*. Arlington, Virginia: Westinghouse, May 1978.

Whitcomb, D. *Focus on Robbery: The Hidden Cameras Project — Seattle, Washington*. Cambridge, Massachusetts: Abt Associates, 1978.

White, R.C. "The Relation of Felonies to Environmental Factors in Indianapolis." *Social Forces*, May 1932, *10*, 498–509.

———. *Consequences of Population Density and Size in Baltimore*. Baltimore, Maryland: The Center for Metropolitan Planning and Research, Johns Hopkins University, November 1977.

———. *Crime Prevention Through Environmental Design: Final Report on Residential Demonstration, Minneapolis, Minnesota*. Arlington, Virginia: Westinghouse, June 1978.

———. *CPTED Commercial Demonstration Evaluation Report*. Evanston, Illinois: Westinghouse, 1979.

Williams, E.N. (ed.) *The Social Impact of Urban Design*. Chicago: University of Chicago, Center for Policy Studies, 1970.

Wilson, J.Q. and Kelling, G.I. "Broken Windows" *The Atlantic Monthly*, March 1982, pp. 29–38.

Wilson, J.Q. and Kelling, G.L. "Making Neighborhoods Safe," *The Atlantic Monthly*, February 1989, pp. 46–52.

Wright, R. *Study to Determine the Impact of Street Lighting on Street Crime: Phase I, Final Report*. Ann Arbor: University of Michigan, May 1974.

Index

LaVergne, TN USA
27 July 2010
191110LV00004B/4/P